I0622925

WHO IS MAX LEWIS?

© Copyright 2021 – by **Max Lewis**

All rights reserved. This book is protected by the copyright laws of the United States of America, and no part of this book may be copied or reprinted for commercial gain or profit without the expressed written permission of the author.

To contact the author:

Info@WhoIsMaxLewis.com

Disclaimer: This is a work of creative nonfiction. The events are portrayed to the best of the author's memory. While all stories in this book are true, some names and identifying details have been changed to protect the privacy of the people involved. Although the publisher and the author have made every effort to ensure that the information in the book was correct at press time and while this publication is designed to provide accurate information in regard to the subject matter covered, the publisher and the author assume no responsibility for errors, inaccuracies, omissions, or any other inconsistencies herein and hereby disclaim any liability to any party for any loss, damage, or disruption caused by errors or omissions, whether such errors or omissions result from negligence, accident, or any other cause. This writing is not intended to provide legal advice, for which an attorney in all circumstances should be consulted.

ISBN 979-8-9853596-5-7 (Hardback)

ISBN 979-8-9853596-0-2 (E-book)

ISBN 979-8-9853596-1-9 (Paperback)

37 CHAPTERS | 37 LESSONS

$37 MILLION

WHO IS MAX LEWIS?

MAX LEWIS

Table of Contents

Author's Note

This book is based on a true story. Throughout this book, I reference things and quotes you may have heard before. That's because my character and intellect are shaped by the influences of many great and wonderful minds: people I admire. Their wisdom has been imparted in me. It has become the very essence of who I am. Countless people have contributed to the person I am today. Every one of them left a mark on the pages of my life. That was their gift to me, whether they knew they were giving it or not. If I happen to reference you or someone you know; whether I do it knowingly or unknowingly, it's because that person or quote eternally influenced me. It was something that helped me along my journey and bolstered my transformation. So, whether you knew you were helping or not, I thank you.

With Gratitude,

Max Lewis

Preface

This book was written for a variety of reasons. Here are just a few: First, to motivate the average person, like me, to look at life's obstacles differently. Second, to strengthen, and embolden at least just one person to act on faith instead of just thinking about an idea they have or something they want all the time. Third, to encourage that person to stay persistent, even when there doesn't appear to be any reason to do so. Finally, to inspire you to access and strengthen your ingenuity today, to live a better life tomorrow.

Not everyone who receives a formal education becomes a millionaire, and not everyone without a formal education is fruitless. The truth is, what separates successful people from unsuccessful people is the effort they put in and the faith they apply. Working toward the things you want is not always fun, and such things are rarely easy. Especially if what you're trying to achieve is monumental. My hope is that this book will serve as proof that you can start with nothing but a desire and end up with whatever it is you seek, if you stay consistent in achieving your intent. So make the tough decisions and do what needs to be done. It's all possible. My hope is that you learn some lessons from this book and obtain whatever you're looking for.

May God bless you on your journey!

Dedication

I dedicate this book to Tony Robbins, Keith Cunningham, and the late Napoleon Hill. These men have had a tremendous impact and influence on my life, and I will be forever grateful to them.

I also would like to thank my father, brother, and Francesca Morello. This book would not be possible without them. Most important, almighty God, who has guided me and been with me throughout my entire journey.

"The mouth speaks what the heart is full of." Matthew 12:34

Hold on a second!

Before you begin reading, I'd like to take a moment to encourage you to answer the questions at the end of each chapter. I promise if you make the extra effort to look inward, by the end of this book you will be rewarded with the gift of self discovery. To what extent, I do not know, however, I do know making a habit of looking inward was the quickest way to finding my **gold**. Let's give it a try with these first three. Go ahead and write in this book.

1. *What* do you want?

_____

_____

2. *Why* do you want it?

_____

_____

3. *What are some of the things you can do to get what you want?*

_____

_____

Chapter 1:

Money Doesn't Grow on Trees

After my parents' divorce when I was around 8 years old, my father began to teach me about money. It all started when I asked him for a new bicycle, and he said he couldn't buy me one because he couldn't afford it. He told me he didn't have enough money, which wasn't true. The truth was, he decided it was time to teach me a lesson: a money lesson. "What's money?" I asked. "Money is what we use to buy things like the bicycle you want," he replied. He then explained that it also was used to buy the things we needed, such as food, clothing, and shelter. But most importantly, he said it should be used to invest into opportunities when they present themselves, so it could multiply into even more money. Although he didn't try to explain finances, assets, or investments, he kept it simple. He told me I had to earn my money, and that saving money was a good thing. That little talk aroused my curiosity. He was making me aware of this money thing, how to respect and value it, the role it played in my life, and all it could do for me.

The lesson continued. Not long after that, he handed me $10 in singles. "Here, this is 10 dollars; I want you to count it," he said. *Wow, here was that money he was talking about.* I was excited. *This can get me the things I want; this is great!* I thought. I began counting "1...2...3... 10!" "Is it all there?" my father asked. "Yes, Dad!" I replied. "Good, you always need to count your money and keep it organized. Keep the presidents facing up, all bills in the same direction, unfold any creased edges, and keep them in numerical order. I prefer the smallest numbers to the biggest. It's best to keep it organized so you know what you have," he said. "Okay, Dad." I replied. "I want you to save it in this." He handed me a blue cookie tin that used to hold about 30 Royal Dansk Cookies.

"Every time you get some money, I want you to put it in this tin. I want to see how much you can save. Let's see if you can fill it to the top, Son!" he challenged. "Okay…where do I get more money, Dad?" "Well, you need to earn it somehow," he said. "Um…how?" I asked. "Well, Son, you can do many things to earn money." He paused, "We have a mango tree in our backyard; how about you start by picking some mangoes so you can sell them to the neighbors?" "Okay!" I exclaimed. With a spring in my step, I hopped up and ran to the backyard. I immediately began picking mangoes off the ground. My father arrived shortly after me. He had gone to the kitchen to get me an empty plastic bag he had saved from the supermarket. "*Esperate!*" (Wait!) he yelled in Spanish. "You need to get the good ones; they need to be ripe and not damaged. If not, people won't buy them." With my father's help, I soon had a bag full of beautiful, ripe mangoes. They were red, yellow, had a hint of green, and an unmistakable sweet smell.

We began walking down the sidewalk toward our neighbor Maria's house. As we walked, my father began giving me instructions. "Okay, we're getting close. When we get there, I want you to knock on the door and tell Maria you're selling mangoes for $1," he said. "Okay, Dad!" I replied. I was excited but also shy and nervous. As we approached the entrance, I could hear Spanish television blaring in the background. The wooden front door was open, and all that stood between me, and my first sale was a weathered aluminum screen door that was shut. It was designed to allow a cool breeze in and, at the same time, keep mosquitoes out. The screen allowed sound and sight to transmit quite clearly. I extended my arm outward, and my tiny knuckles lightly tapped on Maria's screen door. Although I had my father by my side, I was still a bit hesitant, "knock, knock, knock." Maria immediately called out in Spanish, "*Quien es?*" (Who is it?). I could hear the shuffle of her sandals on the floor as she made her way toward me. *"Es Maxie!"* (It's Maxie!) I answered with my childhood nickname. "Hola Maxie," she replied. "I'm selling mangoes for $1 each." I raised the plastic bag so she could examine my produce. "Oh, how nice. I love mangoes, and they look great! I'll take three," she replied. As she turned to grab her wallet, I looked back at my father, who smiled and gave me a big thumbs up. "Great job," he said. I was ecstatic! I had a grin that could light up a room. This was fun. We were having fun together. I didn't realize it at the time, but it was at that moment that I associated making money with making my father proud. It was the leverage I would inadvertently use on myself for years. Making my father proud was now my motivation to succeed.

Throughout the next few weeks, I became more experienced in the mango business, I learned I could sell the larger mangoes for $2 instead of just $1. Accompanied by my father, I gave people all over the neighborhood a visit. I was an 8-year-old mango tycoon. I barely left any mangoes for my family to eat. I had nearly become an expert with the fruit picker, a long wooden stick with a metal claw and basket attached to the end. I would use this innovative tool to harvest the hanging fruit from the parts of the tree I couldn't reach. That helped my sales, because less fruit would hit the ground and run the risk of getting damaged, spoiled, or eaten by birds and ants. I couldn't sell the mangoes once they were damaged or half-eaten by vermin, so the goal was to pick them the moment they looked ripe to prevent that from happening.

Not only had I become an expert with the fruit picker but selling had started to become second nature to me. Neighbors now expected to see me, and I developed more confidence when trying to sell to them. I began to notice people's buying habits, their different personalities, and what was important to them. Some customers were more interested in the size of the mango, others the color. Some wanted their mangoes to be very colorful and ripe, and others wanted them green, firm, and less ripe. Some wanted mangoes delivered as often as possible, and then some didn't want mangoes at all but probably felt bad turning me down, so they bought some anyway. I became very familiar with customers' requesting a discount for purchasing several mangoes at a time. The query would be something along the lines of: "If I buy three mangoes instead of just one, may I have the fourth one for free?" Or sometimes: "How about six mangoes for $5?" The questions were very similar, and I got them quite often. At first, I needed to run these deals by my dad. Mainly because I didn't understand why I would lower the price or what the purpose of doing so was. After a few of those transactions, I began to catch on. It made sense to me: more money! After all, it was either striking a deal and turning these mangoes into cash to put in my cookie tin; or having my dad eat the mangoes, and I'd get nothing. If there happened to be any unsold mangoes, he'd freeze them so they wouldn't spoil, then use them to make mango milkshakes later in the year when there wasn't anything to harvest. So, why not make a deal? It didn't take long for me to feel comfortable bartering with people on my own. I no longer wanted to just sell a single mango to anyone. It was like a fun game. I tried to sell as many as I could to every person I spoke to. Soon after, I began to offer wholesale discounts without consulting my dad. Sometimes I made great deals, and sometimes I didn't. Nonetheless, I was having fun, and I always learned something. Undeniably, the money lesson was working.

At the end of each day, my father and I would count the money I earned from my mango sales. Then we organized the newly earned money into numerical order as he had taught me — each time announcing the new grand total and writing it down on a paper we kept in the Royal Dansk cookie vault.

The tin was filled with 1's, 5's, 10's, and 20's, but my favorite denomination was the singles. In the beginning, I'd often ask my dad to exchange all the money I earned into singles. It made it much more fun for me.

Although a $20 bill is worth the same amount as 20 singles, it was just not as exciting — even if it held the same value. I still preferred the visual stimulation of those singles piled up. It felt like progress. Besides that, the cookie tin would fill up so much faster. Funny enough, that still stands true for me today. No matter how much money I have in the bank, there's just something about having a big wad of cash in my pocket. It gives me a sense of abundance.

Reflection Point 1

Money is one of the most essential tools in modern life. It's a resource used to get the things we want and need. The sooner we know the role money can and will play in our lives, the better we can position ourselves for financial success. It's never too early to raise your awareness around money and learn good financial habits. It's a foundation to build upon throughout one's life; and it's a useful skill that will always be available.

Additionally, setting goals is extremely important. Besides giving you something to strive for, goals help keep you on track. Documenting your progress along the way will not only keep you organized but also will affirm you're headed in the right direction.

There are opportunities all around you to make money, sometimes even in your own backyard. I encourage you to find a mango tree of your own as a way to instill good money habits in your life and to inspire those you love. By the way, you're never too old to start learning good money habits either!

*Please take the time to write out your answers to the questions on the next page and at the end of each chapter.

What are your beliefs around money?

How has money helped you?

In what ways do you keep track of your finances,
and how could you improve them?

Chapter 2:

Planting Seeds

After our mango tree stopped bearing fruit, I no longer had a product to sell, though technically, I didn't need one. At that point, I had saved enough money to buy my own bicycle: about $200 or so, mostly singles, of course. But the bike was no longer my main priority; making money was. If I were to use my money to buy a bike, it would drain my cookie tin of all I had saved, and I didn't want that to happen. I wanted to see my blue tin can overflow with cash. This was now a fun game for me. I told my father I no longer wanted the bike, and I would continue to save. This money-making behavior was being rewarded. So, naturally, I wanted to do more of it.

I had a newly found respect for *money*, and I was being responsible with it, which pleased my father greatly. For that reason, he gave me an opportunity to make more of it. Continuing to reward my behavior, he decided to incentivize me by offering me a sweet deal. "I'll tell you what; I'm going to buy you the bicycle because of how great of a job you've done saving your money and, from now on, whatever money you save by Christmas each year, I'm going to match it," he said. The thought of that excited me. I was getting the bike, and I knew my cookie tin would be bursting at the seams by Christmas. So, I once again asked my father what I could do to earn more money.

My grandfather Leo, who lived with us, kept a small rose garden on the side of our house. My dad suggested that if I pulled some weeds from the rose garden, Grandpa might pay me to do so. It was another way I could earn some money. Grandpa Leo had lost both of his legs due to severe diabetes, so he couldn't pull the weeds himself. He did, however, thoroughly enjoy a well- pruned rose garden. I walked over to Grandpa's room and offered my services.

He agreed to pay me a few dollars each time I worked in the garden. I took the job. Under my grandfather's instruction, I'd pull weeds and often plant a new rose bush. I quickly learned that I enjoyed selling mangoes much, much more. It was hot, there were many weeds, the roses had sharp thorns, and worst of all, it didn't pay nearly as much money as selling mangoes did. The weeds didn't grow fast enough, so my services were also limited to every other week. My grandfather would give me around $5 for about 30 minutes worth of work. I could've sold around $10–$20 worth of mangoes in that same amount of time. There were no mangoes to sell, so that wasn't an option. As soon as the work was completed, he would palm me a tri-folded $5, smile, and thank me for a job well done.

Although it was hard work, it was fulfilling. I was spending time with my grandfather and helping him. I knew that made him happy. Overall, working in Grandpa's garden was a great experience filled with valuable lessons. I continued to learn the value of a dollar and the hard work behind it. When I think about my grandfather and our relationship, many of my memories involve working in his garden. It was, above all else, quality time we shared — just the two of us. While I would tend to Grandpa's garden, pulling weeds and planting new roses, he'd speak to me. He took the time to ask thought- provoking questions. He'd then pause and allow my mind to work while I tried to come up with answers to his brainteasers. When I drew a blank, he'd offer an insight; often coupled with an explanation. Based on my answers, he'd gauge my understanding and patiently reiterate whatever he felt I may have lacked clarity on. Throughout our time together, he educated me on many subjects, but one thing, in particular, has always stuck with me. He'd often repeat this phrase: *"Hay tres cosas que cada persona deberia hacer durante su vida: plantar un arbol, tener un hijo, y escribir un libro."* Which translated in English means, *"There are three things that every person should do in their lifetime: plant a tree, have a child, and write a book."* I didn't realize it until just now, but he was quoting Jose Marti, the revered Cuban poet. I guess roses weren't the only thing we were planting in the garden back then. My grandfather planted that seed in my mind so long ago, and here it is, bearing fruit. I'm writing a book. One of the very things he said I needed to do. He shaped my mind and planted that in my subconscious without me even realizing it. Wow! Thank you, Abuelo Leo! Although it was hard work, spending quality time with my grandfather and learning from him made it worth it. I'm unendingly grateful for that. I'll always remember my grandfather Leo, the priceless time we spent together, and the beautiful lessons he taught me.

Reflection Point 2

Sometimes we need to sacrifice our short-term goals for our more significant, long-term goals. Ultimately, filling the cookie tin was more important to me than having a new bicycle. Exercising restraint led to an opportunity. My father acknowledged my self-control and rewarded me with the bicycle I wanted. Utilizing positive reinforcement, he gave me a phenomenal opportunity to double my yearly savings. He then proposed I work for my grandfather, who likely taught him the very lessons he was teaching me. He may have done this in hopes that some of grandpa's wisdom would rub off on me, and it did. Being in that environment with Grandpa gave me a different perspective and expanded my understanding of these important life lessons.

The subconscious mind is immensely powerful. What you repeat and what is repeated to you will most likely come to fruition.

What are you planting in your subconscious mind regularly?

_____

_____

_____

_____

_____

What do you need to be planting to get the results you're after?

_____

_____

_____

_____

_____

_____

_____

Chapter 3:

Sweet Tooth

As I grew older, I continued selling mangoes whenever they were in season, but I slowly began to lose interest in it. However, I continued to save the money I made from selling them and any money I made from odd jobs such as washing my mother's car, and cash I received on birthdays and Christmases. The habit of saving money stuck with me. I was around 12 years old then and in the seventh grade. I had no clue I was about to embark on the next phase of my journey.

One evening after school, I overheard my mother speaking to my older brother Danny on the phone. He told her that he and a few friends had begun selling candy at his high school during class. It was against the rules to sell candy at school, and, if you were caught doing so, it would likely result in a suspension. My antenna immediately went up. I continued to listen in on the conversation. Once I learned that Danny was making money selling candy, I had heard enough! I had found my next business venture. I was excited about the idea and asked if I could do the same. With my mother's permission, I asked my father to take me to Costco, where my brother would buy his candies, so I could give it a try. I was ready to embark on this new, exciting adventure. Kids my age were eating similar candy to the ones my brother sold, but some of the candies he was selling were too expensive for a seventh grader's budget. The kids in my class had less money to spend, so I thought I might try smaller, bite-sized candies that were cheaper and easier to sell.

After examining the options in Costco, my father and I decided that Cry Baby Sour Bubble Gum would be the best candy for me to start with. They were extremely popular and inexpensive, perfect for a seventh grader's budget. So, I made the investment and purchased the Cry Babies with some of the money I had saved. Once home, I sat down with my father, pencil and paper in hand and did the math on what I should sell them for to turn a profit. Because I was buying them in bulk, I was getting them for around 5 cents each. This meant I could sell one Cry Baby for a dime (which wasn't much money) and make a 100% profit. If a customer bought two Cry Baby candies, I would charge 20 cents. Instead of charging 30 cents for three, I applied the lesson I had previously learned selling multiple mangoes at a discount. If a customer bought three Cry Baby candies, I'd give them a 5-cent discount and only charge a quarter. This naturally would incentivize the students to buy three Cry Baby candies instead of two. It would also work in my favor because I didn't have to provide change so often. It was more likely kids would have a quarter on them rather than three dimes.

In my bookbag, I carried a bank teller pouch my mother had given me, entirely full of Cry Baby candies. The zipper to the bag would barely close due to the overwhelming amount of inventory I stuffed inside of it. I also had a few quarters, dimes, and nickels in case I needed to provide some change.

I wasn't shy about telling my classmates I had candy for sale; after all, I was an experienced door-to-door mango salesman. I was prepared for this. I started spreading the word immediately, whispering to the students in my first-period history class and, handing out little handwritten notes; {Cry Baby: 1 = $0.10, 2 = $0.20, 3 = $0.25}. I had a strategy: I would wait for the teacher to turn his back to the classroom and begin writing on the blackboard before I'd conduct my business. I sold a few pieces of candy during class, but I quickly learned I'd sell much more during our lunch break. Almost all the kids in the school cafeteria had money in their hands in anticipation to pay for lunch or had just gotten change back from buying lunch. To increase my sales, I'd stand right by the cashier and tell each student paying for his or her lunch that I had candy for sale. When I applied that strategy, I sold much more. I had something the school didn't offer, and the kids wanted. And at the price I was selling the candy, it was an easy sale. I told many people in the seventh grade that I was selling candy. I think everyone knew, or at least it felt that way. I even sold some to teachers (the cool ones who didn't care I was breaking the rules). I began carrying more candy in my bookbag than books. I'd often completely sell out before day's end and made what I considered to be a lot of money at the time, around $20 a day. It felt great. I was rich! I had my very own business, and I could buy just about anything I wanted.

I began to save for such things as a go-kart and video games. Sure, I had money saved, but I wanted to make more and spend the new money I had earned, not take from my savings. That way, I felt that I was progressing. In my mind, my savings were untouchable. I began to save a portion of my daily profits to buy the things I wanted. I'd put 75% of the profit I made into a labeled *untouchable savings* tin. The other 25% would go into a separate tin, labeled *savings for things I want*. For example, if I made $20, I'd put $15 into my *untouchable savings* tin and $5 in my *savings for things I want* tin. If I wanted a $50 video game, I wouldn't buy it until I had the $50 in my *savings for things I want* tin. I did so diligently. I never wavered.

While selling candy in seventh grade, I came across another situation that enlightened me. I soon started receiving special requests from my classmates. They wanted other types and brands of candy. My father and I began to regularly go to Costco to do the math and see if the candies the kids were requesting could be as profitable, if not more profitable, than what I was already selling. If the math was favorable, I'd purchase the candy and add it to my offering to determine what the kids would prefer, and what I could make the most money from. Would kids buy more Airheads than Cry Baby candy? More lollipops than Reese's Peanut Butter Cups? I was testing the Butter Cups? I was testing the market, first based on profit, then based on demand. Some candies had high margins but wouldn't sell as often, like Reese's, which would melt in my bag. Others would sell out very quickly but had lower margins. Which meant more sales but for less profit. I started selling about five brands, and I had my regular buyers who were consistent.

My biggest customer was Henry. Every day, he would spend his entire $5 lunch allowance on candy and every day I took orders and made exceptions for him. I had other friends who never had money but always wanted candy. When I would give them the candy, they would ask if they could pay me back later, but when later came, they never had the money. That quickly turned my little candy business into a C.O.D., cash on delivery, operation. I found myself with a pencil and sheet of paper doing math often, calculating profit margins, and making decisions on what to keep in stock. I also noted that if I didn't introduce a new candy from time to time, whether it was as financially rewarding as the other candies or not, my classmates would get bored. So, I would introduce a new product every so often.

The cookie tin can, which was now overflowing, was on its way out. I had won an art contest at school that awarded me a $25 cash prize in the form of a check from a bank nearby. My father suggested I open a bank account there, which we did. I took the cash from my *untouchable savings* tin along with my certificate and opened my first bank account. I now had a savings account and could make my very own bank deposits. After Christmas that year, while my father was putting away his checkbook, he informed me this would be the last Christmas I could double my money by simply saving it. I think he underestimated how well the lesson would take hold. I guess I had graduated.

Although it only lasted less than a year, selling candy in seventh grade gave me a wealth of knowledge and hands-on experience I wouldn't have learned any other way. It taught me several lessons and gave me insight into things I wouldn't have been exposed to otherwise. It was a foundation that prepared me for things to come. Although it was on an exceedingly small scale, many of the business principles are still the same: buy low, sell high. What's selling? What's not? I continued to learn the value of a dollar, different ways to make money, and the effort required to achieve success. It was a priceless experience.

Reflection Point 3

Once you embark on a new venture, study your audience in great detail. What do they want, and what's important to them? Don't be afraid to test different products or techniques and make adjustments along the way. I let everyone around me know I was selling candy. Everyone around you should know what you do, or what you're selling; this will dramatically increase your chances of success. Then, identify the best time and place to execute your strategy. For me, the cafeteria provided a hungry, captive audience with cash in hand. I had what they wanted, at the right price, which made for an easy sale.

Whether you're selling something or not, we're all trying to appeal to an audience in one form or another. To my pet dog, I'm her target audience. When she rolls over on her back, I give her a belly rub. When she stands by the door, I let her outside. Those are the right strategies to get what she wants, so she continues to use them.

Who is your target audience, and what strategy have you
been using to capture their interest?

_____

_____

_____

_____

Could there be a more effective strategy?
If so, what is that strategy?

_____

_____

_____

_____

Chapter 4:

Creating My Own Magic

Years had passed since my stint as a confectioner; I was in high school, and candy was most likely the last thing on my mind. During the previous few years, I was so consumed by spending time with my friends, playing sports, getting into trouble, and of course, girls, I almost completely forgot about my old pal money. During that time, I didn't have a need for it. It wasn't important. My priorities had shifted, but that didn't last long. I was about to graduate from high school, and, believe it or not; I was sworn to be a professional chef. I had a knack and a passion for cooking. It was going to be my life's work, my career. I had obtained a partial scholarship to Johnson & Wales University School of Culinary Arts, and I would begin class after taking the summer off, or at least that's what I thought was going to happen. I, however, knew that I wanted a nicer car, better clothes, and to be able to go out on the weekends without touching my savings, or asking my parents for a handout. I needed money, and I had all but forgotten the effort that it took to make it. I needed to get some real-world experience. Opportunity struck when a few of my friends told me they got jobs working for a magician on the weekends. The magician would perform card tricks to amuse partygoers at special events. As part of his act, he'd hire my friends to entertain children at the events by dressing up in various costumes. My friends would dress up as clowns, Barney the purple dinosaur, or one of the Power Rangers. However, the pay was only $20 an event. I liked the idea of learning how to perform magic but being in a costume for several hours a day to make such a small amount of money was something that didn't interest me.

Instead, I opted to get a part-time job working at a car wash near my house. Some other friends had gotten a job there and said they were making much more than $20 a day. I thought it'd be a good idea to work with them, have fun, and make a little money at the same time. Boy, was I wrong. It turned out to be the hardest work I had ever experienced. Even worse than pulling weeds in the sun; much worse! It was around 8 hours of labor in the blazing Miami sun; it was humid, and I felt like I'd sweat more than I was able to hydrate. I couldn't drink water fast enough, and the work wouldn't stop. The only upside was being able to occasionally drive a nice car. Granted, we'd only be moving these cars at idle speed, for 10–20 feet up the line, hardly a worthy consolation prize. Especially when the owners of the nicer cars tended to be the most particular customers. It's as if they were gifted with the ability to sniff out the most minuscule oversights. This would likely result in applying extra silicone on all four of their tires for a second time, or even worse, having to re-vacuum their entire vehicle after finding a microscopic piece of lint that could barely be seen by the human eye. Which would likely lead to no tip. I'd get home at the end of the day exhausted, only wanting to shower, eat and go straight to bed — all for $70 a day, which was brutal. There had to be a better way to make money than this. I was wrong; this wasn't fun.

On my way home from work one day, I received a call from my father asking me if I'd be interested in working with him part-time until culinary school began. My father was running a small propane business called Local Propane with my two older brothers. They only had one other employee and needed someone to help fill propane tanks and answer phones on Saturdays. He said he'd match whatever I was making at the car wash, and there was no doubt that the work would be less tiresome. Besides that, I always jumped at the opportunity to help my father in any way I could. It was an easy decision. I would work for him part-time for $70 a day.

I was 18 years old when I started working with my father and time went by quickly. Before I knew it, I was ready to begin culinary school. But I made the decision to hold off and decided to start the following semester in order to help my father a bit longer. He and my eldest brother, Rueben, had gotten into an argument, which resulted in Rueben opting to quit working in the family business. After he left, my father needed even more of my help, which made it easy to stick around. I was answering phones and filling propane BBQ tanks for walk-in customers, and, as an added benefit, I spent time with some of my family. It was fun, but what I think kept me there most of all was that I met a girl. Her name was Jessica, and she worked a few blocks north of my job at a mailing company (which was rather popular before emails took over). We'd have lunch together every day and quickly fell in love. *School can wait*, I thought.

With culinary school on hold, I considered a career in real estate. I was always good at the Monopoly board game, so why not? It couldn't be that much different, right? I signed up for a 30-day course on nights and weekends. Although I passed the real estate course with a 93% on my final exam, I failed the state exam. Believe it or not, I failed the exam by only one point. I needed a 75% to pass, and I scored a 74%, which was unimaginable. I studied for the test again and retook it. This time I scored even lower. I got a 63% out of 100%. It was discouraging. I took it as a sign that becoming a realtor wasn't for me.

A few months later, while I was visiting my grandmother, she casually mentioned she had inherited a house from an old friend who had recently passed away and was planning to sell the house to a man who offered her $60,000 in cash for it. Purchasing a home wasn't something I was planning on, but when I heard the amount she was selling it for, it felt attainable for me. It sounded like a great investment opportunity. I mentioned I might be interested in purchasing the house at that price and would match the offer if she would sell it to me. I just needed some time to figure out how to pay for it. She agreed to hold off on the sale and allow me some time to try to come up with the money.

I then spoke to my father, and he encouraged me to pursue it. I began to think of ways I could raise the cash to buy the house. I asked my grandmother if I could pay her in monthly installments. She mentioned that it would be an inconvenience for her because she needed the money upfront to pay some bills. So that option was off the table.

I brought it up to my brother Danny to get his take on it. After brainstorming for a bit, we decided to make a cold call to a realtor we had seen in an advertisement to ask if he had any advice. On the phone, I gave him the rundown. When I told him I could purchase the house for only $60,000 and was looking for a loan, he was surprised. He asked if I would consider selling the home, because he had an investor who might be interested in purchasing it from me for much more than $60,000. I told him I was open to that possibility. He reiterated that he could make me quite a bit of money from the sale of the home. In fact, if his investor was interested, and assuming I had an executed contract. I wouldn't even need to come up with the money to purchase the home, because we could simply assign the contract to the investor. I was familiar with this concept since I had learned about it in real estate school. And with no other realtor involved in this transaction, he could charge a reduced commission of 3% instead of the industry standard 6%. That would be his fee for putting the transaction together. That sounded fair, so I asked him to speak to his investor and get back to me.

The realtor called me back not long after our initial conversation. He playfully suggested that I sit down before hearing his offer to purchase the home. "Is it a good offer?" I asked. "Better than good," he replied. He said his investor was willing to pay $139,000 in cash for that house. I couldn't believe it. I quickly agreed to sell him the house for that amount. I told my grandmother about the deal. She was as surprised as I was and only asked that I give her an extra $5,000, considering how much I'd be making from the transaction. I thought that was generous of her and agreed. I then had the realtor prepare a contract between my grandmother and me for $65,000; then, I assigned my right to purchase the property to the investor for $139,000. The transaction was over in just a few weeks. I made $69,830 without investing even one penny. All I did was make a few phone calls. As a thank you, I gave Danny $10,000 for helping me.

It was quite an achievement. Before that transaction, my savings account balance was $16,007.27. That was every penny I had. I had saved money from mango sales, candy sales, birthdays, Christmases, and most of my paychecks. After depositing the check from the sale of the house, I remember calling the bank again and again, just so I could hear the automated voice announce my account balance. Each time, I followed the prompts and entered my account information. I had done it so many times; I memorized my 11 digit account number. After successfully inputting my information, the first option was, "*Press 1 to hear your account balance.*" I dial 1. The automated voice very slowly dripped out the words one at a time. "*Your account balance is now, Seventy...Five... Thousand ...and... Eight... Hundred...Dollars ...and ...Twenty... Seven...Cents.*" It never got old! I could've listened to that recording a thousand times. I probably did. It was captivating. Truly, a wonderful experience. Apparently not all magic was performed by a magician using sleight of hand. Sometimes, we can create magical experiences for ourselves.

Here's the breakdown:

The purchase price for the house was originally $60,000.

Plus, an extra $5,000 I agreed to give to Grandma.

My cost was = $65,000.

I assigned the contract and sold the house for $139,000.

Paid the realtor a commission of 3% = $4,170.

$134,830 – $65,000 = $69,830. Profit.

$69,830 – $10,000 I gifted Danny = **$59,830.**

I quickly used the majority of the profits made from this transaction to buy my first income-producing rental property, a warehouse. It helped create a steady stream of income, which I still enjoy to this day.

Note: A real estate assignment contract is a wholesale strategy used by real estate investors to facilitate the sale of a property between an owner and an end buyer. That means the person in possession of the contract can assign their rights to buy the house to another buyer.

Reflection Point 4

Stay true to yourself. Running with the pack isn't always the best way to get ahead in life. We are not all on the same journey, so it's important for each of us to do what feels right for ourselves.

If you truly want something, you can find a way to achieve it. You don't need to have it all figured out from the onset; just give it your best effort. Explore the resources available to you to find creative solutions.

Is there a situation, person or environment that leads you to continually compromise on what you feel is right for you?

_____

_____

_____

_____

How will things be different next time around?

_____

_____

_____

_____

Chapter 5:

Sensing Opportunity

It was a hot, dull Saturday afternoon at *Local Propane*. A man walked in and asked me to fill some BBQ tanks. That wasn't unusual. It was basically 50% of my job description, it was that and answering phones. I walked outside to his Ford Sport Trac pickup truck and found 10 BBQ tanks. Now, that was unusual. Most customers only came with one or two tanks. "Wow! That's a lot of tanks!" I said. "Yeah, we do a lot of grilling at the hotel," he responded. I proceeded to help him unload the empty BBQ tanks and fill them with propane, one at a time, taking about 25–30 minutes. Once finished, I helped him load the now-much-heavier tanks back in his truck; then, I asked him to join me inside so I could charge him for the refills. As I was handing him his receipt, he asked, "Hey, do you guys deliver these things?" I laughed and shook my head. "Sorry man, nobody delivers these; they're too cheap to refill, so we can't make any money delivering them," I replied. "That's a shame; bringing them here is a pain in the neck," he said. He paid for his propane refills and went on his way.

The following week, the same man returned to Local Propane; again, with an impressive 10 empty BBQ tanks. We had a conversation that was almost identical to the one the week before, only this time it was a little different. He suggested that I fill and deliver 10 full BBQ tanks to him at the hotel. He would then give me his empty tanks in exchange. That way, he wouldn't have to drive to the fill station I worked at and refill them himself. I'd be saving him the trip which would be very convenient for him, but not for me. It made sense but sounded like a lot of work on my part, with no added benefit to me, a/k/a money in my pocket. I think his name was Jose, but honestly, I can't remember. "We don't do that," I said.

"Please, I'll pay extra," he pleaded to me. "Do you always use 10 tanks a week?" I asked. "Yes," Jose replied. "Where to?" I asked. "The Victoria Hotel in Miami Beach," he replied. I didn't even know how to get there, but I presumed I could drive there within 20–25 minutes. I had a rough idea of how far away Miami Beach was from my job. I did some quick math in my mind and made him an offer. "I'll do it for $15 a tank, 10 tanks minimum," I said. I figured I could buy the propane at full retail, which was $10 a tank, and then sell them to Jose for $15 each. If he committed to a 10-tank minimum, I'd make a quick $50, which was almost a day's pay. "No way! That's too much money. How about $12?" he proposed. "I'm sorry, man; I can't do it for less than that. I don't think anyone would drive that far to make 20 bucks." I said. I could see the disappointment on his face. His shoulders noticeably slumped forward as he began to walk back toward his truck. He looked defeated. *Strange*, I thought. *What's the big deal?*

The next Saturday, Jose arrived at my job for the third time. "Fine!" he said as he came walking through the entrance door. "I'm tired of bringing these BBQ tanks over here. I'm willing to pay you the $15 a tank to deliver them." He smirked. We both laughed. After refilling his propane tanks, we exchanged information. Considering his consistent use of 10 BBQ tanks a week, we confirmed plans for me to make his first delivery the upcoming Saturday. I was to pick up his 10 empty BBQ tanks at the Victoria Hotel, where he worked and replace them with 10 refilled BBQ tanks. That would alleviate Jose having to bring the tanks in for a refill, and I would make $50 for the delivery. We both win. I wouldn't need to return for my tanks because he'd be giving me the empties he had. Simply put, I was exchanging empty BBQ tanks for full ones.

Overly excited, I called my father the moment Jose left. "Dad! Guess what? I have a guy who's going to pay me to deliver BBQ tanks to him. I need to borrow some tanks from you to do the delivery in South Beach.

I'm going to exchange refilled BBQ tanks for his empty ones and charge him $15 a tank. I'll pay you full price for the gas, $10, and earn $50 just for making the delivery." "That's great, Max! Look around the yard and see if we even have 10 BBQ tanks." He chuckled. I looked around his shop and barely came up with the 10 tanks. Most of them had been outside for quite a while; covered in dirt and a tad bit rusty from being left out in the rain. I washed them all one at a time, wiped them down, and added touch-up paint to any tanks that needed it.

The following week, the call came to my cell phone. It was Jose. I took down some details and was excited to embark on my first delivery. I then asked my father for directions to the beach. He photocopied a page out of a map book and handed it to me, along with some verbal instructions. I was a little intimidated because I was bad with directions (what I would've given for Google Maps or an iPhone back then). Nevertheless, I set forth to make my first delivery.

Once I arrived at the hotel, I was instructed by the valet as to where the empty tanks were, which was also where I needed to leave the full ones. I quickly learned why Jose found it to be such a *pain in the neck* to transport these things. Now it all made sense. He was carrying two tanks at a time, through an unpaved alley from Collins Avenue, where the hotel parking was, all the way to the sand on Miami Beach, where the hotel's BBQ grill was (about two city blocks each way). Each BBQ tank weighed approximately 37 pounds when full and 17 pounds when empty. So, he was carrying roughly 74 pounds one way and 34 pounds the other way, making five separate trips. Altogether, he was lugging approximately 1,080 pounds, over a two-mile distance. Not to mention the time it took him to drive to my filling station and back. When it was all done, it took me about 40 minutes to unload and complete the delivery. My shoulders were on fire. *$15 a tank was a gift!* I thought. *I should've charged him more!*

Pleased with his new delivery service, Jose handed me a check. "I'll see you next week," he said. "Yeah, sure!" I replied. Once I got back to work, I asked my dad to cash the check for me, keep his $100 and, to please give me the $50 I had earned from making the delivery. "No, Son, keep it. That was a great idea!" he said. "What do you mean?" I asked. "You saw an opportunity and took initiative. Keep the whole $150. Here," he said, as he handed me the $150 in cash. "I wouldn't feel right doing that, Dad. He's technically your customer, and you'd be losing money. I can't do that." I said. "Okay, so just pay me for the propane you used," he said. "How much is that?" I asked. "Each BBQ tank holds four gallons of propane; multiply that by 40 cents a gallon, which is what I pay for the propane, and it comes out to $1.60 a tank. Multiply that times the 10 tanks you exchanged, and you owe me $16," he explained. "Whoa! That's it? I only owe you $16!" I exclaimed. "That's right," he replied. I thought about it for a second. "It's still not fair; I still want you to make money, Dad. This isn't a good deal for you." I said. "Okay, I have some commercial accounts that pay as little as 10 cents over my cost per gallon. How about that? I'll charge you the same rate. 50 cents a gallon of propane. That way I make something, and we both make money," he said. "Deal!" I handed him back a $20 bill.

It wasn't the most marvelous deal for him, but it was fair. I was delighted. *Wow! I just made $130 in about an hour and a half* (minus gasoline and my time, of course). *That's almost two days of pay!* My mind began to race. *Who else could use this kind of service?* I thought to myself. *Could there be other people out there like Jose? If I could deliver just 10 tanks a day, I would be making $500 a week!* That's what my mom was making at the time as a travel agent. So, it felt like a significant amount for me.

Later that night, while having dinner at our studio apartment, I shared my triumphs with my girlfriend, Jessica. She was excited for me. I casually mentioned I could turn this into a business. She loved the idea. The imaginary gears in my head were turning. That night before bed, I began to write down all my ideas in a college ruled notebook. I started to design a logo, a smiling BBQ tank on wheels, suggesting rapid delivery. I also came up with a name, *Speedy Tanks 2 You*. I was essentially putting together, without knowing it, a business plan. After about an hour of brainstorming, I closed the notebook, gave Jessica a kiss goodnight, turned off the lights, and went to bed. In that quiet and dark room, almost as soon as I closed my eyes, thoughts and images began rushing through my brain. My mind had become flooded with almost endless insights and possibilities. It was almost as if I could achieve a higher state of consciousness once the lights were off. I had to write these ideas down. I

jumped up, turned the lights back on, and began to write. After jotting down several revelations, I turned the lights off again. But it felt as if every time I laid back down, I'd have a new idea; so, I'd sit up and turn the lights back on again to continue writing. This happened repeatedly. Needless to say, I don't think Jessica got much sleep that night.

A couple of weeks had passed, and I had made three more deliveries to Jose. His consistent orders reassured my conviction about the potential of this service. I'd often mention my business idea to Jessica, but I hadn't done anything about it. I just talked about it. Then one day, she finally looked at me and asked, "Why don't you just do it? Why don't you just start the business and stop talking about it? Go make a business card." *A business card?* I hadn't thought of that. I grabbed my notebook and immediately began designing my first business card. It was a bright orange card with *Speedy Tanks 2 You* written across the top. It had the same cartoon-style drawing of a propane tank on wheels, emphasizing a rapid delivery, along with my price of $13.99 plus tax. The next day I went to a local print shop and ordered 5,000 full-color business cards for just under $200. Charging $13.99 plus tax would allow me to cover the cost of refilling each BBQ tank with propane and leave me around $10 in profit on each exchange. I needed to deliver 10 tanks a day to make about $100 in profit and at the time, that was the outcome I hoped to achieve.

Although my little business venture with Jose proved to be lucrative, at that moment it seemed as if Jose was the only person in town grilling so often and in need of that much propane. I asked Jose if he knew of any other hotels in the area that could benefit from a service like mine, but he said he didn't know of any.

I know, I thought. *People grill at home. I can get regular people to use my service. Sure, going to someone's home for one tank is a lot of work for not much money, but it'll add up. I only need to deliver 10 a day.* After doing a little research, I decided to start marketing my services to the middle and upper- middle-class neighborhoods by sending the residents a flyer in the mail. I figured they'd have more disposable income, and a service like this might appeal to them. I also thought I might need a partner to help me cover more ground once orders began to come in. I made a short list of people I thought might be interested in working with me and who would also be good partners. Respectively, I asked my brother Danny, my good friend Sean, and my cousin Jacob to join me in my little business. All three of them turned me down, all for different reasons, and, actually, at the time, I couldn't blame them. It wasn't that appealing. I only had one customer, and even if I could adequately execute my little business plan, it would mean driving all over the city to make only $10 a pop. It didn't seem like much of an opportunity. Although I was a bit disillusioned by being turned down by three potential partners, I didn't let it discourage me. They didn't believe in my idea, but that didn't matter. The only thing that mattered was that I still believed in it and wanted to pursue it. Something told me I had to, regardless of whether anyone else thought it was a good idea.

I felt a need to take action and took initiative. I had a service that people needed to know about and 5,000 business cards, so I did what came naturally to me. I started handing out my business cards to every person I encountered, and I mean everyone. With it came a short elevator-style pitch on the service, the problem it solved, and why they should use it. "I deliver BBQ tanks straight to your door, same-day service on orders placed before noon. You won't have the inconvenience, or need to go out to exchange, or refill them anymore and, it's about the same price you would pay if you had to get it yourself." I told friends, friends' parents, friends of friends, family members, neighbors, strangers in line at the supermarket, people I met at the gas station while pumping gas into my truck, and random people just about everywhere I went. I left stacks of them at restaurants, hardware stores by the registers, and the BBQ section, of course. I would stuff my cards in the BBQs waiting to be sold and by all the grilling utensils. If I parked in a parking lot, I'd put one under the driver's-side windshield wiper on every car in that lot. It didn't take long before I handed most of them out. It made me happy to do so. I was proud to hold that card in my hand. I was in business for myself, by myself. I needed to make this happen. I had created something of my very own, and I truly felt it would work. I saw the need for it; I believed in it.

Most people seemed to like the idea, and some people began to call, but business was still off to a very slow start. I was mainly delivering to homes and sometimes to a few small businesses, hotdog cart vendors, and such. Often, they were completely across town from one another. Sometimes, I would deliver just one in an entire week, or even worse, none. Other times, I'd get lucky and exchange seven or eight tanks a week.

It was never steady or predictable and it certainly wasn't 10 tanks a day. I circled back with many of the people I had solicited, and just about all of them assured me they'd be using my service. *So, what's the problem? Why isn't the phone ringing?* Jose's orders, however, always stayed consistent. It became clear to me that I needed bigger customers. I needed volume. I needed to exchange 10 tanks a day, every day, to be making what I considered good money, that was my goal. Although I knew what I wanted, doubts started to set in. *Is Jose the only person using this many BBQ tanks? Is it ever going to pick up?*

Note: One thing I didn't know was that the average household refills a propane BBQ tank once every three months, on average. I would've needed approximately 900 residential accounts to hit my 10-tanks-a-day benchmark. I probably only had around 50 potential customers.

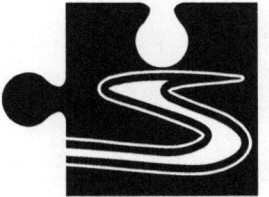

Reflection Point 5

You know what is best for you, better than anyone else does. Don't put your happiness or future in anyone else's hands. If you feel strongly about something, pursue it. If it doesn't pan out, at least you tried, and it was your choice, your decision. We rarely regret decisions we feel are right for us deep down inside. What we do regret are the opportunities we let pass us by. Jose's delivery was hard work, but I saw the potential opportunity and focused on the future. I was solving a problem, and it made me happy.

When forming a business relationship with someone, think long-term. It's important to consider the benefit or effects to all parties involved. I refused to take free propane from my father because I knew that the deal wouldn't benefit him. Not to mention, it likely would be short-lived. My considerate approach led to another opportunity when my father offered to sell me propane at 10 cents over his cost. That gave me the ability to purchase and sell as much propane as I wanted without a negative impact on him. On the contrary, he would now make money off me. Had I thought short-term and taken free propane, we would've never had that conversation. I paid for my candy; why wouldn't I pay for my propane?

Rest assured, when you follow your intuition, you're making the right decision.

Have you been ignoring a gut feeling?
If so, in what area of your life?

What's something your intuition has been trying to tell you?

Chapter 6:

Cold, Hard Cash

It was a chilly night in December, about three months since starting my little business venture, and I had agreed to go out with Jessica and some friends of ours for a drink. They wanted to go bar hopping on South Beach. Once we parked, we began walking down Ocean Drive, in an area commonly referred to as *The Strip*. It was cold (for Miami anyway) when I suddenly felt this intense wave of heat. "What is that?" I asked out loud. "It's a space heater," replied my friend Jeff. I had never seen one. It was about seven feet tall and shaped like a mushroom. Several were strategically placed by the dining tables outside to keep the customers warm while they ate. There must have been 20 of them there that night. I saw a bright orange and blue glow of flames at the top of the heaters and immediately became curious about what powered them. *Does it run on propane?* I wondered.

I knelt down and began to look for the power source. I lifted a metal shroud at the base, and there it was, a BBQ tank. My eyes opened wide, and I immediately sensed the opportunity. "I need to get this account!" I exclaimed. I reached for my wallet to pull out a business card, but I didn't have one. *What? How could I, of all people, not have a business card on me? Impossible!* I was anxious. I felt as if I was going to miss out on the opportunity. I wanted to give a business card to a waiter and explain my services, but how could I if I didn't have one? *What do I do now?* The desperation was setting in. *I can't just tell the waiter about my service. That would be unprofessional,* I thought. *If I don't have a card to hand him, he's probably just going to nod his head, say something polite, and walk away.* Jessica looked in her purse; she didn't have one either. I couldn't believe it. My friend Jeff began rifling through his wallet, and, as luck would have it, he had one. I guess the idea of handing out my business cards to everyone I knew paid dividends that night. I exhaled a huge sigh of relief.

"Thank God!" I exclaimed. I reached my arm over his shoulder and pulled him in for a hug. I continued, "You're a lifesaver, bro! Let's go find a waiter to give it to." My friend Jeff then insisted that we speak to a manager instead of a waiter. "Managers make the decisions, so don't waste your time with anyone else," he said. I agreed with him, although I instantly became extremely nervous. A part of me thought it was crazy, mainly because it was already past 10 p.m. and I didn't think a manager would be present or even want to speak to us. Thankfully, I was wrong. We went inside and were introduced to the manager at Oceanview restaurant, Gaston. He was well-dressed and speaking to a waiter in a thick French accent as I approached him. Once I had his full attention, I extended my right arm to shake his hand and then presented my business card with my left.

"Hello, my name is Max, and I work for a company that delivers propane BBQ tanks just like the ones you have outside for the space heaters," purposely omitting the fact that I was the owner. For some reason, I thought it was important that the company seem larger and more established. "*Vraiment?*" (Really?) he questioned in French. As he raised my business card to examine it, he slowly began reading it under his breath. "*Speedy Tanks 2 You*. BBQ Tanks Delivered to Your Home or Business for $13.99 plus tax. Delivered 7 Days a Week!" He then raised his voice and addressed me. "This is great," he responded enthusiastically. He was happy to meet me. "I've been using our company box truck to get our tanks refilled weekly in northeast Miami. What's your restaurant pricing?" he asked. "It would be the same low price that's on the card, $13.99 plus tax per tank," I confidently replied. He shook his head in disappointment. "I'm getting them filled for less," he noted. "How much are you paying?" I asked. "$12," he replied. "Well, how many tanks are you refilling each week?" I asked. He paused for a second, then said, "Uhm, around 70 a day when it's cold." I countered with a quizzical expression. I couldn't believe what I was hearing; I was sure he misspoke.

"You mean 70 a week?" I asked, confident that he made a mistake. "No, 70 a day between 3 restaurants I manage here," he confirmed.

My jaw must have visibly dropped. I could barely find anyone who used 10 tanks in a week, so the fact that the man standing in front of me was claiming to use 70 tanks in a day was mind-blowing. I never imagined that could happen. I could've easily matched his price and gotten his business, but before I could even think, my excitement got the best of me, and I blurted out, "I can do it for $10!" I later realized that I lowballed him, but I wanted to guarantee I'd get his business at that very moment. Thankfully, I knew my numbers and was confident the price I blurted out would leave me about $7 or $8 gross profit per tank. "Great!" he replied cheerfully as he continued in his thick accent. "I want to test your services; bring me 25 tanks tomorrow; if it goes well, I'll give your information to nine of my other restaurants." *What?! Nine other restaurants, like this one? There are more customers like this?* I contemplated. Had I crossed into an alternate dimension? I couldn't believe what he just said. It felt as if I had just heard someone call out the week's winning lottery numbers, and I was holding the winning ticket in my hand! I thanked Gaston for his time and assured him I'd return the following day to make his delivery. My friends and I carried on with our night out. Now we had a reason to rejoice. The celebratory drinks ensued.

The next day was Christmas Eve, and I was up early. I knew I needed to get my hands on 25 BBQ tanks, and I only had 10. I called my father, filled him in on the good news, and asked if he'd help me make the delivery. He agreed, of course. We managed to gather the 25 tanks we needed from various sources and filled them one by one. I meticulously hand washed and dried each tank. They had to be perfect. I nearly polished them. They were spotless. I found a pack of around 50 ridiculously small stickers, which were about 2 inches long while looking through a drawer for a marker. With a black Sharpie, I wrote my company name *Speedy Tanks 2 You*, along with my phone number on 25 of them.

I placed a sticker on each tank, perfectly centered. Looking back on it now, it was comical, but it was better than nothing. I wanted to make sure they knew whom to call for more tanks. We began loading the tanks into the bed of my 1998 Ford F-150 Flare-side pickup truck, but they didn't fit. We had to load some inside the cabin to transport them all. My father and I headed out to Miami Beach to make the delivery. We arrived at the restaurant on 10th and Ocean Drive; it was cold out. We began to unload the gleaming propane tanks onto the sidewalk. Under the on-duty manager's direction, a small army of waiters and busboys began to help us offload my truck. We formed a chain line; the full tanks went out; empty tanks came back. It was kind of hectic but also exciting, it all happened so fast. Once we finished exchanging the tanks, I went to the manager's office to collect the payment. I received the money in cash and went on my way. As soon as I got back in the truck, I began to do the math.

I charged the restaurant $10 for each tank exchanged and there were 25 tanks: That's $250. Then I needed to subtract my cost for the propane. Each tank held four gallons of propane, which cost me 50 cents a gallon. Four gallons multiplied by 50 cents a gallon = $2 worth of propane in each tank. $2 multiplied by the 25 tanks I filled came to $50 of cost. That's what I owed my father for the propane. I subtracted the $50 from the $250 I charged the restaurant and, *voila!* $200. *Wow! I just made $200!* My mind was off to the races again. Sure, I'd later need to consider my time, gasoline, tolls, sales tax, etc. But who cares? This was still huge. *What if he assigns me all his other restaurants? What if there are more people, and even more restaurants that need this service?* I was overflowing with excitement; my mind was flooded with optimism. *What could this become? What could it mean for me?* I dropped my father off and thanked him for helping me. I went to my room, grabbed all the business cards I had, and headed right back to Ocean Drive. I knew more restaurants had to be using these space heaters.

I parked my truck and walked up to every restaurant I could find that had space heaters outside. I met several managers and pitched them on the service, gaining several new clients. I wrote down all their information. If the managers were not in, I'd ask for their names and when they were expected to return and later circled back. With every new person I spoke to, I grew more excited. It seemed as if they were all interested. This opportunity was turning out to be greater than imagined. I then drove to Lincoln Road, which is another popular locale in Miami Beach, to try my luck there. The beach was packed with snowbirds from up north who came down south to enjoy the warmer climate. This was typical. All the restaurants were open, taking full advantage of the business to be had. I again stopped at every restaurant that had space heating outside. I wanted to get every account, and I told myself I wouldn't quit until I did.

I began working feverishly. On days it was extremely cold, I got swamped, working 12-to-16-hour days until all deliveries were completed. At times, it was so intense I needed Jessica's help to complete my deliveries. I made myself available to my customers 24 hours a day, 7 days a week, and wanted to create a reputation for that. My business grew rapidly in a brief time. I bought an abundance of propane tanks with the profits I made and then purchased another Ford F-150 pickup truck more suitable for work, with a larger bed that could transport more tanks. It had manual roll-down windows, manual door locks, and about 150,000 miles on it, but it only cost me $5,100. I was extremely busy on days it was cold, until March, when it became warm again, and my business came to a full stop. I went from often working all day long, whenever the weather cooperated, to having nothing to do. The restaurants didn't need heat in the summer, so they didn't need propane, and they didn't need my service. I would have to wait until the following year to sell to them again. After all my expenses and reinvestments into my little business, trucks, tanks, more cards, better stickers, and some paint to touch up worn-out tanks. I had made $32,000. I thought that was amazing, especially considering that I started unprepared and late in the season. Had I known, I could've begun in November. I had about three months of what we South Floridians consider winter. In addition, Miami's winters are inconsistent. Many days are quite warm, so I only had about 30 great days of work, when temperatures would drop into the 60s or below. I now had around 200 BBQ tanks of my own, two trucks, and an excellent reputation for service with all South Beach restaurants that use space heaters, and I was the guy they'd call next winter for their propane needs.

I spent the summer planning for the upcoming winter. I made flyers, bought even more tanks, and offered seasonal jobs to some of my high school friends; $65 a day to work with me next season. I was as prepared as I knew how to be. Even though it was now hot, and space heating was probably the last thing on their minds, I still went out and spoke to as many restaurant managers as I could. I wanted to ensure I would earn their business the following winter. As I'd explain my services to restaurant managers and their staffs, their reactions were generally positive, many expressed relief. I'd study their faces and body language as they read my business card, front and back. The majority of responses were consistent. Smirks, nods, and small grins would dominate their facial expressions, as if to say, *the solution has been right here this whole time. Why have I been going through all this trouble?* It was very satisfying to watch. They no longer had to be inconvenienced with having to solve this problem for themselves. The problem was solved; I was the solution.

Managers continually reassured me that they would be calling in the upcoming winter to service their accounts, and they did. I made sure to solidify myself in the restaurant community as the go-to vendor. Little did I know how important this positioning would be for my next big opportunity.

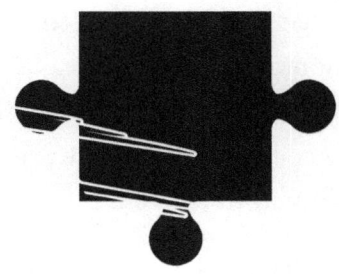

Reflection Point 6

Sometimes opportunities present themselves when you least expect them to. I went to South Beach to have a drink with my friends, not to get business. That night changed my life! Surround yourself with people who motivate you and encourage you. My friend Jeff not only had one of my business cards on him but motivated me to speak directly to the decision-maker. That's a lesson that has stuck with me ever since: Always speak to the decision-maker! He encouraged me to grow at that very moment. Had I not been with Jeff that night, things could've gone much differently.

Know your numbers! Because I knew my cost, I was able to quote the restaurant manager on the spot and make a deal.

No matter the day, the time, or the obstacle that stands before you, if you want something, you need to go for it! I know plenty of people who would've made excuses not to work on Christmas Eve and definitely wouldn't have spent the entire day trying to get accounts. I got every account I spoke to that day.

Be prepared. If you stay ready, you don't have to get ready! In the summer, the restaurants no longer needed my service, but I still pursued them with the same intensity. I wanted them to know that I existed and would be there for them when the time was right.

Who are the people in your life who motivate and encourage you?

How could you spend more time with them?

Chapter 7:

Bringing the Heat

The following winter was off to an impressive start, thanks to my preparation. The phone began ringing non-stop. I started doing deliveries at the very first sign of winter, which was in mid-November. On days it was cold, and whenever they could work, I would hire part-time help: my friends. With their support, it was a lot easier for me to service my customers. But getting their help was often challenging, because it's tough to predict the weather; hence, I couldn't get them on a set work schedule. As the calls would come in, I would take down the order details from the customer: name of the restaurant, address, number of tanks needed, and contact person; then, I would make a handwritten invoice on a receipt book, put that customer into a route sequence, and give roughly half of the workload to whoever was helping me that day. Generally, there was a route for Lincoln Road and a route for Ocean Drive. Although they are only about two miles apart, you didn't want to go out of your way and drive to Lincoln Road if you were doing deliveries on Ocean Drive, and vice versa. So, we would divide and conquer. One truck on Lincoln, one truck on Ocean. On days I had help, I was covering twice as much ground, much more efficiently.

I was servicing 40–60 restaurants. We were about halfway through the winter season and doing great. Ironically enough, while I was making a delivery at Oceanview restaurant, my first heater gas account and where I initially met the general manager, Gaston, the daytime manager Sophie approached me and asked if I knew where she might buy more of the space heaters they had. "Hey Max, I was wondering, do you guys sell space heaters?" she asked. "Yes, we do." I replied without any hesitation. "How many do you need?" I asked. "We need eight of them," she replied. "I'll get you a quote," I said. I walked up to one of the heaters she had and casually inspected it. I memorized the brand name and model number and hurried back to my truck. I kept repeating the information to myself, so I wouldn't forget it. *Endless Warmth…Model 372620… Endless Warmth…Model 372620.* Once at my truck, I immediately wrote it down. *Endless Warmth Patio Heaters Model Number 372620.*

When I arrived back home, I urgently began to think of how I might contact the company. I decided I would call the operator: just by dialing "0" and asking for the company's phone number. (Writing that makes me feel old.) While not that long ago, it was still common practice to get information such as phone numbers and addresses this way. I didn't have a computer at the time or even know how to use one. I didn't have an iPhone either. So, this was my course of action. I gave the operator the name of the business and asked her for its phone number. She gave me the phone number of the company. It was in California. I hung up with the operator and called the company right away. I told the gentleman who answered that I was a licensed propane distributor in South Florida (even though I wasn't). I mentioned that I was looking for wholesale pricing on space heaters to retail them to my customers. The gentleman was eager to help. He was upbeat and polite. I immediately heard him shuffle through paperwork as he muttered to himself. "Price list…Heaters…Oh, here it is!" he said. I couldn't believe he was giving me this information so easily. He hadn't even asked me for any credentials, which was a good thing because all I had was a business card. "$250 each drop-shipped to anywhere in the U.S., and they retail for $389.99. We give you 30 days to pay the invoice." he explained. I thanked him for the information and informed him I'd be calling back to place an order. I hung up and thought about what I would say to Sophie, the restaurant manager.

How could I incentivize her to buy? $389.99 Sounds like a lot of money to me, but maybe it's because I know I could get them for $250. I continued to think it over, *I guess I'll tell her the retail price of $389.99 and then offer* *her a minor discount before she might ask for one. I'll convey that I could apply a discount because she was an existing customer and was buying eight of them at once. That way, she'd feel appreciated and know she was getting a good deal. I liked this approach. Her special price would be $349.99. Maybe that'll incentivize her to buy.* At that price, I would make about $100 on every heater she purchased. If she ordered all eight heaters, I would roughly make $800 with minimal effort. The heaters would be drop-shipped directly to the restaurant, and all I would have to do is pick up a check, make a payment to the supplier for what was owed, and keep the difference. I quickly decided that this was going to be my strategy. I then called Sophie, told her the price, explained the discount, and informed her I'd only need a 50% deposit to place the order. "Perfect, thank you for the discount. Come by my office tomorrow, and I'll have a check ready for you to pick up," she replied.

I couldn't believe it. With just a few phone calls, I managed to make $800. I saw this as an opportunity to make more money and grow my business. I wanted everyone to know I now sold these premium, high-quality space heaters at a discount. I designed and mailed a flyer to every restaurant in Miami Beach, current customers, and non-customers. To reinforce that, I even went as far as hand-delivering one to every propane customer I delt with. This helped me make more money by selling space heaters to my existing accounts, and when I sold them more heaters, they used even more propane. It further multiplied my business by giving me the opportunity to open several new accounts. Most restaurant managers didn't know where to buy them, and once I pointed out that people weren't dining outside at the restaurants that didn't have them, I didn't need to say much else. It was an easy sale. Adding to that, if I sold some space heaters to a restaurant that didn't have them, they'd need a propane supplier, right? This was a home run.

Note: I went on to sell dozens, then hundreds, then thousands, of these space heaters. Fast forward a couple years in, and I remember speaking to the same representative I placed my first order with, as we had developed a good rapport. I casually asked out of curiosity who was the largest distributor they had in all of Florida. To my surprise, he said, "Well…it's you. You buy more of these in Florida than anyone else." He said it as if it was obvious. I was shocked. After we hung up, I took a moment to reflect. I couldn't believe I had come that far. I was so busy working and growing the company I didn't realize how much I had accomplished.

After the end of my second winter, I had managed to make around $180,000 exchanging BBQ tanks for my seasonal winter customers in South Beach. To me, this was another monumental achievement. Without question, it was the most money I had ever made, and in a relatively short time. It had only been a bit over a year since I struggled to make just $100 a day. During this busy winter season, there were several times that I would make over $3,000 profit in a single day. While I pondered on that, it amazed me how much I could accomplish, using not much more than my imagination and a burning desire to prosper. I thought that was remarkable. I had never put this much energy into anything before. The results were proof that I was being rewarded for doing so. I received money in an equal exchange of my energy, creativity, and faith.

This second, much more profitable winter gave me hope. I had continuing aspirations of this becoming what I referred to as a real business. Although I had made a good amount of money, the fact that it was only seasonal income left me unsettled. It gave me thoughts of doubt and uncertainty. *What if it doesn't get cold next year? I would have no business, no income. I can't depend on it getting cold a few months a year to have a legitimate business, especially in Miami.* I thought. I needed to solidify the success of this thing but still didn't know how I was going to do it. In addition, the long hours and lack of sleep made it painfully clear that, even when things were great, the business needed more structure. I tried partnering with my brother Danny during the busy season, but ultimately it didn't work out. We had different approaches to business, which led to several arguments. We decided the partnership wasn't going to work. He continued working with my father at Local Propane, and I remained on my quest.

I needed full-time employees, better equipment, bigger, more specialized trucks, more tanks, and my own location to have an office and store my equipment. At the time, I was still using my truck as my office. With not much more than a cell phone, some propane tanks, and a receipt book, I was essentially, a one-man show. I was the receptionist, the salesman, the manager, the router, the delivery driver, the tank filler, and any other job title required of me. I was occupying a small space at Local Propane, rent- free. I had become a good customer for them. I kept my mind focused on the future. I saved every penny I earned. I knew I would inevitably need it. Whenever there was work, I would work, by any means necessary. It didn't matter the day or the time. If it was freezing cold and extremely busy or warm and business was scarce, it all felt the same to me. I wasn't doing it for the money, really; I just loved what I was doing.

My typical hours of operation ranged anywhere between 6 a.m. to 11 p.m. Whether it was Saturday, Sunday, Mother's Day, Father's Day, Christmas Day, New Year's Day, Thanksgiving Day, Valentine's Day, Labor Day, Veterans Day, Memorial Day, someone's birthday, special occasion day, any day. It was all the same to me. It was a workday. Work came first. The business came first. No matter what, no exceptions. I valued this opportunity immensely and I didn't want to risk losing it. I kept full propane tanks in my truck at all times. My cell phone remained the business line. If a customer would call me at 10 p.m. on a Saturday, which they often did, I'd immediately stop what I was doing, get in my truck and head straight to the customer to complete the delivery. I never turned them down or gave excuses for why I couldn't provide service, even when they called after hours. It wasn't the most efficient system, but it's what I knew how to do. Get it done. At no point did I ever take my customers for granted. I knew no one could compete with the quality of service I was providing, but I still didn't want to risk them getting their tanks filled somewhere else. I wanted them to count on me. It was exhausting, but at the same time invigorating. While most of my friends were out partying, getting drunk, and doing all kinds of fun stuff I definitely wanted to participate in, I was investing. I was a slave to the business, but I was also a student of it. I learned from it every day. It was rewarding and filled my soul. It was a different kind of fun.

After the winter season, I had nothing to do. So, I concentrated on expanding in other areas related to propane. I began to research and think of ideas. *Who else could benefit from this propane exchange type of service?* I had taken note of some large propane companies that were doing "Forklift Tank exchanges." These tanks were used to fuel forklifts, which are mainly used in warehouses and loading docks to carry and move things such as cargo, merchandise, and produce. It was the same product, propane, just in a different tank, one that held twice as much propane, eight gallons instead of four, and was used as motor fuel to power the forklift's engine, instead of being used for heating or cooking like the BBQ tanks.

As I began to research and become more familiar with the concept, I discovered a sizeable need for it. This could very well be what I was looking for. So, I made a run at it. I bought about a dozen used forklift tanks, crunched some numbers, made a flyer, and tried my luck. It was hard. I applied the same strategy I had used previously at the beach. I walked door-to-door through many warehouse districts all over the county, trying to convince people to buy their forklift fuel from me. I quickly learned that this was no easy task. The market seemed impenetrable. This wasn't a new service for them. Several large propane suppliers would exchange or refill customers' forklift tanks on-site at their place of business. Companies had been buying and selling forklift fuel for many years before I came along. There was fierce competition for these accounts. I couldn't believe some of the prices these people were getting.

One company, in particular, appeared to be the most aggressive and had the majority of the customers. The name of that company was Stonewall Propane. How Stonewall was making any money with the prices its customers were paying was beyond my understanding. From my viewpoint, they were outrageous. Razor-thin margins, by my calculations. Most of his customers were paying pennies above cost. Sometimes, even below cost. *Maybe I should be buying my propane from him,* the thought crossed my mind. *How does he make money this way? What am I missing?* I was unquestionably stunned by this way of doing business. It was foreign to me.

Warehouse after warehouse, I kept seeing the same thing over and over: a yellow forklift tank with big red letters that read, STONEWALL. I quickly understood that whoever this Stonewall guy was, he had a stranglehold on the forklift market. I guess I just wasn't ready for this opportunity yet. Stonewall was living up to his name. I couldn't get past him. He was too big; the competition in forklift propane tank exchange was too intense. I didn't understand how I could make any money from it. I needed to search for a better opportunity — an opening. My time trying to earn forklift business didn't feel like it was well spent. After a few months, I stopped actively pursuing forklift accounts. There wasn't much progress. It seemed pointless. I only managed to get half a dozen accounts or so, none of which used that much propane. I scarcely profited from any of them. It was time to look else where for customers...

Reflection Point 7

If you can't do it alone, get some help. Refusing to hire staff when you need them is a great way to deteriorate your customer service, stunt your growth, and ultimately lose customers. Most small business owners don't want any more employees; you can add me to that list! Although, if adding an employee or employees will help you make more money and get more customers, that's an investment worth making. My one objective was to get as much business as possible. I was succeeding by solving as many issues as I could for my customers. Always put your customers first. Think about their needs, not yours. Even if I lacked the resources to accommodate their requests, I always would find a way to get it done. I didn't hesitate to tell Sophie I could get her some space heaters. I knew I could find space heaters; I just didn't know how. Figuring that out led to plenty of money and enormous growth for my small business.

When you plan for success, you're more likely to achieve it. I had planned to get as much of the winter business as I could, almost a year in advance. If I would have given up or lost focus while things were slow, I would've never reaped the benefits of this very profitable second season. What propelled me forward and made all the difference was my desire to put in old-fashioned hard work.

I know of no universal strategy for success. I used the same, highly effective, door-to-door strategy trying to earn business exchanging forklift tanks as I had used in South Beach. The beach was wildly successful, but my attempt to get forklift exchange business was a complete flop. Applying the same strategy to a different type of customer was ineffective. Think things through independently. Furthermore, sometimes we need to shift gears and look for other, more profitable areas of opportunity. Timing is everything. Not now does not mean not ever!

Are you giving up at the first sign of an obstacle
in a particular area of your life?
How could you become a part of the solution?

What steps are you taking right now to ensure a better future?

What else can you do?

Chapter 8:

Mr. Reed

One of my high school friends, Tommy, heard that I was exchanging BBQ tanks for people at their homes during the summer. He asked if I was interested in passing by his father's business, where he also worked, to give him a quote on exchanging some tanks. His father owned a Shell gas station in South Miami, not far from where we grew up. He had a display cage outside of his store filled with propane tanks for customers to exchange their empty tanks for filled ones. I knew about these display cages, but I never made the correlation between their service and mine. *Hello? It's the same product! Why haven't I thought of this?* It reminded me of Biff Tannen in Back to the Future, when he's knocking on Marty's head saying, "Hello, Hello, anybody home? Think McFly! THINK!" I guess I never saw myself as being able to get accounts like these. Maybe, I subconsciously told myself doing business at that level was beyond my reach? It could have been why my mind filtered them out, and they weren't important to me. I automatically categorized them as background. Well, from this day forward, they would become foreground. This is the opening I had been looking for.

Tommy's father wasn't there when I arrived, but Tommy was. He explained what he knew about the retail BBQ exchange business. He said the company that serviced them provided the display cage and all the tanks in it. The cage he had in front of his store held 12 BBQ tanks. Tommy would pay a wholesale price to the distributor for the tanks and resell them to the end users at a higher price to turn a profit. It was an added convenience to their customers, and Tommy's gas station made money from it; that was the appeal. The distributor would visit them about every two or three weeks to swap out the dirty, empty tanks customers had brought in to exchange and replace them with clean, filled tanks. Tommy indicated they would swap out around six to eight tanks each time they refilled the display cage. The distributor then would bill Tommy for whatever they exchanged. Sound familiar? The company that serviced them was called Atlas Propane. They specialized in retail BBQ tank exchange. I knew nothing about them.

Note: I later learned that Atlas Propane was well known and trailblazers in the industry, particularly in this business model. They didn't invent it, but they were well-established. They also happened to be the largest independent retail BBQ tank exchange distributor in the state of Florida at the time.

I assumed Tommy was getting a great price from the supplier, and it was going to be tough to compete with them. After educating me, Tommy handed over his most recent invoice from Atlas Propane. I looked it over, and to my surprise, he was paying a whopping $14 a tank! I was in disbelief. This was truly unbelievable. If I could sell him these tanks at $14, with my cost at the time being only $2 to fill each tank, I would have a gross profit of $12 a tank. That's a healthy margin. I couldn't believe it. I took a moment to let it sink in. *$14 a tank? Seriously? That's a lot more than what I'm charging the restaurants*. I was overrun with optimism! To top it off, Tommy was reselling each tank for $22.99. We both make money, and the customers get what they want. Everybody wins. I instantly fell in love with this concept. This was the opportunity I was waiting for; I needed to get accounts like these; if I did, I would no longer be a seasonal business. I would be solidified year-round. Stable. Confirmed. Legit.

I learned from Tommy that he needed to obtain a resale license and provide proof of insurance to the state of Florida to resell propane gas to the public. Truthfully, my license and insurance still weren't in order at the time. To save money on insurance and other expenses that came with opening my own business, I was ill advised to open *Speedy Tanks 2 You* as a DBA of my father's company, Local Propane, and not my own corporation. The intention was to disassociate myself from them while providing me a risk-free trial period to test my own, independently run concept. It was like putting training wheels on a child's bicycle. I wasn't paying Local Propane for anything other than the propane gas I bought from them. I kept 100% of my profits. I was assured that this would be the most cost-effective approach until I was certain I wanted to take on the expenses that came with owning my own corporation. If proven successful, I would then formalize my own entity. That's when the training wheels would come off. (This was horrible advice and ultimately a huge mistake.) I was flying under the radar and being cheap. I didn't have my own proprietary insurance or resale license, but I benefited from their legitimate corporate structure. My corporate status was nebulous. This frugal approach ended up costing me a lot of money in the future. You will learn about that later. (Know, for now, that this was not the proper use of a DBA.)

The meeting with Tommy made it all too clear that I needed to address this ongoing concern. I was a little out of my depth, so I expressed to Tommy I would get back to him. The last thing I wanted to do was overpromise and underdeliver. I thought to myself, *this will be simple. I would:*

1st. *Open my own, separate corporation.*

2nd. *Apply for the license.*

3rd. *Get independently insured.*

4th. *Celebrate, because I would have my first account!*

I would have it all hammered out within a week. It's just as easy as that, right? Wrong! Before opening my own corporation, I decided to call the state of Florida and gather as much information as possible. I was informed that this wasn't going to be so easy. The onslaught of requirements at the time was intimidating, to say the least. I was a negligible business with little experience and no credit. The state of Florida required me to provide $1 million of insurance coverage for my business, in the event of an accident. Along with an additionally insured certificate of $1 million of insurance coverage for Tommy's gas station and anywhere else I might be retailing propane to the public. That meant I would need one of these certificates for every single account I might get in the future.

I began calling insurance companies, every insurance company in existence; at least that's what it felt like. At the time, I couldn't convince any one of them to take me seriously. The state's insurance requirement scared them. $1 million of general liability insurance coverage for my business and every account I opened. If I opened 10 accounts, that would mean I needed $10 million of insurance coverage. If I opened 100 accounts, I would need $100 million of coverage! That's alarming. Insurance companies couldn't see past that. They couldn't underwrite it, or at least they didn't want to. They didn't want to expose themselves to that amount of liability. In that respect, I didn't blame them. They were probably envisioning shelling out tens of millions of dollars after some kid makes a completely avoidable mistake and blows up an entire city block. It was very safe, in all reality, but people heard the word propane and there was an immediate sense of trepidation. Now add to that, 22 years old, $1 million per location, multiple locations. And the response from the insurance company would most likely be, "No thanks!" This made it nearly impossible to even get one retailer.

At that point, it seemed I was left with only one option: I would need to convince every retailer to add an additional $1 million of insurance coverage to their existing policy. That would result in their insurance premium increasing anywhere from $600 to $2,500 a year, on average, depending on their provider. I phoned Tommy and a few other prospective retailers and explained the requirements to them. To no surprise, none of them were willing to add the extra coverage, understandably. If I were a gas station owner being presented that information, I wouldn't sign up for it either. It was confusing, hassles they didn't need. I understood their hesitation. It was too much friction and a lot to explain. Not sexy. Not an easy sale. I needed to make this effortless, a no-brainer, almost risk-free if that were possible. But how?

I continued to search for options and insurance companies, because I was determined to make this happen. In the interim, I was able to find a company that sold the display cages to house the BBQ tanks, similar to the ones Atlas Propane had, but, in my opinion, better. They were priced at around $450 each. They were painted white and held 20 BBQ tanks instead of only 12. I thought this was great because if the retailers had almost double the inventory, they would require deliveries less often, which would result in fewer trips to refill their cages once empty. It seemed much more efficient. I would exchange more tanks and make fewer deliveries. They were much better than Atlas Propane's 12-tank display cage. The company that manufactured the cages was based in Alabama. I placed an order for just two of them; I guess that was my version of dipping my toes in the water to check the temperature before jumping into the deep end. I was naturally still somewhat hesitant. Although I couldn't do much with only two, I was setting the tone for expectancy. I would be licensed and insured someday. Having them would do me good. They would be a constant reminder of what I was attempting to do. They would motivate me to see this through.

Despite my being eager and confident of finding a resolution, the display cages didn't see much action. All in all, my ignorance pushed me back almost a year. No luck getting insured; it was a tough time for me. Without insurance, I was stuck. I hit a roadblock. How was Atlas Propane doing it? At that moment, I didn't know how to go about overcoming this challenge. It was just something I couldn't understand. Those two white display cages I ordered sat so long they turned gray from dust accumulation. It was humiliating. To make things worse, Tommy sold his gas station. Now I couldn't even get him as a customer. I started to feel I had no chance at success. After some time, my enthusiasm began to wane. I felt hopeless.

Right before I was ready to admit defeat, I caught a lucky break. A young lady I had previously spoken to in the state licensing department called me. She knew from my many conversations with her that I was looking for an insurance company. She recommended I call a Mr. Reed at Miller & Reed Insurance Agency. I did. I explained to him what I was looking to do and how each retail location I would put a display cage at would need $1 million of insurance coverage, respectively. As luck would have it, Mr. Reed was familiar with Local Propane and expressed interest in earning my father's business. I mentioned I could facilitate an introduction to aid him. This helped my case. I was able to use that as leverage, a carrot, if you will. He also knew of other propane businesses that were providing this type of service up north. He was familiar with the concept, not scared of it. Mr. Reed inevitably agreed to write me a policy. Finally! I couldn't believe someone said yes. I was so accustomed to getting rejected; I would almost look forward to it so I could hang up the phone sooner and not get my hopes up. But not this time. I broke through. I was talking to the right guy. I finally found a yes in a sea of no's. Someone who understood the business and was willing to take a chance on me.

Mr. Reed quoted me a very reasonable $200 a year for every $1 million additional insured certificate required by the state. This would enable me to comply with Florida's requirements every time a gas station or supermarket agreed to retail my propane. The way I looked at it, if I could get good accounts, the income I would make from the retailers would offset the insurance expense at the end of the year. Either way, I couldn't complain; he was putting me in business.

I was elated and, at the same time, totally nauseous. I was a ball of nerves, but in the best, most exciting way. The obstruction, which had become my everyday reality, was now gone. It was clear skies ahead. There was no longer a reason or excuse for me not to succeed. No more roadblocks. This giant barrier was coming down. Life finally gave it up. Now, it was up to me to make this happen.

Note: DBA stands for "Doing Business As". You file a DBA registration when you want to conduct business under a name of your choosing. This action allows your company to legally operate under a trade name, also known as an "assumed" or "fictitious" name. For example, business owner "John Smith" might file the "Doing Business As" name "Smith Roofing."

The main benefit of filing a DBA registration is it will keep you in compliance with the law. For sole proprietors, a DBA allows them to use a typical business name without creating a formal legal entity (i.e., corporation or LLC, limited liability company).

Reflection Point 8

Keep the end result of what you want to achieve in the forefront of your mind and demonstrate confidence. Taking shortcuts can be costly and most likely will set you back in the future. Try to do things the right way, from the onset. It may not be as easy, but in the long run, you will be rewarded.

Find a way to make things effortless for your customers; put yourself in their shoes. What would sound appealing to you if you were them? Does it seem convenient or beneficial? How would you like to be treated?

Set a tone of expectation and always look for ways to improve. I knew where I could find and buy the same equipment as Atlas, but I want-ed something better, and I found it. Use whatever leverage you have available to you. I used Mr. Reed's desire to gain Local Propane's business to my advantage. That information became a bargaining chip to help me achieve my goal.

Where have you taken a shortcut that can eventually lead to a setback?

What can you do to correct it?

Chapter 9:

St. James

My friend Tommy had long ago since sold his Shell gas station, but I was in luck. I had another acquaintance, James, who owned a Chevron station. After having a quick call with him and giving an overview of what I was offering, I drove to his business. Upon arrival, I briefly described the concept and asked if he would be willing to become my first retailer. With little to no convincing, he agreed. He mentioned he needed to make a 30% margin on all the things he sold in his convenience store. For example, if he sold a pack of gum for $1, he made at least 30 cents from it. I hadn't done the math but assured him the margins would be there. I then suggested where I thought the BBQ exchange display cage in front of his store would look best. He liked my suggestion. With his permission, I filled out all the necessary licensing paperwork, requested an insurance certificate from Mr. Reed at the insurance agency, and mailed it in.

A few weeks later, I received a letter from the state, referencing James' license application. His gas station was now approved to resell propane tanks. A few short moments after reading the approval letter, I got out a water bucket, soap, and sponge and began to handwash the dust-covered display cages I had purchased almost a year ago. I wanted everything to be flawless.

After arriving at James' gas station, I proceeded to unload the display cage and BBQ tanks with the help of my brother, Danny. I alerted James of our arrival and asked him to come outside to explain the details of the exchange program. Although James was my only retailer and had no knowledge of Atlas Propane or their exchange program, my competitive nature wouldn't allow me to charge the same amount to exchange BBQ tanks as Atlas. I had to be better in every way from the onset — the clear, preferred choice. I explained what I knew of Atlas Propane's program in detail to James and what they charged their retailers. I then pointed out the benefits of my program in comparison to theirs. I wanted James to perceive the value. I decided to charge him $12 a tank and suggested he retail them to his customers for $19.99. That would make me a tidy profit and allow him to make around $8 from each exchange. This would be a 40% margin — much more than what he was looking for, so I had exceeded his expectations.

I continued to oversell it. I wanted to reassure him of his decision. I explained that if he exchanged just one BBQ tank for $19.99, he would basically be making $8 selling just one product, to just one customer. In comparison, this was far more profitable than selling a pack of gum for $1 and only making 30 cents. But that's not all. James also would benefit from the additional sales of items associated with grilling, such as ice and beer. Here's what I told him: "James, think about this for a second. You'd have to sell 26 packs of gum, probably to 26 different people, to make the same amount of money you'd make exchanging just one BBQ tank to one person. While those customers are here, you can upsell them by asking if they need ice or beer. They most likely will. Your gas station will now be a much more convenient place to shop. Propane is going to attract many people who were going somewhere else to buy these items. You're going to make a lot of money off this." He nodded in agreement. The look of contentment and excitement on his face confirmed that I didn't need to sell it anymore. He was hooked. At that moment, I decided to try my luck and squeeze in a little extra. Before handing him the invoice for the BBQ tanks, I wrote, *Licensing fee $100 a year, Insurance fee $200 a year*. If he refused to pay, it would have been my cost to bear, but I figured it was worth a shot. He accepted without any hesitation. I collected the money and told James I would be back in a couple of weeks to check on his inventory.

It had been less than a week since I set up my first retailer, James. Quite honestly, I hadn't given it much thought. I was most likely preoccupied preparing for the upcoming winter, and I didn't know what to expect. I guess I was in the *let's just see how it goes phase, set it, and forget it!* I was at work when my phone rang. It was James on the caller ID. I thought that was strange. *What could he want? Maybe I forgot to explain something to him?* I picked up. "Hey, what's up, James?" I asked. "Hey bud, whenever you have a chance, I need you to come by the station and refill my cage with full BBQ tanks, please," he said. "What do you mean?" I asked, confused. "Well, I already exchanged 10, and I don't want to run out." he replied. "You already exchanged 10? How?" I questioned. I was baffled. "You were right; a bunch of people came to exchange their BBQ tanks. They all filled their cars with gasoline while they were here, and I upsold ice and beer to most of them." I couldn't believe my sales pitch had worked! "I'll pass by today," I said. As I jumped in my F-150 and immediately made my way to James, I thought back on my conversation with my friend Tommy at his gas station. *Didn't he say he was selling six to eight tanks every two to three weeks? How is it possible James had sold 10 tanks in under seven days?*

When I arrived, I inspected his inventory and, sure enough, there were a bunch of older, dingy-looking tanks in the cage that I didn't recognize. Definitely not the hand-washed and pampered tanks I had left him a week ago. What a sight! It was a euphoric moment. It felt as if a ray of sunshine came gleaming down from heaven and cast its light right on me and those filthy BBQ tanks. Nothing could have been more beautiful to me at that moment. Nothing compared to the sight of those empty, greasy tanks. They were almost gilded; in my opinion, they were exquisite. I felt an overwhelming sense of joy. I couldn't contain myself. Dollar signs, growth, expansion, wealth, alarm sounds, flashing lights. It was all going off at the same time. This was it. I knew exactly what this meant. Opportunity! *10 tanks at one location in a week! In the dead of summer? This is insane. I would have been happy with 10 in a month!*

James had no marketing material, no advertising whatsoever; he didn't even offer BBQ tank exchange the week before this one. Yet, he exchanged 10 tanks in the middle of summer, in just one week. While I thought to myself, I stared into nothingness and let it register, *how is this possible? I wonder if the other gas stations sell this much propane? They have to! If I could go to one location and exchange 10 tanks a week, I could make a gross profit of around $100, from only one customer, making only one stop. Just one, one customer! This is colossal. Beyond that, even. It's light years better than driving all over town to different people's homes to exchange a single tank to make $10.* I continued thinking, *There are hundreds if not thousands of gas stations in South Florida, and this is just one of them! I need to do something, now!* I had an incredible sense of urgency flow through me. I scurried back to Local Propane and, with my brother's help, immediately began designing a sales flyer, specifically targeting gas stations.

My parents were divorced, so I called them separately to give them the great news. I called my father first and filled him in on this small but, in my eyes, symbolic victory. After filling him in on the details, I said, "Think of how many accounts I can get, Dad! This is going to be awesome!" He chuckled and encouraged me, "Good, go get them!" I called my mother right afterward at the travel agency where she was working and shared my plans with her as well. I explained why I thought the future of my company could be so bright. Being the playful mother she was, she also encouraged me to "Go for it, boy!" "I'm going to get every account in Miami!" I replied. I was happy to have their approval and vote of confidence.

Here's how I calculated my investment in setting James up as a retailer:

Display cage = $450

Empty BBQ tanks (retailer pays for the propane) = $400

Insurance (if I had to pay) = $200

State license (if I had to pay) = $100

A buffer for miscellaneous items such as stickers = $100

Approximate Investment per account total = ***$950–$1,250***

If I could exchange just 10 tanks a week at a $10 gross profit, I would make $100 a week from each account. Multiplying that times 52 weeks would mean I'd be making a potential profit of $5,200 a year. If I were able to acquire 100 accounts, I could potentially gross $520,000 in just one year!

After drawing up my plans on my trusty college ruled notebook. I decided that the training wheels were ready to come off. I had the money and now the reassurance that there was a bright future ahead. It was time for me to become fully independent. I needed to buy my own property to be self- sufficient, my own place to do business; store my propane tanks, trucks, and equipment, etc. So, I began looking at properties near my father's business and found a perfect fit for me. It was in my price range and not far from home. Around this time, my mother called and asked if I could meet her, my father, and my brother at my dad's office on Sunday morning, when his office was closed, to have a family meeting. I thought it was strange. We had never had such a meeting before. "Meeting? For what?" I asked. "You'll find out on Sunday when you get there; just be there by 10 a.m.," she said. "Okay, see you Sunday," I confirmed.

Reflection Point 9

There is always more than one option. Although Tommy sold his station, I quickly replaced him with James. I still was able to get a feel for the business by testing the waters with his gas station.

Presentation is key. You should take pride in your work and your appearance. Know what your competition is doing, but ultimately you should compete with yourself. What could you be doing better? I knew Atlas' pricing and program, so I improved wherever I could.

Don't be afraid to ask for things; you only can get what you have the courage to ask for. I took a chance when adding the license and insurance fee expenses to James' invoice, and it worked. I would have paid for that myself had I not mustered up the courage to go for it.

What closed doors in your life have led to better doors' opening?

Have you reached your full potential? What else are you capable of?

Chapter 10:

Family Reunion

Leading up to meeting Mr. Reed and acquiring insurance, my brother Danny had been upset that I wasn't independently licensed or insured. On more than one occasion, he indicated that I might be a liability to Local Propane, which he now was an unofficial partner of. Admittedly, I most likely was, in fact, a liability for them. However, I still didn't appreciate him regularly pointing that out and giving me grief about it. This led to quite a bit of controversy. It was a recurring theme for us. We would have pointless arguments, yell, and curse at each other.

Outside of work, my brother and I had a good relationship. I had previously contemplated involving Danny in my business and becoming partners with him before and during this business endeavor. It made sense to me. I wouldn't have to do all the work on my own. He was brilliant, maybe genius-level, and he knew a lot about propane gas, which I didn't. He also had a commercial driver's license, which I didn't have at the time and would need to haul around large quantities of propane gas, if this little business idea were to take off. In addition, and maybe the best reason of all, he was my brother. Who better than to share work and profits with? The unfortunate reality was, we didn't work well together. We're different people when it comes to business. Through several attempts, Danny and I tried to work together, only to end up with the same result, each time: arguments.

I decided early on, it would be best if we didn't work together. I treated my business as if it were my child; it was all I cared about, all I thought about. It had to succeed, no matter what. I would do anything, on any day, at any time, for my business, whether I was making money or not. It had become my passion. I guess I expected Danny to feel the same way about it as I did. He didn't. His priorities were different, and he had a family at home. He wasn't wrong, and I wasn't right.

But, to be on the same team, we would need to be aligned. We weren't. However, our mother still had hopes we would one day work together, so she devised a plan.

I arrived on Sunday morning at my father's office for the family meeting my mother had arranged. My father, brother, and my mother Josephine had all arrived before me. She thanked us all for coming and then directed her attention toward me. In her straightforward manner, she said, "The reason I asked you to come here is to see if you and your brother can work together." "What? What are you talking about, Mom?" I asked. "I think it makes perfect sense for you and your brother to partner up in this business together," she replied. I immediately retorted. "No, I'm not going down this road again, Josephine! (I would call her by her first name sometimes.) Listen, Danny's my brother and I love him, but we don't see eye to eye when it comes to business. I'm not doing this again." "I know, but your father and I spoke, and we both feel it doesn't make sense for you to do this on your own. You're going to spend all that money buying a property when we have more than enough space for you to run your business here. It would be better for you just to use this property, save all that money and focus on getting customers. You could be growing the businesses together. Plus, you guys are brothers." "No. I'm doing it on my own. End of story." I said. "Your father and I have an idea. Will you at least hear me out?" she asked. "Go ahead," I said as I crossed my arms in protest. Your father is willing to sign over 100% of Local Propane to you and Danny if the two of you agree to work together. You and Danny will be the owners and split the profits evenly," she said.

On the surface, and to some people, this could have appeared to have been a good deal for me, but I wasn't convinced. My father's business had more customers, more resources, and was larger than mine in proportion. He had a few employees, two propane bobtail trucks used to refill propane tanks at his customers' locations, and one service truck used to install propane gas lines. He owned the property where he parked his trucks, stored his equipment, and kept inventory. I, on the other hand, didn't have much more than my idea, some seasonal customers, very few assets, and the money I had made from my business, which was now around $220,000. However, despite resource comparisons, my business proved to be as profitable, if not more profitable, than his and appeared to have greater opportunities for growth, or at least that's how I saw it.

"I don't want anything to do with Local Propane. I'm honestly not interested in owning any part of it. I don't like it! It's the same product, but we have entirely different business models." I stated firmly. "What's the difference?" she asked. "Local Propane installs large propane tanks and propane gas lines at homes and businesses. The propane tanks he installs are used to power stoves, water heaters, dryers, pool heaters, and other utilities. After he installs them, he needs to drive a huge, slow truck with a massive propane tank on it, which holds about 3,000 gallons of propane to the customer to refill the propane tanks he previously installed. My company strictly exchanges BBQ tanks. It's that simple. I don't need any specialized equipment, knowledge, or huge, slow trucks to install propane gas lines in the blazing sun to obtain customers. Instead of driving around filling propane tanks on-site like Dad, I deliver the small tanks, already full. Not only is it faster, but I make more money. It's also less of a headache, and most important, it's not complicated," I replied. "And, as we already know, Danny and I don't get along well when it comes to business; I don't want to argue with him. I've been doing my own thing; I have my own money, I want to continue to make my own decisions, and I don't want anyone to get in the way or tell me how to run my company." I stood my ground. "Well, hold on, I think we have a solution for that. What if Danny and your father continue to run their business and you continue to run yours separately but under the same roof? No one will get in your way. At the end of the day, we'll be working together on the same team, one company. That way, we can all work together. I'm willing to quit my job to come work for you guys. I'll make sure to keep the peace between you and your brother." "What?! You and Dad have been divorced for like 15 years now and barely get along. This might even be the first time the four of us have been in the same room together. How do you plan on working alongside each other all day long, every day? Dad?" I questioned, as I turned my attention toward him. "Your mother and I have spoken about it, and I'm fine with her working here; I think it's a good idea," he said.

This wasn't just an old run-of-the-mill curveball they were throwing at me. This was a major league curveball! I was confused. It was quite a bit to consider; however, it was appealing to me in several ways. One: My family would be together, even if in a weird way. I had not experienced that before. Two: I'd avoid investing a large chunk of my money, probably all of it, to purchase my own property and buy equipment I'd need to become fully independent. Three: I wouldn't have to do this all by myself. I wanted my independence, but that doesn't mean I wasn't a little apprehensive and nervous. Four: I'd get partial ownership of their business. Five: I could immediately focus on growth and lastly, Six: I was getting the reassurance that I could run my business without the potential threat of arguing with Danny. I also had the guarantee that my mother would mediate if ever a problem were to arise. That had a certain appeal to it. It felt safe. Sure, I would need to share all my profits with them, but they were also willing to share their profits with me. And in all sincerity, the money was not as important to me as succeeding was. I just wanted to grow. I wanted to see my dream come true, I knew it was possible. I thought it over for a few moments.

"Okay, so whatever my company makes, and Dad's company makes would be split equally between the two of us, but we're running two completely separate businesses. How does that work?" I asked. "Yes, your company will be like a separate division. We can keep your DBA under Local Propane, and you won't have to get any extra licenses or insurance; it'll all fall under Local Propane. Which will eliminate any additional expense for you," she said. "I'm getting 50% ownership of everything Local Propane owns. The land, the business, and 50% of the profits? The company's going to be in my name and Danny's name but not Dad's? Why?" I asked. "Your father was planning on leaving Local Propane to you and your brother as part of your inheritance. He is getting older, and he also feels like it'd be a good idea for the two of you to work together. If you guys agree, he will transfer the ownership of his business to both of you now. That way, if anything would ever happen to him, it would all be done already. Think about it, it makes sense," she said.

I mulled it over again. "What about all the money I've spent investing in my business? I've bought tanks and trucks and spent a lot of time getting customers." I asked. "We can work it out so you get whatever you invested back before you have to share profits with your brother," she replied. I thought about it some more. "If I agree to this, no one is ever going to tell me what to do, ever, right?" I asked. "Yes. You have my word. That's the deal. You can run your business, and no one is going to interfere with it," she said. My father and Danny nodded in agreement. "And I wouldn't have to do anything for their side of the business at all, correct?" I added. "Correct. Danny and your father will run their own shop, and I'll answer phones and do office work for both brands," she replied.

I saw some value in this proposition; it began to grow on me. I went from being completely opposed to this offer to kind of liking it, even though, inherently, I didn't want to like it. I think, more than anything,

I wanted to know what it felt like to be a family. That may have been the biggest allure and motivating factor for me. I didn't want to be the one dividing my family again. My parents had done a bang-up job of that the first time around when they got divorced. That very well may have been what influenced me to make an emotional decision. Whatever the case was, I went for it. "Okay, I'm willing to give it a shot, but, if this doesn't work, I'm taking my things, and I'm outta here!" I said. "Okay, deal," my mother replied. She smiled and with her arms outstretched motioned for me to give her a hug. We embraced. She spoke softly in my ear: "Everything's going to work out just fine honey; you'll see. This is the American dream. We are all going to be working together under one roof. I love you, Maxie." Any noticeable tension in the room subsided. We sealed the deal with a family hug and began planning our roles for the future.

A few days had passed since I agreed to the partnership with my family. As promised, my mother quit her job. Danny and I were now destined to officially be business partners. To legalize our agreement, Danny hired an attorney to combine the assets of both businesses and document it. My tanks and trucks, plus their land and equipment, everything would be split equally. The document would need to state that Danny and I would own Local Propane and, consequently, *Speedy Tanks 2 You* in a 50/50 partnership, as agreed upon. He also would need to draft a new operating agreement.

The attorney asked for a meeting, which I wasn't a part of. I didn't give it much importance. I thought it was just a formality. In this meeting, it was suggested to Danny that one of the partners should have 51% ownership of the business and be a majority owner, to resolve any partnership disputes that may arise. Basically, whoever has 51% is ultimately in charge unless stated otherwise in an operating agreement. I was not made aware of that fact. The paperwork went on to state that Danny would be 51% owner and I would be 49% owner, the minority owner. Whether it was done purposely or in good faith, that's not what I signed up for. When the agreement was interpreted to me, I was under the impression that someone needed to have 51% and having a 50/50 partnership was simply not possible. And naturally, because Danny was the older sibling, it made more sense that he be the one to have 51%. It didn't seem like a big deal to me. After all, it was only 1%, right? I naively went along with it. I was a layman. I never sought my own legal advice because, honestly, I was dealing with family. I never questioned the fairness of any documents presented to me nor sought counsel from someone who may have known better. I felt that because we all had verbally agreed on our partnership, that is what would take place — nothing else. Well, I was wrong. Had I hired my own attorney and spent just $500 on a consultation, I might have been able to save myself a truckload of money and avoid plenty of heartaches for our entire family. I signed the documents without even giving them a second thought. I didn't realize what I had done. I never thought for a moment that those seemingly insignificant pieces of paper would come back to haunt me.

Reflection Point 10

This arrangement inevitably turned into a nightmare. Are you surprised? They say that when you mix family and business, it's a recipe for disaster. While I'm sure it's not always the case, that statement rang true for my family and me. Sometimes making decisions with your heart is the right way to go, but you should take your brain with you. Just because someone is close to you, whether it be a family member or a friend, it doesn't mean they're going to be great business partners. Quite often, it's the complete opposite. Even if your heart is in the right place, that doesn't mean it's all going to work out.

This deal wasn't necessarily the problem. It was the shareholders' agreement that I eventually signed that became the problem. It listed me as a minority shareholder. It also lacked clearly defined roles and deliverables from each partner. No one ever stopped to think and consider, *hey, you guys fight all the time; what if Mom can't keep the peace between you two?* Or *what if she does, but one day isn't around for some reason?* Both my parents had the best intentions for Danny and me, but they failed to realize the huge mistake they made. Danny and I would now be in a business partnership, knowing full well that we had a history of continually arguing about business. It was like being part of an arranged marriage, while certain that the person you are marrying isn't a good match for you but getting the reassurance that you'll be the benefactor of free marriage counseling. Not smart.

You should be a part of every discussion that involves you, your well-being, or your business interests. If you don't understand something, you should gain clarity on it. If necessary, hire your own attorney or get advice from a well-educated fiduciary. Seek full understanding before agreeing to anything and educate yourself to make an informed decision.

Does your paperwork show what you believe you agreed to?
Have you gotten proper legal advice?

What important documents should you personally review?

Chapter 11:

The New Kid on the Block

Our companies were now merged. Things were off to a good start and operating smoothly. I was running *Speedy Tanks 2 You* as I saw fit, mainly with the help of my mother, without being questioned or challenged in any way. I was making my own decisions and running my own shop. A proverbial line had been drawn in the sand, and it was being respected by everyone, as promised. Danny and my father continued to run Local Propane. I received assistance from them when I required it and now had the benefit of Local Propane's resources, which I hadn't freely had beforehand. In return, I shared all profits with them, as we had agreed.

After things settled down and we got into a routine, I asked Danny to help me design some eye-catching flyers to attract new business. The plan was to send them directly to our target audience, which were gas stations, hardware stores, supermarkets, pool-supply centers, and quick marts. I was able to do this by purchasing a list of all the businesses that fit those descriptions, in specific Zip Codes I had previously selected. I ordered the list through my girlfriend Jessica's mailing house. This was common practice, just as email lists are sold today. Once mailed, our flyer began yielding impressive results. On our flyer, we explained in detail how the BBQ tank exchange program worked and how they'd make money from it if they became retailers. We offered and guaranteed the best pricing on the market, seven-days-a-week service, and most notably, the ability to provide retailers with insurance for only $200 a year. Which, up until that time, had been the biggest hurdle. Now it was a no-brainer in the eyes of the consumer. Getting business was a lot easier. If I saw value in a retailer, I'd commonly offer to pay for their insurance myself as an added incentive, especially if we were taking over an existing, proven account from another supplier (i.e., Atlas Propane, Empire Gas, or Black Bull) This was appealing to me because I wouldn't have to wait for the account to mature, due to the fact that they already had obtained a license from the state and had a history of exchanging BBQ tanks. Taking over an account instead of opening a new one meant instant sales. It was a significant head start. Nonetheless, all of our retailers were provided with marketing material to help increase sales, such as large "PROPANE SOLD HERE" corrugated yard signs, and "PROPANE SOLD HERE" double-sided stickers to place near cash registers and entrance door handles. I knew everyone had to look toward the door handle to enter the convenience store, and, by placing it there, when they reached for the handle, they saw my sticker.

One after another, gas station and convenience store owners began to call about retailing propane BBQ tanks. Most were first-time retailers, but many of them were potential takeovers from Atlas Propane and the two other national players, Empire Gas and Black Bull. Each potential retailer received a personal visit from me and would be given a full-color, detailed brochure. I gave them all the same short sales pitch on how great this was going to be for their business and how much money they would make selling propane gas. I made my interactions with retailers as brief as possible because these people were busy. They didn't have all day to talk about this, or anything else, for that matter. They had businesses to run, and, frankly, so did I. I sensed that and adjusted. The easier I made it for them to decide they wanted to sell propane, the easier it would be for me to get accounts. I designed my sales routine to have the least possible amount of friction. I began noticing a pattern in the questions people would have. I wrote them all down and came up with the best-possible answers for each. In anticipation of the impending inquiry, I gave the answers to those most commonly asked questions before they'd even have a chance to ask. I was prepared. For the times I was caught off guard by a question or request I wasn't ready to answer, I came up with a way to call a timeout in mid-conversation. I did so by simply deflecting to someone, usually a fictitious person, who wasn't present, "my boss." As an example, if I was dealing with a hard-nosed customer who wanted a better price, I would say I needed to run it by "my boss" (even though he didn't exist) and ask if I could step outside so that I may give him a call. I would then walk outside or at least out of hearing range, grab my phone, making sure the ringer was off, then press it to my ear and pretend to make the call. I never called anyone; I just held the phone to my ear. Once on the phone with my imaginary supervisor, I would think it over. I knew I needed to give the customer a discount, but how much of a discount? When I was ready and had made a decision, I would pretend to hang up and return to update the customer on what we could do for them. Which typically started with something like, "I have great news, my boss is a tough cookie, but I was able to get you a better price..." This also worked to my benefit, because it made the customer feel as if I was on their side.

I then would quickly pull out a contract that stated they would be doing business with us exclusively for the next three years, which was always pre- filled with their information, of course. Next, I would say, "I already filled this out for you to save you the trouble." But, in reality, I was saving myself the trouble. If you hand someone a blank contract, they immediately begin scanning the document, more questions get asked, and it generally doesn't go over as smoothly. I would always previously highlight or mark an X where I needed their signature. Once I had it in front of them, I would point at the highlighted area or X with the pen in my hand. After a while, I began noticing that their eyes would go wherever the pen went. It was pretty funny, actually. Here's the routine: "I just need you to sign the service agreement, and we're good to go," (present service agreement, a/k/a contract). "There's your name," point with a pen. "There's your address," point with a pen. "And that's where I need your signature, please," point and then hand them the pen, cap off, ready to sign. While handing them the pen, I kept talking, reassuring them, and basically distracting them, until they signed, so I could leave quickly. While they were signing, I'd rattle off something like, "You should be approved within the next couple of weeks…I'll call you…Nice meeting you…You have my cell…Have a great day!" Smile, and I was gone; on to the next one.

A couple of months had passed, and we began getting more accounts than what we could service. Specifically because we didn't have enough display cages for the amount of business we were gaining. What a nightmare! Here was this incredible opportunity, everything I had prayed for, and I was not prepared for it. The company I was ordering my cages from in Alabama couldn't build them fast enough. Retailers I had acquired began to get upset, and we were losing opportunities to get new business, because we were unable to deliver on what we promised, and that began to upset people, understandably. Too much demand and not enough supply. What a problem to have. Unfortunately, it was still a big problem and it needed to be solved. We tried building the cages ourselves, but it wasn't our strong suit. Plus, it was far too time-consuming. We began ordering display cages from different suppliers. I found a company that had a large stock of them, but they were all painted blue. I already had been using white, so I wasn't too thrilled about using a different color and changing the business's image, but it was that or nothing! Blue it is. When the first truckload of cages from the new supplier arrived, it was stacked to the very top with these absolutely gorgeous displays. Never would I have imagined that mere metal objects could look so beautiful. They brought a smile to my face. I was in complete admiration. The blue was so remarkably distinguished; I never went back to using white display cages again; it felt regal. It instantly became our new company color. A second truckload arrived soon after the first. We got to work immediately. The display cages would get unloaded from the transport truck directly onto our delivery trucks, to continue on their journey to their new homes, which so desperately awaited their arrival. No time was wasted. They went out just as quickly as they came in.

The company was doing well. We were making money, and our partnership with my mom playing referee, was actually working. It was the peak of summer, and every day was busy now. I got my wish; my dream came to life. I was just as busy in the summer months as I was in the winter. I spent many days on the prowl, soliciting business door-to-door, trying to sign up as many retailers at gas stations, hardware stores, and convenience stores as possible. Other days, I'd be making deliveries or setting up display cages at accounts I recently had signed up, most of which had never sold propane. We were growing very quickly, organically. We continued taking business from Atlas Propane and other suppliers. We were more aggressive with pricing, had more style and had better service, across the board. My never-say-no attitude became the foundation of our company culture. These customers were not accustomed to getting this quality of service. Our reputation for price and reliability grew as quickly as our business did. We were the new kid on the block, the talk of the town, a disrupter, but I was faced with a new nagging concern: *How do we maintain this level of service and high-growth rate?*

Reflection Point 11

Be on the lookout for low-hanging fruit. Takeovers were a great way for us to make money instantly.

When it comes to gaining customers, know your business and be respectful of people's time. Get to the point; they'll appreciate it. Lastly, there's nothing worse than having an opportunity and not being prepared for it. Think ahead!

What is your biggest opportunity?

Why do you see it as an opportunity?

Are you prepared for it? If not, what do you need to do
to be prepared for it?

Chapter 12:

Fuel to the Fire

It was late afternoon on a regular, routine workday. I arrived back at my office to reload my truck with full BBQ tanks to exchange for my retailers. After making several deliveries, I had run out. I was exhausted but cheerful and in good spirits as usual. I noticed someone sitting in a chair across from my desk. Our office had an open layout, so you could see everyone in the room. There were no walls. My mother informed me that the man sitting there was waiting to speak to me about wanting a job. He was an older gentleman. If I had to guess, I'd say he was in his late 50s.

I made my way toward him then extended my arm to shake his hand and introduced myself. "Hello, I'm Max." "Hi, I'm Raul," the gentlemen replied. "How can I help you today, Raul?" I asked. "I wanted to know if you'd be interested in hiring me; I can be a salesman for your company," he said. "Well, to be quite honest, Raul, we have more work than we can handle at the moment," I replied. "I know, I used to be a propane salesman. I've been watching you guys and it seems like you're taking over the market," he chuckled. "I know all about BBQ exchange and I can help you get five times the amount of business you have now. If you give me the opportunity, I'll prove it."

"Are you working in the propane industry now?" I questioned. "No, but it's what I love to do," he replied. "Well, if you love it, why aren't you doing it?" I was curious. "Honestly, I was fired from the last company I used to work for, but not for stealing or anything like that. I had a personal disagreement with management, and they decided to let me go," he said. "Okay, that's fine, I'm not concerned about that, but do you really think you can get us five times the amount of business we have now? That's a pretty big claim." I replied with skepticism. "I know I can. I was a salesman for many years. I like your aggressive approach, and how you're doing things overall. You're different. You're giving great service, offering insurance, and you have better prices. It'll be quite easy for me to grow your business," Raul said. "How much are you looking to make a week?" I asked. "How about $500 a week salary and a commission of $100 for every account I land?" he asked. "I'll tell you what, I'll give you the $500 a week and $100 for every existing account you convince to switch over from another supplier, but only a $65 commission if you open new accounts with no pre-existing sales history," I said. "Okay, that sounds good. I guarantee I won't let you down," Raul replied. I smiled and said, "Well, it looks like you made your first sale; you've convinced me to give you a job! Let's see what you can do!"

Was I too hasty? This was a large commitment for me to make at that time. Here I was, barely able to handle the workload I already had, and I was about to put myself in a position to potentially get five times busier. Had I lost my mind, or did I see an incredible opportunity to hire someone with industry-specific knowledge and grow my business even more? I remember feeling like it was a total blessing. Fate dropped this man right at my doorstep. How could I say no? It was an incredible opportunity that I needed to capitalize on.

As I previously mentioned, I preferred taking over accounts from other suppliers because those accounts already were generating sales. They had a pre-existing history of making money because people already knew they could exchange their BBQ tanks at those locations. My experience with setting up new retailers with no sales history typically revealed a grace period in which we had to wait for them to mature, if they matured at all. Some didn't. I wanted to maximize my investment by only getting the best-quality accounts first. It was worth paying the extra money to get an account that would begin producing instantly. But either way, I paid the salesman's commission with the profits made from the first delivery. Which brought my cost to acquire the account almost to zero. In a way, it was a risk-free trial period to test the quality of the account. If it didn't produce after some time, we would simply pick up our equipment and redeploy it elsewhere.

Hiring Raul proved to be a wise and profitable decision. He consistently brought in new business, almost daily. It was like pouring gasoline on a bonfire. We were already the aggressor in our market, acquiring the majority of the business to be had. Then we added rocket fuel to our already-infectious momentum! Though Raul didn't grow my business five times, he definitely assisted in doubling or even tripling the business we already had.

After about a four or five-month run, Raul began to fizzle out and lose impact. Atlas Propane and the other suppliers became much more competitive. They started to lower their prices; it was a battle for market share. To avoid losing business, Atlas Propane began to pressure their retailers with civil lawsuits citing a breach of contract if they stopped doing business with them and switched over to us. It was their defense to our vigorous offense — a clever countermeasure. That left many customers eager to do business with us once their agreements expired. The other suppliers fought back but weren't as determined to keep their accounts. I think it would be fair to say, we quickly became the preferred supplier in our market. With Raul's help, we were able to capitalize on the opportunity in front of us and fast-track our success. *Speedy Tanks 2 You* had firmly planted roots and established itself as a leading BBQ tank-exchange company in South Florida.

I don't exactly remember how much time had passed, maybe it was two or even three years. What I do remember vividly is constantly daydreaming about buying out Atlas Propane. It was a recurring fantasy of mine. They were our biggest competitor, and I didn't want to compete — I wanted to dominate. I wanted to supply the entire market and for everyone in South Florida to buy their propane from me. They were the biggest obstacle, which meant they had to go. If we could only take over their business, we would be the undisputed, largest, independent propane tank-exchange supplier in Florida.

Just thinking about that would get me excited and I thought about it often. It had become all I wanted. I discussed it with people in the industry, friends, and family members. I remember mentioning it to my brother Danny and wondering how much money Atlas might want for their entire operation. Based on the number of accounts Atlas Propane was servicing, I assumed the company was probably worth around $4 million. I came up with that estimated value based on how many accounts I had and how much money I was generating. I had no clue. It was just a shot in the dark. That's what I would have valued it at. I definitely didn't have $4 million; I didn't even have $100,000. We were aggressively reinvesting every penny earned back into the business; I was cash poor, but it didn't matter. If I could get Atlas to agree to sell their company, I knew I'd find a way to get it done.

Reflection Point 12

Most people would think it's a good idea to take a break when they're already doing well and keeping busy. I would disagree. I feel that the absolute best time to step on the gas and increase the intensity is when you have already built up some momentum. Keep that energy flowing in the right direction, drive it home, get it done!

Your dreams should be so big they don't seem possible to you; they should excite you and almost scare you! Now, that's something worthy of your time.

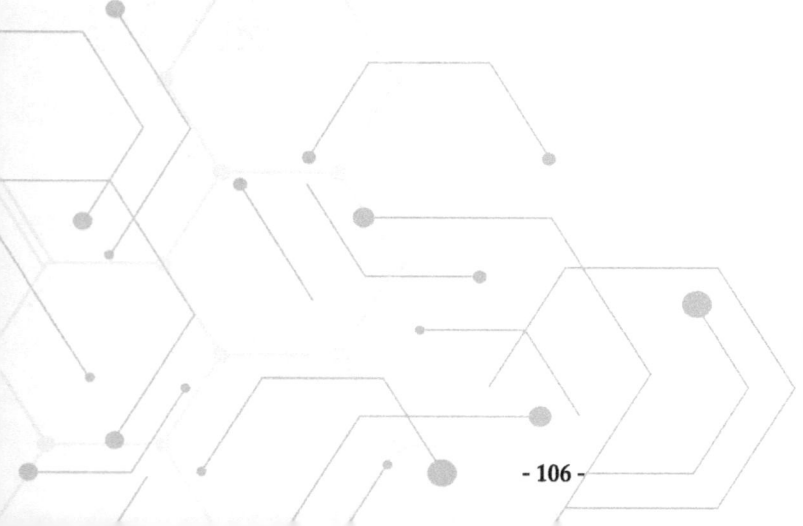

Are your dreams BIG enough?

What dream do you have that is so BIG it scares you but at the same time EXCITES you?

What are some things you can do to get a few steps closer to that dream?

Chapter 13:

Blindsided

I was 26 years old when my mother, Josephine, was diagnosed with breast cancer. I believe I didn't know much about her medical condition because she had shielded me from the full details. I don't think she wanted me to worry. Adding to that, part of me blocked it out and didn't want to believe she was sick. I chose to remain optimistic during that time and encouraged her to think of a positive outcome for the future. I genuinely never thought anything would happen to her.

She had chemotherapy treatments for almost a year, and they seemed to be working. Some days she felt great; others she didn't. She had been in and out of the hospital and was barely able to come to work; however, I was still hopeful and honestly believed she would be okay. I supposed her weakness was just part of the healing process.

One morning, my father called me and suggested I go to my mother's house before coming to work, because she had called him and said she wasn't feeling well. After hanging up, I urgently drove over to see her. When I arrived, Danny was already there. I was worried, anxious, and confused, primarily because she didn't call me personally to inform me she wasn't feeling well. I felt like I was out of the loop and wanted her to rely on me if she needed anything. With emotions running high, we got into a little tiff, and I left hastily, upset. Had I known that was the last time I would ever speak to her, I would have handled things much differently, exercised more patience and understanding, and told her how much I loved her. The next time I would hear news of my mother was later that same day. While I was at work, my brother called to let me know she was in the emergency room on a respirator. She would never gain consciousness again and died a few days later. I was in total shock and disbelief. I still don't have words to describe that experience. I was depressed for months and lost a lot of money at work, partly from making poor decisions and partially from just not caring. All in all, I self- isolated for about six months. I lost my mother, my best friend, my business partner, and my referee, all on the same day. Things would never be the same again.

Reflection Point 13

Nothing in life is guaranteed, and you never know when your time is up.

Be grateful for what you have and take nothing for granted. When was the last time you told your family, friends, or coworkers how much you truly care about them and appreciate them? Even if it was recently, there is no limit for how often you can express yourself. Don't leave things left unsaid.

Whose presence are you taking for granted?

How can you express to them how much they truly mean to you?

Chapter 14:

At Last

After my six-month stint in self-pity and depression, I rebounded. Feeling sorry for myself got old, and I wanted to get back to work. I wanted to take better care of myself. I had done away with the whole "I don't care" attitude I had been brandishing. I was sick of applying poor judgment to just about everything. I was once again clear and focused. I decided it was time for me to learn more about propane in general and made an effort to learn a little more about the trade. To operate a complete propane company like Local Propane, you needed a Master Qualifier's License. To get one, you would need to complete a course administered by the state, in Ocala, FL. This required a great deal of specialized knowledge and was heavy in science and math, knowledge I didn't have. It was confusing to me and partially why I was not interested in Local Propane to begin with.

Many people fail and never have the privilege of passing this test. I wasn't greatly confident in my ability to do so either. For Danny, learning and retaining this information came very easily. It truly was something to behold. State inspectors would call Danny regularly for his take on unique situations they encountered in the field. Danny came to their aid so frequently they would offer him a position at the state's office after almost every call. Although his extensive, propane-specific knowledge was well regarded in the industry, Danny still hadn't been officially certified by the state of Florida, but there was absolutely no doubt he would ace the exam. What better study partner could I ask for? If I were ever to have a shot at passing this thing, this would be the time to do it. We took the drive together so I could try my luck.

On orientation day, Danny and I signed in as attendees to take the Master Qualifier Course. We received a couple of books and lanyards that had our full names on them and the company we represented. We then immediately made our way into the auditorium-style room. I was surprised to find quite a lot of people there. I would never have imagined that many people would be interested in becoming an officially licensed propane nerd. It felt like there were 100 people in attendance, though it probably was much fewer in reality. As we were directed toward our seats, we politely greeted everyone we walked past. Each of the attendees was pre-assigned to a specific table and seat for the entire course, which was several days long. I remember wondering who decided where we should sit and what metric they used: *Was it alphabetical order by name? County of employment? Area of expertise? Age, maybe? Or was it just names selected at random?*

Upon arriving at our table, I noticed little A-frame cards with our names and company information on them. Danny and I spoke casually and made small talk as we glanced over the room, pointing out and waiving at a few people we knew who were also there. Danny was sitting to my left, and the chair right next to me was empty. After our little game of point and wave, I glanced at the A-frame card on the empty seat next to me. It read, *Andrew Atlas, Atlas Propane.* "Holy crap!" I yelped. I almost jumped out of my chair as I frantically slapped Danny on the shoulder. "Look!" I pointed at the A-frame piece of paper on the desk next to me. "Are you looking at that? Do you think it could be the owner of Atlas Propane? It has to be! I cannot believe the owner of Atlas Propane is sitting right next to us. I don't think he's going to be too happy about this!" I said chuckling. Danny laughed and agreed. "What are the odds of this happening, Danny? This can't be a coincidence. We need to convince him to sell us his company. This is our chance; we have to buy his business. We won't have any real competition if we do. We will basically control the BBQ exchange market," I said. "Let's do it. Let's make it happen," Danny replied. I nodded with confidence. "We will," I agreed.

Out of all these people in attendance, how could they sit two rivals literally right next to each other in this huge room? Did they not know we were in intense competition for market share? Maybe they did and wanted to see a fistfight. Or perhaps it was purely coincidental. Either way, I viewed sitting next to our biggest competitor as a great thing. Even though I figured he would most likely hate me, this was a sizable opportunity, once in a lifetime. If I could convince him to sell to us, I would achieve my version of world domination. Now, I'd have a few days sitting next to this guy; that was certainly enough time to win him over.

About 45 minutes had passed. Everyone had now settled into their seats, everyone except Andrew Atlas, and class had begun. There was no sign of him. I spent the majority of those 45 minutes deep in thought, mentally rehearsing what I would say to him and what his reaction might be. Mental role playing, if you will. I needed to be prepared if he were ever to arrive. *Hi, I'm Max. I want to buy your company. No, too straightforward. He might get offended,* I thought. *How about… Hi, I'm Max, do you own Atlas Propane? Would you be interested in selling me your business? No, he probably isn't interested; consider… that might be a better word. Hi, I'm Max. Would you consider selling me your business?* Over and over, I kept thinking about it and pre-analyzing my subsequent introduction to Andrew from Atlas Propane. *What do I say to this guy?* I thought. I was nervous, but I knew I had to pitch it to him. I needed to observe his reaction. *Would he be appalled? Offended? Think I'm utterly crazy? Or would he think it was a good idea? Worthy of consideration and further discussion?* The truth is, I wouldn't know until I asked. I needed to look him right in the eyes and ask. Then I would know where I stood. Either way, it was starting to seem like he would be a no-show.

About 20 more passed, and I had pretty much accepted that Andrew Atlas wasn't attending. I guess I wasn't going to get the opportunity to express my interest in buying his company, if it was his company, after all. Perhaps the rehearsal was an exercise in futility. Even if he said yes, I didn't have the money to make it happen anyway. I had all but accepted this fact and had begun to rationalize internally. *Maybe it's better that he doesn't show. That way I don't make a fool of myself by offering to buy a $4 million business with only $50,000 in the bank!* I chuckled at the thought, *ambitious would be an understatement!*

I was doing a relatively good job of talking myself out of it. I was mid-thought, looking at the front of the room, in the direction of the man speaking, although not listening to a word he was saying, when I felt the chair to my right move. I was still in a trance, rehearsing, evaluating, playing mental chess. When I looked to my right, and there he was, Andrew Atlas at last, fashionably late and smelling like he had just smoked an entire pack of cigarettes. I was so caught up in self- deliberation, I almost forgot he still could potentially show up.

He wasn't at all what I had pictured. He was young, maybe 30 or even younger. *This can't be him*, I thought. *He's a kid. There is no way this is the owner of Atlas Propane.* Well, it was either him, someone mistakenly sitting in his chair, or someone who worked for him. He had blonde hair and blue eyes. I nodded at him as to say hello. He nodded back, and that was it. Over an hour of rehearsal for a nod. No words exchanged. He still had not yet noticed who was sitting next to him. His biggest rival. After just a few minutes, he glanced over at the A-frame sign on my desk and caught on. He was probably just as shocked as I was when I had gotten there. I had over an hour to digest the fact that someone from Atlas Propane could and would potentially be sitting next to me. He, on the other hand, just had this dumped on him and had to have been caught off guard. He had stepped into a lion's den. I'm sure it was an awkward feeling. I would have paid money to have known what he was thinking at that very moment.

He was probably wondering how we had the nerve to sit right next to him. Had I not desperately wanted to buy him out, I would probably have preferred to be seated on the opposite side of the room from him, or anyone from Atlas Propane for that matter. I guess that's just my antagonistic nature. It was quiet, and everyone was focused on the instructor at the head of the class. It definitely wasn't the time for me to strike up a conversation with Andrew. We had previously been informed we would be getting a 15-minute break a few hours into our lesson, so I decided to wait until then to chat with him.

It was now break time and not a single word had been spoken between Andrew and me. After being dismissed, everyone spilled out into the courtyard. There was a lot of chatter; people were buying refreshments and snacks out of vending machines and talking about the things they had just learned. Danny and I bought a couple of sodas and some chips. We joked about how Andrew might have felt when he realized he was sitting next to us and shared a good laugh. I continued expressing to Danny how important it would be for us to buy out Atlas Propane. As we were talking about it, I noticed Andrew in the distance smoking a cigarette, no surprise there. I gestured to Danny that we should go over and speak to him. "Now's our chance. Let's go," I said. We walked up and introduced ourselves. "Hi, my name is Max, and this is my brother Danny. We own Local Propane and *Speedy Tanks 2 You*. I was wondering if you would be interested in selling your business?" I asked straightforwardly. "It's not my company; it's my uncle Stanley's business. But I think he might be interested in something like that," he replied. "Okay, great. I'd love to speak to him about it," I said. It literally couldn't have gone any better. Short and to the point. I remained composed as Danny continued having small talk with Andrew. I stood there, smiled, and pretended to be interested in their conversation, but, in reality, I was checked out. My mind was elsewhere. I already was daydreaming and thinking of my next move. I was reanalyzing Andrew's body language and choice of words. I knew what they meant. *When Andrew quickly nodded and confidently said, "I think he might be interested in something like that," what he really meant to say was, he is DEFINITELY interested in something like that! They must have had a conversation about this at some point, how else would he know his uncle might be interested in selling?* I had no doubt about it. What a rush! I felt completely supercharged; overflowing with anticipation but remained completely calm on the surface. This was it. It was actually happening.

After chit-chatting for a bit, we invited Andrew to eat dinner and play pool with us after class at a local billiard; he accepted. Later that night, while playing pool, I learned a lot more about Andrew. He was friendly. He didn't hate us, or at least he wasn't acting like he did. It turned out that Andrew's true passion was architecture and he only had been working with Atlas for a short time. He wasn't too interested in propane; he was merely getting his license to help out his uncle Stanley, who was the true owner of Atlas Propane. Throughout our conversation, Andrew revealed that Stanley had some health issues and had just about had enough of running the business. I'm sure the contentious nature of it had a little something to do with that as well. Either way, it appeared as if there were no hard feelings. The next day before class, Andrew handed me a small piece of paper with his uncle's phone number scribbled on it. He mentioned he had spoken to him and suggested I call him after we returned to Miami the following week.

Reflection Point 14

Mental role-playing or role-playing in general can be extremely helpful to stay prepared for any conceivable or inconceivable outcome.

Make the most of every opportunity life gives you, even the unexpected ones. Don't assume that you know the answer to everything. If you never ask, you'll never know.

What is something bold you wish you had the courage to ask someone?

What could you be missing out on by not taking that chance?

Chapter 15:

The Art of Negotiation

We were back in Miami, and I was getting ready to make the big phone call to Stanley from Atlas Propane. The anticipation was killing me. I don't know if I had ever been so nervous in my entire life. My overly ambitious desire to purchase Atlas Propane was starting to weigh on me. Doubt began to take root in my mind. *Is this too bold of a move? Am I way out of my league here? How much is he going to want for the company? Is he going to be rude? If we agree to something, how will I pay him? I don't have the money.* I worked through the doubts as best as I could. I was pacing back and forth in my office, going over as many different possible scenarios as I could come up with, before making the call. This was a big moment for me. I asked my father and my brother to please be in the room during the call. I felt their presence would give me a little more confidence. I was a ball of nerves and wanted support. "Okay, no more thinking about it. I'm just going to do it!" I said.

I grabbed the paper with Stanley's phone number on it out of my pocket and began to dial. A young lady picked up on the first ring. "Hello, this is Roxy; thank you for calling Atlas Propane. How can I help you? she said. "Hi, this is Max from Local Propane. I was calling to speak to Stanley, please." I said. "Oh, hello, um…just one second. I'll get him for you." She sounded confused. She left me on hold for what felt like an eternity. It was a strange moment. I felt out of place, almost as if I had crossed into enemy lines. How dare I? I wondered what the lady who answered the phone was thinking while I was on hold. You could hear the surprise in her voice when I had introduced myself. Her response might as well have been, "Um… do you have the right number? You do realize you're calling Atlas Propane, right? Your nemesis."

Moments later, he picked up. "This is Stanley," he said. "Hello Stanley, this is Max from *Speedy Tanks 2 You*. I had spoken to your nephew Andrew about possibly purchasing your company. Is that something we can talk about?" I asked. "Well, yeah, we can *talk* about it." he said, as if to emphasize talking would be the only thing taking place. I didn't let that deter me. "Okay, great. When would you like me to come by?" I asked. "Why don't you come by on Thursday? That'll give me some time to get some information together," he said. "Sure, that sounds good. What time?" I asked. "I leave every day around lunchtime, so, any time before noon will be fine." "How about 11 a.m.? I'll call you in the morning to confirm," I replied. "That works." "Perfect, see you then, thank you." I hung up the phone and immediately threw both my arms straight up in the air, followed by some fist-pumping. "Yes, baby! This is awesome!" I was ecstatic, giddy even. I hugged my dad and my brother. I was one step closer to securing this. How exactly? I still didn't know, but it felt right.

Thursday morning had quickly arrived. This was the day I finally would meet the owner of Atlas Propane and attempt to persuade him to sell me his business. I ditched my daily blue-collar delivery attire I regularly all but slept in and put on something more presentable: black pants with a white, long- sleeved, button-down-collar shirt, tucked in, with a belt. I rarely dressed like this, but I felt the need to present myself as someone who should be taken seriously. I wanted him to know I wasn't just some punk trying to waste his time. I meant business. Essentially, I was dressing the part. In an abundance of caution, and to aid my posturing, I also asked my father to accompany me to the meeting. I just wanted him to be there, not to talk. I figured having someone closer to Stanley's age present would improve my chances to be taken seriously. After all, this man was about three times my age. My father agreed to join me and, for the most part, stay quiet while I negotiated. I called Atlas

Propane's office to confirm our appointment and advise them I would be on time. The receptionist who answered confirmed that Stanley, the owner, was expecting me. My dad and I hopped in my truck and made our way toward Atlas Propane's headquarters.

As we pulled up to Atlas Propane, we were taken aback by the great magnitude of their operation. The business was on an exceptionally large piece of property. It turned out Atlas Propane was also in the self-storage business. They had an impressive amount of land — at the very least, 10 acres, right in the middle of a bustling commercial area. Their property was filled with tractor-trailers, boats, commercial and personal vehicles, along with several other unique items people needed to store. It appeared that exchanging BBQ tanks may have been the smallest part of their operation. Near the entrance, a man filled propane tanks for walk-up customers using a propane dispensing unit, just as I had been doing when I met Jose from the Victoria Hotel.

I parked my truck, waved at the man filling tanks, and we made our way inside. Once there, I began to take in my surroundings. It was a well-organized, relatively small workspace, especially when considering the amount of activity going on outside. Much like our office, it had an open format. Upon entering, you could see everyone in the room. There were only three visible employees working, two older women at their desks and a younger woman at the register behind the counter. They had a handful of propane- related products lined up against the wall and a few smaller items beneath a glass countertop, which was under the cash register. New tanks, grills, spatulas, and other barbecuing accessories were all on display. I walked up to the counter and introduced myself to the young lady working there. "Hello, my name is Max. I'm here to see Stanley." "Hi, yes, he is expecting you. Give me one quick second and I'll let him know you're here," she replied. The young woman stood up and walked toward

The Art of Negotiation

a closed door near the back of the room. She knocked lightly with the knuckle on her right index finger and simultaneously opened the door with her left hand, confidently, not waiting for permission to enter. She peeked her head into the room and mumbled something. She then looked at us and said, "Come on back, guys," gesturing for us to walk behind the counter to join Stanley in what presumably was his office.

We walked in and saw Stanley sitting at his desk in the far-left corner of the room, facing the wall. He had to turn back and to his left to see us in his doorway. It was an odd configuration; he was giving his back to the rest of the room. Stanley appeared to be in his late 50s, maybe early 60s. He was wearing a white, short-sleeved, button-down collar shirt. He had blue eyes just like Andrew, light brown hair, and wore thin, gold-framed glasses. He was a tad pudgy and not very tall. He turned and stood to greet us. I extended my arm to shake his hand. I introduced myself, then introduced my father. "Hello, Stanley, it's very nice to meet you. I'm Max, and this is my dad. His name is Max also," I said. "I'm Max Sr.," my father added as he smiled. "Oh, nice to meet you. I assumed you would be coming alone," he said. "Well, I figured it couldn't hurt to bring him along. I hope you don't mind," I replied. "Not at all. Please have a seat," he pointed at the two open seats by the entrance. "Okay great, thank you." I replied. The chairs he pointed at, which were the only two chairs in the room apart from his, were now behind us. They were catty-cornered to his desk, up against the wall, directly in front of the doorway we had just walked in through. We passed them on the way into the room and now had to take a few steps back toward the entrance to sit down. So, it was the doorway, my dad in chair #1, then me in chair #2, and Stanley diagonally across the room from us. I was technically closer to him but still felt a world away. We were only about three feet into his office; I guess we still weren't officially invited all the way in. He may have wanted to make it easier on himself to kick us out if this meeting didn't go so well.

It was rather unusual and kind of funny, now thinking back on it. He sat back down and turned in his chair to converse with us. "So, do you work for your father?" he asked. "No, I don't, actually. I started my own propane- exchange business a while back, which I ran for a couple of years separate from my father's brand, Local Propane. Then, as a result of a family meeting, we decided to merge both companies; however, we still operate independently as two separate brands. I'm 100% in charge of the propane exchange business, and my father and brother run their conventional side. It's weird, I know," I replied. "Well, that's certainly an interesting arrangement," he noted, with a quizzical expression on his face. The door to his office had been left wide open by the young lady who showed us in. I was sure he'd want some privacy to discuss this sensitive information we were about to get into. I know I did. "Should I close the door?" I asked as I confidently arose from my chair. "No, leave it open," he firmly replied. I sat back down, mystified. His response caught me off guard. With the door open, the employees in the adjoining room could hear our entire conversation. *Why would he want that?* My mind began to race. *Does he want them to listen in? Maybe he just wants their opinion? Or what if he's going to try to embarrass me in front of his staff to make an example out of me? Is this a setup? But why would he go through the trouble? This doesn't make sense.* Setup or not, knowing that there was an audience made me uneasy. I thought I'd be having a private conversation with Stanley behind closed doors. Not the case. The stage had been set, and I was on it. We were, in essence, sitting at an intersection between one room and the other. I didn't exactly understand his reasoning behind it, but I wasn't going to let that stop me. The fact was, if I needed to appeal to him and anyone else who was within earshot of Stanley's office, I was going to do so — I was committed.

It was awkward. I didn't know what to say, so I just started talking. "Thanks for taking the time to meet with me, Stanley. I want to start by saying I hope there are no hard feelings; I know we've been aggressively competing with each other for some time now. I just want you to know that I respect you and admire the business you've built. As you know, the reason I'm here is because I'm interested in purchasing your propane-exchange business. What information can you share with me?" I asked. Maybe not the best way to start, but I think the apology/compliment softened him up a little. "Well, thank you for saying that. And yes, you guys have been a royal pain in my ass!" he said as he smirked. His small display of humor put me more at ease. I felt the tension in my shoulders slowly release. I was more comfortable now. "Let me show you some reports," he said as he turned in his chair, facing back toward his desktop. "Why don't you bring your chair over here?" He motioned for me to place my chair next to his desk. I did. I guess I had passed his initial test. I didn't get kicked out of his office and was actually invited farther in. Odd, yes.

My father remained seated and silent in chair #1 toward the entrance of the room. Stanley continued, "Just to be clear, if we work something out, I can't sell you the name of the company. Not only is it my last name, but I use the name Atlas for other things I own with my family. Like this storage business," he explained. "Yes, I understand that. I just want to purchase your customer list," I replied. "Okay, good. Let's start by looking at the customers we service and our different weekly routes," he said. He then pulled out a three-ring notebook that held several laminated sheets of paper, with different routes for different days of the week. Four routes for Monday, three routes for Tuesday, four for Wednesday, and so forth. Below the days of the week were customers' names and addresses, Shell Gas Station, Mobil, etc. Stanley proceeded to describe his business: "We're delivering to around 200 retailers right now. I'd say 5–10% of them aren't that great," he candidly admitted. "I'll probably remove a few cages within the next couple of weeks from the retailers that aren't selling that much propane. You know, we had better accounts before you came along," he jokingly said. I began to appreciate his seemingly quirky personality. I smiled and continued to press on. "How many BBQ tanks are you exchanging a week?" I asked. "We're averaging around 1,500 to 2,000 tanks a week," he replied. (At the time, I was exchanging around 2,000–3,000 BBQ tanks consistently with about 240 retailers.) "Some days are better than others, and, as you know, we sell more on holidays and long weekends because everyone is grilling," he added. "How much are you charging each retailer per tank? I asked. "Many of them are paying around $12 a tank. Some are paying less, again, largely thanks to you," he replied. Consistent with his joking demeanor, he was almost being silly now. It appeared as if he had totally lightened up at this point. It was refreshing.

He continued, "Large-chain accounts we service like Ace Hardware get discounted pricing. They all average around $10–$11 per tank exchange." "How many trucks do you use to deliver to your customers?" I asked. "We have four trucks in service. One of them is almost new, and the other three are old and beat up, but they're all reliable.

"We deliver all the way down to Key West and as far north as Jupiter," he said. "Wow! That's a pretty broad territory. You deliver down to Key West. That's over three hours away without stopping. That's unbelievable," I said. "Yeah, we had to expand to land some of the bigger accounts. Most of the larger retailers wouldn't give us their business unless we agreed to service all of their locations in South Florida," he replied. "I still can't believe you guys go all the way down to the Keys. How do you do that?" I asked. "For the Key West route, we go down on Fridays. The driver must get here at 4:30 a.m. and does the entire route with a helper. They usually get back around 5 p.m.

It's a long day, and I have to pay them both around four hours of overtime, but they get it done," he noted. Intrigued, I continued to probe. "That's quite a bit of work. How many tanks do you exchange on that route? Is it even worth going that far?" "We usually exchange around 70–100 tanks. On a great day, which doesn't happen that often, we empty the truck and exchange all 128 tanks, which is what our biggest truck holds. If the driver runs out of tank inventory and has to cut the trip short, we then need to drive back to the Keys the next day and service the retailers we couldn't get to," he said. I was perplexed by that statement. It seemed surprisingly inefficient. Why did his biggest truck only hold 128 BBQ tanks?

At that time, I was running three large, flatbed-style trucks locally. All of them held more than 140 tanks; actually, my biggest truck held 264 tanks, and we never had to travel much more than an hour away. If I was delivering as far south as he was, I would have wanted to carry as many tanks as possible to make fewer trips and not run out of full tanks to exchange for my customers. Granted, this was only one of his many routes and most likely his farthest one, but it was a valuable insight. He wasn't running the business as efficiently as he could've. Which meant to me, he was leaving money on the table.

On this route, Stanley was paying two employees, instead of just one, to drive down to Key West. It was a three-hour trip in each direction, not counting the stops the driver had to make to service each customer. The driver could only exchange up to 128 tanks on his best day. That's because his truck didn't hold enough inventory, and the reason he rarely exchanged 128 tanks was because he was going too often, in fear that some of his accounts would run out of full tanks. *Why doesn't he just buy a larger truck, add bigger cages, and go every two weeks instead of every week? He could sell twice as much propane in half as many trips. That would make his company more profitable and efficient.* I took a mental note and continued my line of questioning.

"How often are you visiting all of your other retailers?" I asked. "We visit all our customers once a week," he replied. "So, you're not using routing software and delivering to them based on their average consumption?" I asked. "No. We just use days of the week, depending on what area the retailer is in and visit them on their corresponding day. For example, Monday, we're in South Miami. Tuesday, North Miami. If a retailer's in North Miami, we will see them every Tuesday," he responded. This was another glaring inefficiency. Stanley hadn't taken advantage of innovative tools such as routing software to streamline his business. This was a large oversight.

At *Speedy Tanks 2 You*, all our accounts were on a route system. If a retailer was selling more than average amounts of propane, and needed a delivery twice a week, our software would schedule it, and we would visit them more frequently, and vice-versa. If they weren't selling large amounts, and required service less frequently, our software would make the adjustment and extend their delivery dates. That way, we didn't waste time or energy driving to retailers who weren't in need of a delivery. It not only helped us provide better service but also helped save time and money. A dollar saved is a dollar earned! It was clear to me that Stanley's inefficiencies cost him a great deal of money. He was sending his drivers all over South Florida to customers who didn't need service. Think of all the money he was spending on tolls and diesel, the extra wear and tear on his trucks, and the payroll and overtime he was paying to his employees every week to service customers who didn't require service.

Stanley and I reviewed a couple more of his reports then took a walk around his operation. He showed me some display cages he had in inventory. Many were incredibly old and in bad shape. They had been removed from service because they needed to be repaired and painted, but with a little love, they could be as good as new. He also showed me one of the older trucks not currently on the road making deliveries. It was beaten up, just as he had described. After our tour, we parted ways. I thanked him for his time and said I'd be getting back to him. We never discussed a price for his business, and I never asked him how much money he was making. I didn't even ask him for his financial information, such as a profit-and-loss statement or balance sheet, although they wouldn't have done me any good, even if he did volunteer that information. I knew next to nothing about financial statements at the time. My understanding was just about zero.

I headed back to my office with my father. Once we got back, I sat quietly at my desk, and wrote down some of the things I learned in my meeting with Stanley. I was trying to determine how much money he might want for his company, using my newly gained knowledge. I knew it was valuable, especially to me, but I still couldn't put a number on it. The next morning, I called Stanley and asked him when he'd like to meet again. He said he would be in my area toward the afternoon and could stop by and visit me. I thought that was a great idea. Stanley came by around 2 p.m. I introduced him to some of the staff who were present, gave him the nickel tour, and then asked him to join me in my office so we could get down to business. The small talk was over. I jumped right into it. "Stanley, as you know, I'm interested in buying your accounts, and I'd like to move forward," I said. "Well, we haven't even discussed the price yet," he exclaimed. He was right. I hadn't broached the subject. I was scared to. I was still anticipating an astronomical asking price. If he really did want $4 million for his business or anywhere near that number, it was going to be a very short conversation. It would crush my hopes of buying him out. I guess, in a way, I was trying to save myself the embarrassment of proposing to buy his business with next to no money. I paused for a second, took a deep breath, exhaled slowly, then took the leap. "Tell me what you would like for it?" I asked. "Well, what's your offer?" he snapped back defensively. "Stanley, just tell me what you want for it, and we'll take it from there," I persisted. I didn't want to be the first one to propose. I knew that would be a mistake. Through my experience as a salesman, I had learned it was best not to make the first offer in any negotiation, if I could help it. Instead, I always asked what the other individual wanted first. I was often surprised by what the opposition was thinking, what they genuinely wanted, and some of the things they said. I'd say it pays to listen and be second to act.

Stanley was locked in, glaring at me through his thin, gold-frame glasses. His face had become flushed, and his posture was overall uptight. He held a stern look on his face and didn't break eye contact with me, even for a second. Both of his hands were firmly latched onto the armrests of the chair he was sitting on. I sensed he was wavering and about to give in but still wasn't sure.

He then suddenly, in a semi-combative manner, made his demands. "Well, I want $1,000 for every active account I have. I also want you to buy any excess inventory I have of cages and BBQ tanks from me at the price I paid, and I want Kelly Blue Book market price for the three old trucks. I'm keeping the newer one," he ordered, as if to say, "So there — ha!" To which I replied, "Deal!" Stanley's expression was that of total shock. It didn't even take me more than what felt like a millisecond to accept his terms. I got ahead of myself, but how could I have not, after what he just asked me for? There was no need to negotiate. I would've been taking advantage of an already– unimaginable opportunity. This was a gift. My dream had come true. Possibly sensing a mistake had been made, Stanley immediately began to investigate. "Well, what do you mean deal? Why did you agree to what I asked for so quickly?" he questioned, now exhibiting a look of concern. I needed to neutralize his uncertainty, immediately. I quickly began to explain the reason for my prompt reply. I just started talking: "Honestly, Stanley, you deserve it. You've worked hard in this business; you've built a beautiful company with a great reputation, so it's worth the money to me," I clarified. Self-assured, he replied, "Well, okay." It was a satisfactory response. He was at ease. "I'll have my attorney start drafting things up," he replied.

I walked Stanley out to his car before I came back inside my office, overjoyed. I couldn't contain myself. I screamed. I yelled. I clapped and shouted. I jumped up and down, all over the office. I bear-hugged my brother and even some of my employees, who had no idea what I was even excited about. This was incredible! I couldn't believe that Stanley Atlas had just agreed to sell me his company for essentially $200,000! Are you kidding me? Maybe it wasn't worth $4 million, but I definitely felt it was worth more than $200,000, especially to me, his biggest rival. In my eyes, he was giving it away. This was the opportunity of a lifetime. I probably would have agreed to much, much more. I was buying an already-operating, profitable company, my largest direct competitor, for less than what it would've cost me to purchase the equipment alone. Sure, most of his stuff was old, but it still worked. It was producing money daily. If this deal went through, I would instantly add approximately 200 active, licensed retailers to my business. All the hard work had been done. I just had to service them. My company would quickly double in size. In addition, I would just about control the entire local market. This was truly a quantum leap — an absolute game changer!

Reflection Point 15

It's wise to ask tactful questions and then listen intently to gain understanding. Nothing you say will teach you anything; if you want to learn, you need to listen.

Analyze your situation continually, and never get too comfortable. We can always do better, so never settle for good; it's the enemy of great.

Do you listen to understand, or are you listening to respond?

What could you do to be a better listener?

Chapter 16:

Napkin Math

After coming off Cloud 9 and back down to Earth, I began to think about what I needed to do next. It was time for a little dose of reality. Sure, Stanley agreed to sell me his business for roughly $200,000, but I didn't have $200,000. Most of the money I had made was invested back into the business. At the time, I had only about $70,000. After speaking with my father about it and filling him in on the opportunity, he agreed to lend me $50,000 he had saved in his retirement account, which was just about all the money he had. Okay, so now I had $120,000. Still not enough. The more I thought about it, the more it became clear that I needed Stanley to agree to finance the difference. I was apprehensive about breaking the news to him, but I had no choice. *How can I get myself out of this jam?* I wondered. *What can I do to solidify this deal and put him at ease?* It was vitally important that I find a solution. As I thought, I came across a resource I could use but only if it was absolutely necessary, and right around this time, it was looking pretty necessary. When my mother passed, Danny and I inherited her house. It had no debt attached. No mortgage. The home was free and clear and worth around $235,000. I figured I might be able to use that as collateral to gain his confidence.

Even though I now had a property to offer Stanley as a guarantee, I was still extremely nervous when I called Stanley to inform him I didn't have all the money. I thought it might be a deal-breaker. If he were to get upset and refuse to go through with the deal, it would force me to come up with another option, and quickly. Once I had him on the phone, I explained I could give the $120,000 I had as a down payment and pay the difference, roughly $80,000 over the next two years. If he agreed to finance the deal, I would be willing to put my mother's house up as collateral. That way, he could rest assured he would be getting his money. The home would secure the note. Surprisingly, when I broke the news to him, he agreed with little to no convincing necessary. It was almost as if he had been expecting to finance the deal to me the entire time. What a relief that was. With any potential points of contention now addressed, this looked to be a smooth transaction.

After hanging up the phone with Stanley, I started thinking of ways to pay back the loan sooner than expected. I wasn't a fan of being in debt. Adding Atlas Propane's retailers would make me more money, but how much more? I took out a sheet of paper and a pen and started doing some math to work through it. I knew his prices and the average amount of tanks he was exchanging, which gave me an idea of how much money I would make. I also knew that, by combining both businesses, I could take advantage of synergies and make extra money that way. Additionally, I now would have no direct competition. Sure, the two big national players, Empire Gas and Black Bull, would still be around, but it seemed as if they didn't have an appetite for the type of businesses we were supplying. They also offered their propane at a much higher cost to retailers. They were both charging $16 and $17, respectively, per tank exchange. Essentially, they priced themselves out of the market. I'm not sure if this was done purposefully or if they weren't attuned with the region. Either way, their prices weren't competitive. It appeared as if they were more interested in delivering propane to accounts like Home Depot, Lowes, and other prominent national retailers. As a result of my aggressive price war with Atlas Propane, in many cases, I was selling propane for far less than the $16 or $17 the big guys were charging.

In some cases, I offered propane as low as $8 a tank. I did that to entice a retailer to switch to us or retain a customer who had been solicited. $8 a tank was almost half of Stanley's average price of $12. My overall average price at the time was around $11 a tank. Stanley and I had repeatedly lowered our prices to win over retailers and be the more competitive brand. But, in reality, the real winners were the retailers. They continually benefitted from our price war. By playing both of our companies against each other, retailers were almost always guaranteed to get a discount. But, once I purchased Atlas Propane's accounts, that war would be over. It would all be one company, the same company. If I raised my prices, retailers no longer could threaten to switch over to Atlas Propane and vice-versa. I began exploring this in great detail.

My Current Position:

I was exchanging roughly 104,000 to 130,000 tanks each year, at a median price of around $11 a tank.

Which = $1,144,000 to $1,430,000 in gross sales on average a year. This is what I was selling at the time without including Atlas Propane's accounts. I was making a profit of around 30% of gross sales. So, let's assume I was making around $343,200 to $429,000 in profit a year.

	My Current Position:
Tanks Exchanged Each Year	Roughly 104,000 to 130,000 tanks $11 each
Average Gross Sales a Year	$1,144,000 to $1,430,000
Average Profit a Year	$343,200 to $429,000

Atlas Propane's Current Position:

From what I gathered, Atlas Propane was exchanging roughly 1,500 to 2,000 tanks a week, at a median price of around $12 a tank.

When I multiplied that, it gave me $936,000 to $1,248,000 in gross sales on average a year. I figured this was roughly what Atlas Propane was selling at the time. Although he was charging $12, and not $11, I didn't believe he was making the same 30% margin of profit I was. But I assumed I could make a 30% margin after adding his customers to my business. Looking at it that way, I figured his accounts could make me an additional $280,800 to $374,400 in profit a year.

	Atlas' Current Position: *assumed*
Tanks Exchanged Each Year	Roughly 78,000 to 104,000 tanks $12 each
Average Gross Sales a Year	$936,000 to $1,248,000
Average Profit a Year	$280,800 to $374,000

Note: Taking the low average of $280,800 of profit a year clearly indicated I could pay Stanley back in less than one year; in theory, with his own money. Just by acquiring his accounts. I was paying only around $200,000 for a company that I felt could produce approximately $280,800 of profit each year, on the low end. The math illustrated that I could pay for the entire company and still have $80,800 left over. Keep in mind, that's only the first year's profit. Everything after that would be gravy. This reassured me how great of a deal this was.

I then added both companies' average tanks exchanged a year, average sales, and average profit together to give me a ballpark figure. I knew it wasn't going to be 100% accurate. It was just to give me an idea of what to expect.

Combined Business:

	My Current Position	Atlas' Current Position: *assumed*	Combined Estimate:
Tanks Exchanged Each Year	Roughly 104,000 to 130,000 tanks $11 each	Roughly 78,000 to 104,000 tanks $12 each	**182,000 to 234,000 tanks**
Average Gross Sales a Year	$1,144,000 to $1,430,000	$936,000 to $1,248,000	**$2,081,000 to $2,678,000**
Average Profit a Year	$343,200 to $429,000	$280,800 to $374,400	**$623,800 to $803,400**

This exercise further demonstrated that I would be just about doubling my existing profit by acquiring Atlas Propane. Keep in mind that this was without considering synergies that would enable me to squeeze even more profit out of the combined businesses, another encouraging indication that this was a great deal. Based on that promising information, it became time to turbocharge this plan!

The Markup:

Assuming I kept all of Stanley's retail accounts after the transaction took place, I could expect to exchange roughly 182,000 to 234,000 tanks each year afterward. If I raised prices across the board to all the accounts from the median prices of $11 and $12 to $15, what would that look like?

182,000 to 234,000 BBQ tanks x $15 = $2,730,000 to $3,510,000 ingross sales on average a year! If you multiply that by 30%, I potentially could increase my profit to $819,000 to $1,053,000 a year. Potentially tripling my profit.

	My Current Position	Atlas' Current Position: *assumed*	Combined Estimate:	After Price Increased to $15:
Tanks Exchanged Each Year	Roughly 104,000 to 130,000 tanks $11 each	Roughly 78,000 to 104,000 tanks $12 each	**182,000 to 234,000 tanks**	**182,000 to 234,000 tanks**
Average Gross Sales a Year	$1,144,000 to $1,430,000	$936,000.00 to $1,248,000.00	**$2,081,000 to $2,678,000**	**$2,730,000 to $3,510,000**
Average Profit a Year	$343,200 to $429,000	$280,800 to $374,400	**$623,800 to $803,400**	**Low End: $819,000 High End: $1,053,000**

Which meant I could go from making $343,000 to over $1 million a year in profit! Think it's a good deal? That is an astronomical jump. I didn't need to do any more math; this was the right move.

Note: Gross sales are the total amount of sales a company earned throughout a specific period of time, without taking into consideration any costs involved with running a business. Gross sales don't factor in cost of goods sold or COGS, which get deducted when calculating net sales. For example, they don't account for costs associated with item production, employee wages, building rent, returns, theft or sales tax.

Reflection Point 16

When problem solving, grab a pen and paper to WRITE THINGS DOWN. Getting your thoughts on paper will help you gain clarity and awareness of what needs to be done.

Try to determine the roadblocks and find a solution before taking any action. For example, before even finalizing the purchase of Atlas Propane, I already knew some steps I could take to immediately increase profitability.

What are the top three things you could do right now to become more efficient and increase your income?

What more will you gain from making these changes?

Chapter 17:

Peaks and Valleys

After doing my napkin math exercise, I decided that the moment Stanley would sign and agree on paper to sell me his business, I was going to raise all my accounts to $15 a tank. This was a gutsy move, but where were they going to go? Were they going to stop doing business with me to switch over to Atlas Propane? It wouldn't matter because I would essentially own Atlas Propane. Their only other options would be to switch to Empire Gas or Black Bull, and if they did that, they'd be paying even more money than I was charging, which wouldn't make any sense. In addition to the price advantage we would still have, it was already well known that we gave exceptional service. I had put myself in a position to corner the market, and that is just what I was going to do. The plan was set. With that resolved, I began to think of ways to protect my investment in the purchase of Atlas Propane's accounts. I wanted to do everything possible to mitigate the surprise factor, but how could I do that?

Here's what I came up with:

After Stanley and I established a fair market value for his old trucks and other equipment, I suggested it become a requirement to our deal that Stanley travel with me to every Atlas Propane retailer. I wanted him to personally inform them of the transition. We then would have each retailer sign a new service agreement with my company, acknowledging and accepting the transition. They would officially become my retailer, and from that point on, my company would begin servicing them. Once his retailers signed the new agreement, I would pay Stanley on a case-by-case basis for each account. This would be done by just tallying the number of accounts each day that agreed versus the ones that didn't agree. If they disagreed and refused to sign on with my company, I wouldn't pay him the $1,000 for that account. This worked in my favor because, if his retailer refused to onboard with me, I wouldn't be out of a customer and $1,000. Stanley willingly agreed to my proposal. This was a phenomenal addition to our deal. It made the purchase almost risk- free. It just kept getting better and better.

While I was thinking through the details of this deal, it dawned on me that I would no longer be running a small, local business. Our customer base would be covering a span of more than 200 miles. That was about 150 miles of increased territory coverage. It was a big leap. We would no longer be a mom-and-pop operation, and I didn't want that kind of image anyway. I felt that the name *Speedy Tanks 2 You* didn't represent who we were, or where I was trying to go. The name no longer suited our needs. I felt it was a bit childish — we had outgrown it. It was time to level up. The business needed a better name, one that would command some respect. The name alone needed to imply this was a large, respectable business. I began to think of other potential names by making a numbered list of about 10 candidates. I then asked several employees and family members for their takes on them; by requesting that they initial next to the names, they liked most. *Prestige Propane Exchange* turned out to be the fan favorite. I liked it as well and immediately had our secretary file the DBA name, crafted a new logo, and from that moment on, stopped using the name *Speedy Tanks 2 You* altogether.

After Stanley's attorney drafted all the necessary paperwork, I gave it to Danny so the attorney representing us could have a look. Once he signed off on it, our attorney contacted Stanley's attorney and coordinated a closing date. We needed to have the legal paperwork signed before we set forth to start visiting Stanley's retailers. A few days later, Stanley called to arrange a meeting at his attorney's office to complete the documents. He mentioned Danny would need to attend since he was part-owner of the business.

Although we didn't know exactly how much I would foreseeably owe Stanley, I took with me a cashier's check for $120,000 in good faith. I wanted to reassure Stanley and his attorney that we were serious about seeing this through. The remaining balance would be determined after tallying how many of his retailers eventually signed my service agreement.

Upon arriving at the closing, we were escorted to a conference room, where we found Stanley, his attorney, and our attorney waiting for us. We shook hands, exchanged pleasantries, and sat down opposite Stanley and his attorney. Stanley's attorney began sliding documents across the table for signature, but he wasn't sliding them to me; instead, he was sliding them to Danny. All of them. I didn't think much of it at first until Stanley, wide-eyed and with lifted eyebrows, commented: "Interesting, he negotiates the entire deal, and his brother signs for it. Huh!" Insinuating amusement and disbelief. I'll never forget the look on his face or his saying that. "He's 51%," our attorney replied. I ignorantly smiled and giggled, as if nothing was wrong, not understanding why he found that amusing — it seemed normal to me. I just wanted to get the deal done, to start taking over his accounts.

After the paper shuffling, we got straight to work. Stanley and I traveled all over South Florida for well over a month, visiting every retailer he serviced. At first, it was a little awkward. I didn't know the man or anything about him, yet we were riding alone in a car together for 8 to 10 hours each day. We mainly ate at fast-food restaurants to save time and visit as many locations as possible before heading back home. We typically visited 6 to 10 retailers each day, depending on what area we were in and how far away each location was. Not long after taking on this agonizing task, we started to see the fun in it. It was like a game. It appeared that Stanley and I, to some degree, were cut from the same cloth. We had become quite the team — a dynamic duo. We took turns breaking news of the impending acquisition to each retailer. On occasions when they became uncooperative or difficult to deal with, we'd support each other. Kind of like a good cop, bad cop scenario, only in this case, we were both the good cop.

One at a time, we explained to each customer that I was now the new owner and would be supplying them going forward. We gave them their new delivery schedule based on their needs and had them sign a three-year contract, which acknowledged Prestige Propane Exchange would now be their new supplier. I then took the liberty to personally inform each retailer of their price increase to $15 a tank and suggested that they adjust their retail prices accordingly. Although it could've been perceived as bad news, delivering this information in person had its advantages. Many of these retailers had never met the principals of the companies they were doing business with. Several of them didn't even have a clue who Stanley was until he introduced himself. So, the fact that I was there in-person helped to soften the blow and gave me an edge. Most of the retailers respected that I was there to meet them, look them in the eyes, and shake their hands. It gave me an opportunity to form personal relationships with each customer, address any issues they may have had in the past, and explain the price increase, on the spot. Along with the face to the name they now had, I also gave every customer my personal cell phone number. This comforted and assured them they would be in good hands moving forward. To those who needed it, I often promised better marketing material and new display cages. It's as if I were campaigning for their vote, trying to win each retailer over one at a time, attempting to earn their trust and respect.

Even though it was a long, grueling process, we got it done in roughly a month and a half. In the end, it was worth all the time and energy. Just about every retailer signed and agreed, which helped me and also benefitted Stanley.

Because of the nature of our arrangement, the more people who signed, the more money he made. Throughout this long, adventurous process, I became very fond of Stanley as a person. He was a genuinely nice guy with a wonderful family and a warm heart.

Now that our campaign tour of South Florida had come to an end, it was time to sign the final closing documentation, along with the promissory note that Stanley was going to give me for the difference. It would be remarkably close to the $80,000 I thought I might need, given that almost all the retailers had signed our service agreement. That was the deal and what we agreed upon, but the closing didn't go according to plan. A large part of the deal had subsequently changed during the very short month and a half that Stanley and I visited all his retailers. The decision to increase every retailer, Atlas's, and mine, to $15 a tank worked. In the short month and a half it took to transfer Stanley's accounts over to Prestige Propane, the price increase helped me earn the extra $80,000 I needed to finalize the deal. As a result, a loan from Stanley was no longer necessary. I wrote him a check for the entire amount at closing. I also paid back the $50,000 my father lent me just a few weeks after that. It felt as if we were printing money. During the following year, I paid off every debt we owed: my dad's $67,000 mortgage, the $32,000 loan on his personal truck, and a $300,000 debt we had on the company location. We even purchased a couple of new delivery trucks and bought a parcel of land next to our company for $400,000 to expand the operation. We had just about everything we wanted and the money for things we needed, all paid in cash. I had the money to instantly solve any problems that arose. I wasn't used to this. It was an amazing feeling — abundance. It was immensely satisfying and fulfilling to be able to do that for myself and my family. We now had a stranglehold on the market and were making money to the extent I expected. We were on course to make well over $1 million by year's end, just as I predicted. We were in our own lane with virtually no competition. No one had noticed or contested our reign. We were the undisputed champions of propane; or so I thought.

That high only lasted for about a year. Yep, it was too good to be true. The big boys, Empire Gas and Black Bull, noticed all the success I was having and decided to join in on the fun. Empire Gas began to solicit my accounts at around $12 a tank. This now gave them the price advantage over us. At first, I couldn't believe it. *Why are they doing this now, after all this time on the sidelines? Now is when they're going to undercut me?* I guess they woke up. Empire Gas was the aggressor. They began relentlessly pursuing my business. I was the target now. It seemed as if they had sent an arsenal of salesmen after my accounts. Every day I was bombarded with phone calls, and every call contained a version of one of two general complaints: "I was offered a better price. I need you to match it." Or the second, more impassioned statement: "Come pick up your cages. I'm switching to another company!" It was like playing a telephone version of whack-a-mole. The phone didn't stop ringing — it nearly drove me crazy!

After a while, I started sounding like a broken record. I repeated the same spiel every time the phone rang. I gave them all the same calm down speech, followed by a promise to lower their prices, and quickly rushed them off the phone. Freeing up the phone line for the successive, irate customer. I guess this is what Stanley must have experienced when I was at war with him. I was getting a little taste of my own medicine, I presume. Karma. Though that may have been true, I wasn't about to roll over and be beat. I continued to reduce prices to the retailers who called and complained on an as needed basis but, after awhile, it became overwhelming. If I allowed this soiree to continue, it would damage my company's reputation, and I wasn't about to stand by and let that happen. Never. After much deliberation and a few sleepless nights, I reluctantly gave in. I determined I needed to bring all prices down to debilitate

Empire Gas's upper hand and put an end to this uproar. It seemed to be the right move — the best way to put a stop to this chaos, quickly. If I were to offer a better price than Empire Gas once again, this problem would go away. I would be the undisputed champ once more, and there'd be nothing else to talk about, right? So, I did. I lowered every one of my accounts to $11.50 right away. That decision essentially cost us around 25% of our yearly profits, which was several hundred thousand dollars a year. We'd now be lucky if we even scrapped together $700,000 by year's end. It was a tough decision but one I felt needed to be made. We kissed all that beautiful extra money goodbye. But we did, however, reclaim our competitive advantage.

A couple of years had passed since my short bout with Empire Gas. Nothing else ever arose from it. We were back to keeping our prices just under market to maintain our competitive edge, just as we had done with Atlas. We kept our defenses up, remained unfazed, and settled in nicely to our new normal. It was business as usual. Prestige Propane Exchange steadily progressed, with little resistance.

Around that time, I reflected on my decision to lower all prices. I promptly put an end to the ordeal, and it ultimately was a successful tactic, but I still viewed it as a mistake. By lowering all prices across the board, I won instantly, but I also left a major amount of money on the table. Empire Gas's aggressive, unexpected barrage took me by surprise. I believe this happened because I had become comfortable. I was making money. I was fat and happy. I wasn't trying to attract new business, just resting on laurels. Up until that moment, I felt I was the big fish in this small pond. Erroneously believing I had no natural predators, I forgot what it was like to fight, to defend myself. When they attacked, I was caught off guard. But the reality was, Empire Gas didn't have my customer list, and wasn't going to solicit all my accounts. This meant that not all prices needed to be lowered. Such a dramatic, knee-jerk reaction wasn't necessary. I was simply scared. I made it worse in my mind than what it was in reality. I should've continued to fight and aggressively retaliate by soliciting their accounts with full force. I should've played more offense instead of going into panic mode. All the money I instantly gave up by lowering prices across the board could have been used to finance such countermeasures. I learned from this and applied it in the future.

I continually reinvested profits back into the company. Danny and I were even fortunate enough to take some distributions and purchase a couple of investment properties, which were paid for in cash. Our company bank account consistently rebounded faithfully. It was hovering at around $400,000. Business was predictable and healthy, but I was unsettled. I had become gravely aware of an extremely frightening and important detail, Danny's apparent lack of enthusiasm for increasing sales on his side of the business, Local Propane. He didn't seem passionate about it; it was just work for him. I preferred the challenges of business conquests, but he preferred mastering subject matter. Because he already had mastered the science of propane, it appeared as if he grew bored with it. There was nothing else to learn. Propane was no longer a challenge; therefore, it wasn't exciting. This led to stagnation on his end of the business. It wasn't growing, resulting in our lifeblood being just one product: BBQ tanks. Whether it was for gas station retailers or space heaters, we were fundamentally a one-trick pony. If something were to disrupt the BBQ industry, we would lose it all. The thought of it kept me up at night. BBQ tank exchange was a complete and total blessing, but, at the same time, an Achilles heel. That, to me, was unacceptable. This fear may not have been warranted, but it was enough to light a fire under me and create a sense of urgency. It was time to level up, time to diversify. I just needed the opportunity. Now, what's it going to be?

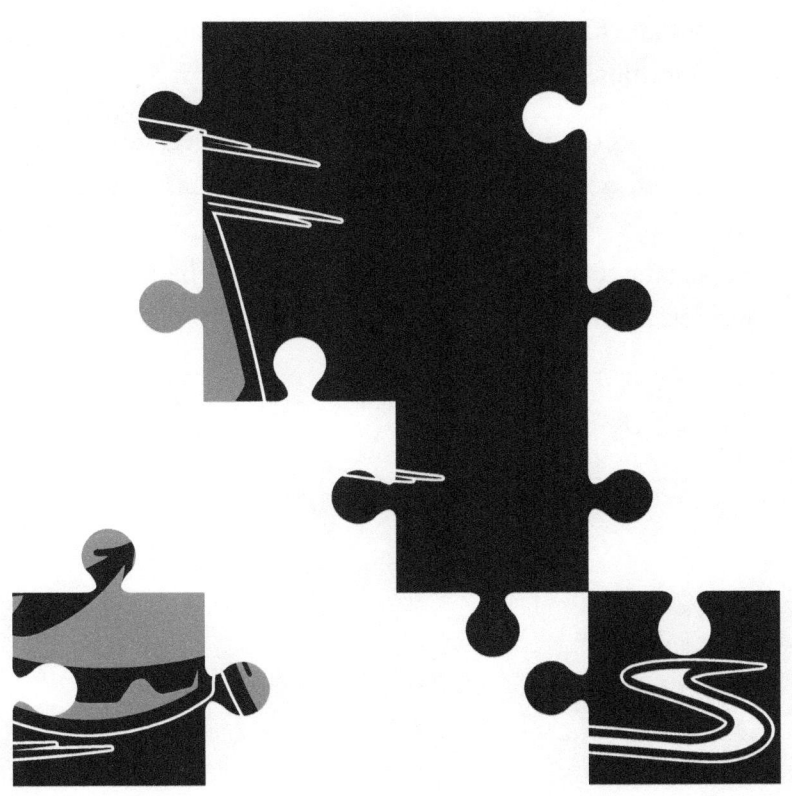

Reflection Point 17

Secure the *gold*. I optimized my deal with Stanley by having him drive around with me to visit his customers, one at a time. In addition to getting the contracts signed, this helped people feel comfortable with the change and transition. There is no substitute for an in-person visit to form relationships, so don't be scared to show your face.

Consider eliminating your debts. I have never heard of someone being foreclosed on or losing it all with no debt! Last, but not least, keep in mind that thinking too highly of yourself can be your downfall. It's important to take inventory of yourself and be aware of what could be lurking around the corner.

How often do you evaluate your financial picture?

Where can you trim some fat?

Chapter 18:

Taken by Storm

Hound Welding was a local gas and welding supply company that thought it might be a good idea to appropriate my entire business model. They re-created the same marketing material I had personally designed for Prestige Propane Exchange, right down to the punctuation. They printed business cards that were identical to mine and made just a few changes. In place of my tank logo, they used a caricature of a dog barking, wearing a cape around its neck. I guess it was some form of superman reference. They also used the same style and color display cages I had. I wasn't amused. They say imitation is the highest form of flattery, but I wasn't flattered either. I was infuriated. I felt like they were trying to rip me off and assume my identity.

While reading some of their marketing material, I felt my heart begin to pound heavily within my chest. I slowly clinched my teeth and my body filled with tension. My heart was racing so fast and pounding so hard I could feel the throbbing in my eardrums. I was familiar with this feeling. It was similar to what I experienced before getting into a scuffle when I was a kid. It was an uncontrollable biological response from feeling threatened, my body's physiological way of telling me I needed to protect myself. Although the propane industry was highly competitive, I didn't like being challenged. As a matter of fact, I took offense to it. It always felt like a life-or-death situation. I needed to defend my business at all costs. If there was a threat to my business, it was a threat to me. We were one and the same.

Immediately after learning of this perceived plagiarism, it was recommended that I phone an attorney for legal advice. I quickly learned the sad truth. Legally, there was not much I could do. It was all very similar but not exactly the same. Sure, I could've sent a cease-and-desist letter, and even have filed a lawsuit. I may have won, eventually, or I may have lost. In either case, that would have cost a lot of money, and even worse, taken a great deal of time. Hound Welding could easily do damage to my reputation and my business during that process. And that was a chance I wasn't willing to take. So, I did what came naturally to me, what I knew how to do: fight back. I had been down a similar road before with Atlas and Empire Gas. I wasn't about to roll over and be beat by Hound Welding, or anyone else, for that matter. I wasn't going to let them into my territory to take market share. How dare they? I was stirring. It was time to act and make a statement. There'd be no competing, no contest. I was going to extinguish this effort immediately. I stopped everything I was doing and personally took the reins. In my opinion, this was an all-hands-on-deck effort. I pulled salesmen, some office staff, and even a few drivers from their regularly assigned tasks to join the battle. I held a meeting and let them all know how serious this was. I asked them to scour the city, find all of Hound Welding's customers, and report back to me. I wanted this done, now! Nothing else mattered; nothing else was important. This was their new assignment, their only assignment, indefinitely. Regardless of how long it took, everything else would take a backseat until it was done. We win or die.

Hound Welding had opened seven new retail BBQ accounts, and even somehow managed to take one of mine in the process. I wanted them all under my banner, pronto. My team and I quickly got to work on it. In some cases, we offered steep discounts to win them over. In other cases, it took some free BBQ tank exchanges with their first delivery. One of the accounts was lucky enough to get three free months' worth of BBQ tank exchanges out of me; that was unheard of. But that's what it took to get it done. Crazy? Maybe. But I got it settled immediately and sent a clear message that I wouldn't be messed with. It was over before it started. By the end of the third day, Hound Welding had been stripped bare of all its accounts.

At day's end, I received a phone call from the owner, Tim. He was startled, scared even. "Hello, this is Tim. Uhm… I'm not sure what happened… but uhm… I'm not sure why you guys are mad…I wasn't trying to fight with you," he muttered. "I don't care," I quickly replied. "This is my market, and every single time you open an account, I'm going to take it! I don't care if I have to give all of your customers free gas for the rest of my life!" I replied, impassioned. "I'm sorry. Uhm… It wasn't personal," he stuttered. "Well, if you're imitating my business and trying to take my accounts, I'd say it's pretty personal. How would you like me to open a welding company exactly like yours and take all your accounts? I might just do that, actually," I spoke arrogantly. "Hey, listen, I'm sorry. There's no need for all of that. I'm not going to sell propane anymore. You have my word," he replied. "Okay, have a nice day!" I hung up. I may have been acting a bit like a bully, but I couldn't help myself. I was overly passionate and protective of my business. The thought of someone trying to take it from me made me a bit irrational.

After the tension settled from my heated quarrel with Tim from Hound Welding, Tim and I made peace and began a dialogue. With the drama put behind us, I began to refocus on diversifying. Maybe my idle threat of selling welding gases could very well have been the diversification I was looking for. Potential customers did happen to call us from time to time asking if we sold welding gasses such as oxygen and acetylene. We turned them down regularly. We weren't capitalizing on the opportunity that was right in front of us the entire time. I figured all we needed to do was stock the welding gasses they were looking for and sell it to them when they called; it could be that easy. Well, it was significantly more intricate than that. It turns out it was much more complicated than propane. It was out of my wheelhouse. The science of it all made me cross-eyed. Tim, however, knew all about it. I began to think about the possibility of purchasing his company, or even partnering with him.

His business was still relatively small, so it could be rather easy. I continued to think this through. *Hmm, maybe I can stake him? Make a separate branch of our company and offer him a partnership? That could work. This new branch would fit nicely into that piece of property I just bought that borders our existing operation. Tim can run the welding-supply business from there, and we could finance its growth. With not much effort, we would be getting a piece of the pie. We would also have our hooks in a new industry and be diversified.*

I ran the concept by Danny. He liked my idea but didn't want to stake Tim. He wanted to run this new division himself. I disagreed; I felt his time could be better spent running his side of the business, which had already been starved of his attention. He didn't need another distraction. After a short conversation, I felt Danny and I were on the same page; so, I phoned Tim to get his take on the idea. I informed him that we were considering going into the welding-gas business and offered him the opportunity to join forces with us. Because his company was still in its infancy, he didn't have much business or presence. I pointed out that he undoubtedly would benefit from all the welding-gas business we were turning down — I was trying to sell him on the idea. We went on to discuss the potential structure of this proposition in detail. I offered to buy all of Hound Welding's assets and then rebrand the company as *Local Gas and Welding Supply*. We'd then relocate them to our recently purchased, vacant facility next-door. Tim would be entitled to a percentage of profits, going forward, based on his performance. That would essentially turn Tim into a glorified employee. This would be a much better deal for us than it was for him. Nonetheless, he was receptive and onboard. He may have just wanted to be a part of a winning team.

I went ahead and gave Tim Danny's phone number and suggested they speak regarding the technical aspects of the business, which I didn't quite understand, before we moved forward. After they spoke, Tim called me, somewhat perplexed. He notified me that Danny called off the deal. Danny told Tim that we had no need for him because he could do it himself. I was stunned. *Why would he do that without consulting me? How could he scrap my idea and this opportunity without even speaking to me about it?* I felt like a fool in front of Tim. I had made it a habit to fill Danny in on what I was doing and take his opinion into account when making decisions for Prestige Propane Exchange, even though I didn't have to. Apparently, that was a one-way street. I couldn't make sense of it. I guess Danny wanted to chase a new, shiny object. Which I understood, because I knew he preferred to learn and be challenged, but that doesn't mean I agreed with it. I just wanted him to focus on holding up his end of the bargain, which he hadn't been prioritizing.

Prestige Propane Exchange had outpaced Local Propane long ago. Thus, our unique partnership had become lopsided. Prestige Propane was responsible for approximately 70-80% of the profits at that time; therefore, it felt as if I was doing all the heavy lifting. I forbade Danny from taking on the new welding task, and I, in turn, denounced the idea altogether. I preferred not to begin a new venture, if it meant he would continue to overlook his responsibilities. It was, undoubtedly, the elephant in the room. I again asked Danny to please focus on his end of the business, and that was that. I called Tim, apologized for wasting his time and for all the confusion. Then, I put it to rest and went back to work.

A little time had passed, maybe a couple of weeks. It was a run-of-the- mill workday. I had just arrived at my office. As I walked past Danny's desk, I caught a glimpse of some business cards with the Local Propane logo on them, but something was different. I stopped and picked one up to check it out. It read, "Local Gas and Welding Supply, Owner. Danny Lewis." The cards had Danny's cell phone number on them. They also listed the address of the property next-door I had just purchased for our company's future use.

Now that is something I didn't expect to see. Apparently, Danny went behind my back, took my idea, dismissed Tim, and was planning to use our property for his own endeavor, all without my consent. Had he lost his mind? To make matters worse, there was another stack of business cards with a name I recognized on them. "Nick Gomez." Apparently, Danny had found himself a new partner as well. He was a mutual friend of ours. What was Danny thinking? As I read those business cards, you probably could've seen the steam coming out of my ears. I felt betrayed, disrespected, and unappreciated. He had gone too far this time. I called on my father to intervene, but he wasn't much help. Non-confrontational by nature, he did next to nothing to resolve the conflict. He essentially called *Switzerland* and bowed out.

From that point on, the arguments intensified. Insults flew back and forth. Sometimes they weren't that bad. Other times they were downright awful. There was major disrespect on both sides. It was destructive. I know I was upset, because I felt betrayed, but I didn't know what Danny was trying to gain from all of this. Maybe he felt the need to assert his dominance over me because he was my older brother. Perhaps he was taking some sort of frustration out on me. Either way, he didn't want to stop, and kept stirring it up. The absence of our referee was obvious. Danny and Max arguing on a daily basis was once again the new normal.

The never-ending story. He continually provoked me. His go-to altercation fire-starter was reprimanding me for not arriving to work promptly at 8 a.m. each day.

Completely overstepping his boundaries and not abiding by the terms our family agreed upon, presumptively acting as if he were my superior, did he forget? I run Prestige Propane Exchange independently and answer to no one. Remember that? I did more than my fair share of reminding him. At first, I would reply with something simple such as, "Leave me alone, Danny. You're supposed to run your side of the business, and I run mine. You're not my boss." But as his little jabs persisted, day in and day out, I became irritated. I began to retaliate with such remarks as: "Maybe if you made us as much money as I have, you could come to work at any time you want." I had never held things like that over his head, but as he continued to provoke me and incite conflict, he brought it out of me. Was he blind to all I had done for our family? The sacrifices I had made and was still making? The money I had made for him? This is what I get? A disloyal business partner who complains because I don't clock in and out? He wasn't complaining about my hours when I shared profits with him. The funny thing was, being at work at 8 a.m. had absolutely nothing to do with my success. I wasn't an employee; I owned the company. In fact, I put in more hours than anyone who worked there, but I chose my hours. I wasn't on a schedule; my timecard didn't matter. What mattered were my results. Customers were happy; business was growing, and we were making money.

Sure, I would arrive late, but I was often exhausted from working after hours the night before. Was I supposed to work 16-hour days for the rest of my life while he dashed out the door at 4:59 p.m. each day? Why harass me with such foolishness? Especially when he was reaping the benefits of all my hard work. It felt petty, as though I was being scolded, picked on. My mother's passing and not being around to interject and keep the peace between us was a reality my parents hadn't planned for. This once-dormant volcano was once again active, and ready to erupt at any second.

Danny and I had another heated discussion about it, and, not surprisingly, we got nowhere. I didn't want to waste any more time and energy arguing with him. At that point, I just figured he had something to prove. Whether it was to me, himself, or someone else, I just wasn't interested in fighting about it any longer. I had work to do, and the continual bickering was a distraction. So, I let it go. Danny went forward with his plans to open the welding business, without me, who had the idea in the first place, or Tim, who had the experience and a majority of the equipment. Nick was to be his partner. This was a significant turning point for us — a devastating blow to our business and personal relationship.

This working-together deal my parents coerced me into turned out to be a horrible arrangement for me. I had kept my end of the bargain, and for what? I worked day and night, earned almost all the money, and still split the profits. Doesn't sound too great for me. This persistent turmoil kept leading me to a simple question that continually loomed in my mind. *How am I benefitting from this arrangement?*

Although I was disappointed and thankless, I chose to push forward. I still was very motivated and had dreams of continued growth for Prestige Propane Exchange. Besides this hiccup, I was having fun. There was still a lot of work to do.

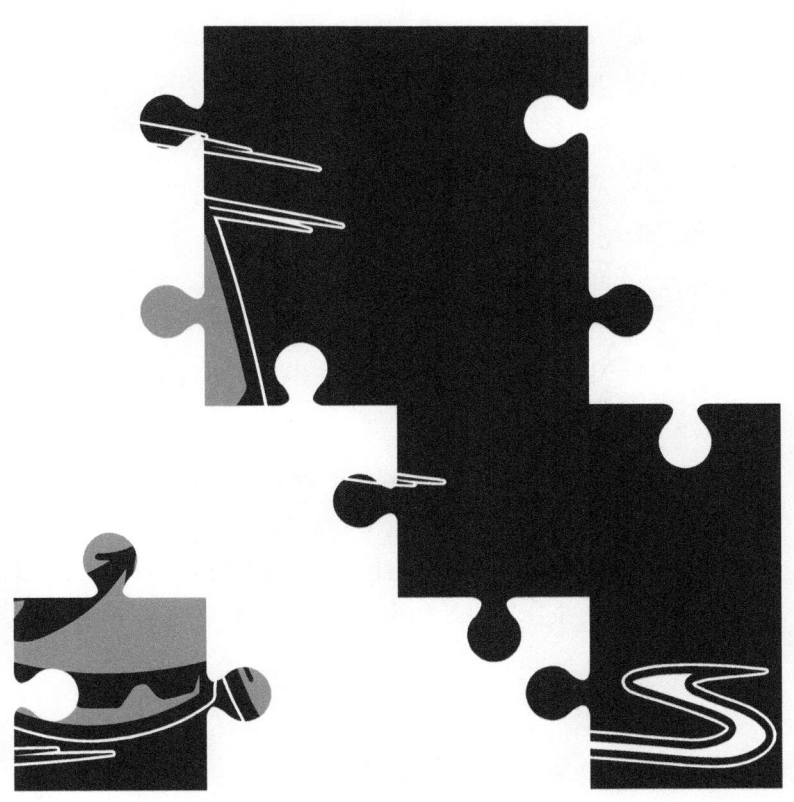

Reflection Point 18

Stay on top of your game so no one can knock you off. I needed to stay aggressive because I had to protect my business. When I came into the BBQ tank-exchange market, Atlas didn't do much about it. Stanley basically let me in. I slowly chipped away at market share until, one day, I was a legitimate player. He basically allowed me to grow into a problem for him. That resulted in Atlas's losing most of its customers and, ultimately, the entire business.

Be ready to address different challenges as you grow. Know when to act and what response would be appropriate and effective. As I once heard… "Kill the lizard while it's still a baby. Don't wait around for it to turn into Godzilla!" Some situations require all hands-on deck; some don't. Know the difference.

There's no clocking in and out when you own a business. It's a 24/7 commitment. If you have partners, always clearly communicate your intentions with them. Say what you mean and what needs to be said. No one likes being left in the dark.

Be honest with yourself. Is all your communication truthful?

How could being 100% sincere improve your relationships?

Chapter 19:

The Underdog

Heartland Propane was now the second-largest propane company in the country, behind Empire Gas. They continually expanded their operations through acquisitions and successfully purchased propane gas companies of all sizes across America. They even attempted to purchase our business, at one point. Though that didn't work out, Heartland managed to make a very strategic acquisition in South Florida. They bought Stonewall Gas, the company that all but controlled the seemingly impenetrable forklift tank- exchange market. When the news first broke, local competitors like us were delighted at the potential opportunity of gaining some of that market share. After an acquisition, it's common for service to lag. The new owners often, and almost immediately, start changing things around. They fire or undervalue key people, with little or no knowledge of how important some processes are or how vital some employees may be to the organization. It's not always the case, but this is why many mergers and acquisitions are unsuccessful.

During those tumultuous times, the customers tend to take the brunt of it. They often experience subpar service, which leads to anger and frustration. Then they begin to look for other options. Other propane suppliers who care about them and their needs. That would be us — on standby, waiting for our turn. Ready to scrounge up any neglected customers that were about to fall through the cracks during all the pandemonium. To almost everyone's surprise, this time, it was not the case. Stonewall, now owned by Heartland, maintained its grip. It appeared Heartland had changed next to nothing in Stonewall's operation, not even the company name. Almost no one outside of the propane community knew that the transaction had taken place. They absorbed their business smoothly, as if the acquisition had never happened.

It seemed as if they merely added the company's assets to their balance sheet and continued running the business without making any changes. It was business as usual. In my opinion, this was extremely well done. They kept the employees and management who had made the company successful up to that point. After all, why would they change them? Those employees were responsible for the success they were buying into. Everything was just about the same. There was no confusion. No chaos. Which for us, meant no opportunity — it was a false alarm.

Heartland/Stonewall maintained their strength, but it was short-lived. Not awfully long after the news of Heartland's acquisition of Stonewall came the real opportunity, the one that sent shockwaves throughout the propane community. That news was — Empire Gas acquires Heartland! What? The biggest guy buys the second-biggest guy. Now, that was news. This was a move similar to my acquisition of Atlas Propane to corner the local market, but on a national level. My purchase of Atlas Propane was microscopic in comparison. Now Empire Gas was the biggest propane company in the country, by a long shot, no question about it. There would undoubtedly be turmoil. This deal was enormous. It was too big a deal to control. Adding to that, Empire Gas didn't appear to have the same strategy Heartland used when buying Stonewall and other businesses. This was no secret. It was well known that this was taking place. It created awareness among the community. A few months after the coupling of the two conglomerates, the buzz died down. The news wasn't really news anymore, and the chatter all but ceased.

Then, one day, the phone rang...it was a Stonewall/Heartland, now Empire Gas customer, looking for a price quote. The call was transferred to me. "Hello, thank you for calling Prestige Propane Exchange; this is Max speaking. How can I help you?" I asked politely. The man struggled slightly to gather his thoughts. "Hi...um. I was a customer of Stonewall

Gas, and now I think they're called Empire, but, um, anyway…I was wondering how much you guys charge to exchange forklift tanks?" he asked. "Exchange forklift tanks," I repeated, "No, I'm sorry, we're not currently offering that type of service. You can bring your tanks here and have them refilled if you'd like," I replied. "Well, I want to switch companies, and I need them exchanged. We don't have anyone here with a pickup truck to take the tanks to get refilled. We need the exchange delivery service," he emphasized. He evidently wasn't taking no for an answer. "Uhm, okay, sir. Give me one quick second, please. Let me see what I can do for you," I replied. I put the man on hold and just sat there staring into space. I was thinking about what I was going to say to him. Although forklift tanks were being exchanged and refilled all over Florida, it was a service we didn't offer. Last I remember, forklift tanks were a waste of time. I didn't even own any forklift tanks. What would be the point? There was no profit margin in it. I thought it over for a second and decided I might as well humor him. *I'll ask him what price he's paying; he'll tell me he's paying pennies for his forklift gas, and then I'll tell him he's got a great price, and he should stick with his current supplier.*

I picked the phone back up. "Hello, sir…How many tanks do you need exchanged?" I asked. "We go through about 12 to 14 every week," he replied. That was a decent amount. He was a good customer. "Okay, what are you currently paying for each forklift tank exchange?" I asked. "Oh, uhm…hold on, let me check the last invoice." I could hear him mumbling to himself as he read his invoice. I patiently waited for his response. Completely apathetic and just going through the motions, I felt this was a waste of time. The man began to speak, "It says here $47 a tank." I chuckled as I responded, "No, I think you're misreading it, sir. It can't be $47 a tank." "Yeah, that's what the invoice says, 12 tanks x $47 per tank is $564. Then there's other taxes and fees," he replied. I was in disbelief. I asked the man if he'd be willing to email me over a copy of his invoice. I promised I'd call him back after I had a chance to review it.

Sure enough, he was paying $47 a tank. The crazy part was, he wanted a new supplier because of the lack of service he was getting. He never had an issue with his pricing. Apparently, Empire Gas raised all their prices to make back as much money as possible, quickly. It sounded a lot like what I did with Atlas, but it appeared they took a far more aggressive approach.

Before calling the man back, I needed to call a local tank supplier and get pricing on some forklift tanks, because I didn't own any. The supplier quoted me $95 for each steel forklift tank, but he didn't have them in stock. He only had aluminum forklift tanks, which were more expensive, $140 each. Ouch! The supplier assured me they were a better option, and I'd be pleased with them in the long term. I thought he was trying to make a sale, honestly, but, either way, he had them, and I needed them. I didn't want to miss out on the opportunity to get this account. If I were going to make it happen, this was my only option.

I then crunched some numbers on how much it would cost to fill each forklift tank with propane, to quote the man a price. The tanks were surprisingly inexpensive to fill. Each tank held only around $8 of propane at my cost. After doing some math, I decided I would quote the man $24 for each forklift tank exchange. There was no question whether he'd be happy with the pricing I was giving him. I was quoting him half the amount he already was paying. Which was more than reasonable, and at that price, I'd make around $16 a tank, which was an attractive margin for me. When I multiplied that by his average consumption, I figured I'd be making roughly $200 a week from this account. I supposed, in theory, I would be paying off one of these tanks every week, at that rate, and, after a few months, I would be making pure profit.

I called the man back and told him I had good news. First, I explained the benefits of aluminum tanks versus steel. Second, I mentioned we could deliver seven days a week if he were ever to have an emergency. To sum it up, I gave him his price quote. He was astonished by the disparity in pricing and asked me to send out the forklift tanks right away. He was hooked. After he requested the tank delivery, I mentioned I would need his company to sign a three-year service agreement, of course. It was inconsequential to him, at that point, after hearing all the benefits and the price being offered.

I still didn't own the tanks, so I informed the customer that his delivery would be scheduled for later that day. I sent one of my employees over to the tank supplier with a check to buy the aluminum forklift tanks. I had him bring the tanks back to my office. Once they arrived, I inspected them. The supplier was right about the aluminum tanks. They were much more attractive than the corroded steel tanks I was accustomed to seeing. Steel tanks would often rust; once they started rusting, whatever company owned them would typically paint over it, but painting them rarely had the desired effect. They always looked horrible. Most steel forklift tanks I came across were half-rust, half-fresh paint. That wouldn't happen with aluminum tanks; aluminum doesn't rust. Another disadvantage to having steel tanks was, they were heavy. A full steel tank weighed around 75 pounds. These new aluminum tanks weighed only 59 pounds when full, making them a preferred choice if you ever had to lug them around regularly. They were a much more appealing option. It was a quality product, worth the extra money.

I began researching everything about forklift tanks — the different designs, the different materials they were made from, and how other companies were operating their exchange programs. After some research, I listed all the ways I could improve on what the competition was doing or not doing. I designed cutting-edge marketing material, developed an aggressive pricing schedule, and hired a dedicated salesman with experience in door-to-door sales. We quickly began to attract business. We had a competitive advantage — exceptional equipment and aggressive prices. It was an opportunistic time. Accounts came in steadily. It almost felt easy — a far cry from my previous experience with Stonewall. Forklift tank exchange was officially on the menu!

Note: A balance sheet is a financial statement that reports a company's assets, liabilities, and shareholders' equity, at a specific time. It provides a basis for computing rates of return and evaluating its capital structure. It's a financial statement that provides a snapshot of what a company owns, owes, and the amount invested by shareholders.

Reflection Point 19

If you're not 100% sure of what needs to be done, maybe you shouldn't do anything! Sometimes the best move, is no move. When entering a new environment, take some time to observe before invoking any changes. Heartland understood that, and their acquisition strategy was flawless.

Stay curious and open minded. You may find *gold* where you never thought it existed. Selling propane to forklift tank customers wasn't an opportunity before, but a lot had changed. When I realize there was now an opportunity to profit from it, I made the adjustment and immediately seized that opportunity.

Don't get greedy. I could've quoted the customer a higher price but, I felt I already could make very good money at $24 a tank. If I had quoted him just a few bucks less than the $47 he was paying, it would have been only a matter of time before someone came along and undercut my price.

Lastly, investing in quality equipment can save you time and money in the long haul, which will, in turn, put more money in your pocket. Don't just go with the cheapest option. Do some research and make an educated investment. If it looks cheap to you, it's going to look cheap to the people you were trying to impress.

Are you doing the appropriate amount of research before
entering an unfamiliar environment?

How should you be mentally and physically preparing yourself
for a new opportunity?

Chapter 20:

Forced Furlough

Danny was off to a start with the welding business, but it was a slow start. I secretly hoped he might lose interest in the idea. I thought he might see how great I was doing with the forklift exchange opportunity at Prestige Propane and get inspired to refocus on his side of the business. This development proved there was still plenty of money to be made in the propane industry. But unfortunately, that didn't happen. He appeared to be in some sort of distress. When I would casually run into him at the office, I noticed he often wore a long face and didn't seem happy. After a few weeks of watching him mope around, we finally had a conversation about it. Danny said he needed to take some time off. He said he might need a few weeks or maybe even a couple of months away from work, to clear his head. He wasn't quite sure if he ever wanted to return.

Business aside, I asked him some personal questions about his mood. I wanted him to be happy. He was my brother, and even though we fought most of the time, I loved him. From our conversation, I couldn't discern what specifically was troubling him. He did mention, however, that he still was partially grief-stricken over the loss of our mother. Whatever the case may have been, I offered to support him in any way I could. Danny asked if I could cover for him and run Local Propane until he figured out what he wanted to do. Of course, I agreed.

During Danny's absence, I took a hands-on approach to learning more about Local Propane. It was a little challenging but not impossible. For the most part, it was no problem. There were no arguments in the office, and everyone was focused on growth. I began to make some minor changes to his side of the business. I was able to implement efficiencies and increase profitability. It was going well. About a month into this arrangement, Danny called to check in on things. In that conversation, he again mentioned he might not ever come back to work. It appeared that he was at a crossroads and not sure what he wanted to do with his life. I assured Danny that he had nothing to worry about. Things were under control, and he could take all the time he needed to come to a conclusion. I continued to pay his salary and maintain all his company benefits, which included: health insurance, car payments, his cell phone bill, and some cash distributions.

The naked truth was that things were running smoothly with only one of us there. There was no bickering, no friction. Our office had become peaceful again. I didn't know much about Local Propane or the specifics of propane itself, but it didn't matter. I didn't need to be a propane expert to be successful. I just needed to know how to run a business, which I did. Although I was doing much more work, I didn't mind it at all. Danny got his time off, and I got to do what I liked to do, which was work and grow. All was well.

About three months into Danny's leave of absence, he showed up at our office, midday, unannounced. The employees were surprised to see him. I wasn't there but also was surprised when I heard of his visit. There obviously was nothing wrong with his being there, but there was one issue. Almost as soon as he walked through the door; after being absent for nearly three months, Danny began to give marching orders to the employees. Many of his orders were in direct conflict with what I had instructed the employees to do.

When I arrived back at my office, the staff filled me in on the details of Danny's drop in. Although happy to see him, they expressed how it disrupted our workflow. They were confused as to who was in charge. I sympathized with them. Concerned that Danny's visit would hinder our progress, I called him to have a conversation with respect to this. I pointed out that his stepping in, after a three-month hiatus and ordering people around might not have been the greatest approach, especially without speaking to me first or understanding that he had no knowledge of our priorities at the time. He wasn't up to speed on what was going on or any of the changes I had made, or the reasoning behind those changes. Everything was under control. He asked me to manage Local Propane for him, and I was doing just that. In fact, I was able to increase Local Propane's profitability within those three months, just by keeping an eye on things and making small changes — raising prices and adding minimum delivery charges for all deliveries, to name just two. I explained to Danny that everything was working fine in his absence and, if he were interested, I would be more than happy to bring him up to speed. I then expressed if he wanted me to continue running both companies that he please not disrupt the workflow again.

Before this minor incident, things were running very smoothly. We were making money, and there were no issues. Considering this, I offered Danny a proposition: I gave him the option of not having to come to work anymore, ever. It was clear that his heart wasn't in it. I proposed he could continue to draw his same salary and same distributions going forward; I only asked that he make himself available if ever I needed him and that he not interfere with my management of both brands. Danny seemed to be receptive to this idea. Who wouldn't be? You basically don't have to do anything. Just go home and relax. I'll send you your money. It seemed a superb deal to me. He said he'd think it over and get back to me.

After a few days, Danny showed up at work again. This time I was at the office. He asked to speak to me privately and mentioned he was interested in coming back to work. I informed Danny that if there was one thing I was absolutely certain of, it was that we couldn't work under the same roof together. His time off proved to me that I could handle just about anything on my own. I had outgrown our mismatched partnership. Things were peaceful and I liked it that way. I informed Danny that if he would be coming back to work, I would definitely be leaving. I didn't want to regress to the way things once were, and the extra work wasn't bothering me. I found it fun and very fulfilling to clean things up. I was happy now. I knew if we continued working together, it was only going to poison our relationship further. I'm sure it wasn't the response he was expecting, but it was the truth. I needed to draw a line in the sand.

I didn't hear from Danny for a few days. I'm not sure what he thought about during that time or whom he spoke to, but I believe he got some very bad advice. Arriving at the office on an ordinary weekday, my then secretary, Desiree, stopped me at the entrance to my office. "Don't be mad," she said. I was confused. "What are you talking about, Desiree? What's going on?" "Just trust me; try not to be upset," she said. "Um… okay. Can we get to work now?" I asked. I walked past her into my office. What I found was a camera pointing directly at my desk. Not in the direction of my desk, it was staring right at where my face would be if I were sitting down. In addition to that, there were a handful of new cameras in my office. "What the hell is this about?" I asked out loud. "Your brother called me this morning to see if you were in. When I said you weren't, he had the camera guys show up shortly afterward. He said he wanted to keep his eyes on things from home. I know it's not cool, but I didn't want to argue with him. I didn't tell you because I don't want to get in the middle of it," she explained. "Is this a joke? Do I require 24/7 parental supervision now? I don't understand the need for this. This is disrespectful!" I said. I called Danny.

There were a few rings before he picked up. As soon as he answered, I immediately questioned him. "What's this bull about Danny? You're going to put a camera right over my desk? Pointing right at my face? What the hell's your problem, man?" I yelled. He calmly replied, as if he was expecting this reaction out of me. "Well, If I'm not going to be there, I want to be able to keep an eye on things," he replied. "And you're going to do that by pointing a camera at my face? When have you ever cared about what's going on here? I've been doing you a favor by running your side of the company, Danny, and I've been doing a great job of it. I've never needed your supervision, and I don't need it now!" I slammed the phone back into the cradle, walked out to my truck, grabbed a hammer out of the toolbox, walked back inside, and smashed the camera right off the wall. I guess you could say I was just a little bit upset.

I left the office and went home. I didn't want to be there in that moment. I felt Danny was back to pushing my buttons again. I didn't get it. What'd I do to deserve this treatment? Here I was, now willingly doing 100% of the work, his and mine, still splitting every penny with him, and somehow, he still felt the need to belittle me. It was never enough. He still needed to have some sort of control over me. Why was he treating me like this? I was hurt and, once again, felt unappreciated. I was out of answers.

The next day, I arrived at work refreshed. I had slept off the argument from the day before and was ready to get back on track. Upon arriving, I greeted several employees as I made my way toward my office. When I opened the door, I discovered that Danny had yet another camera installed above my desk. In disbelief, I just stood there for a moment and stared at it. My nostrils flared as I took in as much air as I could through my nose, before slowly releasing it through my mouth as my puffed cheeks deflated. I was doing my absolute best to remain calm. He had pushed me to the breaking point. This was the last straw. I took out the giant set of keys I had in my pocket, which opened just about every lock, door, and gate to both companies, and calmly tossed them on my desk as I walked around it to pick up the phone. I began dialing Danny's cell. He picked up on the second ring. "Hello," he answered, as if nothing were the matter. "Hey, if you think you can do a better job of running the companies, why don't you come over and do it yourself?" I asked. Not waiting for a reply, I slammed the phone back into the cradle and walked out. For once, I had finally stood up for myself. I knew my value and what I had done for him and my family. I wasn't going to let Danny, or anyone else, for that matter, undermine me for even a second longer.

Reflection Point 20

It would be wise not to have two primary decision-makers in a business. Ultimately, one person should have the final say.

Communication is key. I have no clue what was going through Danny's mind at the time, but I do know his decision to install cameras above my desk crossed the line. Know your worth. Don't be afraid to remove yourself from situations that no longer serve your best interest. Instead, surround yourself with people who have the best intentions at heart. You don't have to allow people to take advantage of you or treat you unfairly. Whether it's friendship or family, don't settle for less than you deserve.

Are you appreciated for what you bring to the table?

Do you need to remove yourself from an unfavorable environment?
If so, why?

Chapter 21:

Silver Lining

As I drove away from my office and my life as I knew it, fear started to sink in. I thought to myself, *What did I just do? Working on the business is pretty much all that my life is about, and I basically just quit.* A sense of great anxiety accompanied my fear. *How am I going to make a living now? Should I start over, maybe start another company? I probably shouldn't, but who am I without the business? Geez, I don't know. What am I going to do?* Lost in thought, I drove a few miles down the road without even noticing it. *Where am I even driving to right now?* I had a million questions and not many answers. I was undoubtedly scared but going back wasn't an option.

While I drove, I began to rationalize and comfort myself. Yes, I'm scared right now, but is this fear real? I continued to think it through in detail. After re-evaluating my current financial position, I found the truth. The fear existed, but only in my mind. In all actuality, I was doing quite well. I had planned for my future and had done a great job of preparing myself for the unexpected. I was going to be okay, even if I never received a single penny from my company again. My house was small, a little over 1,200 square feet, but it was paid off. I had a healthy amount of money saved, roughly $500,000. Apart from that, I owned several rental properties that were making me over $100,000 of profit a year. I honestly didn't need any more money. I wasn't spending what I was earning anyway — just investing and saving it. How much money do you need to be happy anyhow? With this improved outlook, I began to think about retirement. Ironically, I had always said I wanted to retire by 32, and I was 31 now. Maybe this was a self-fulfilling prophecy. This wasn't how I pictured it but what the heck? Sure, I was still young, but are there rules to retiring? Do I have to work relentlessly until I turn 65, just because everyone else is doing that? No, I don't. I get to decide what path I'm going to take. It's my life, and I can make my own rules. Besides, I had been on call, seven days a week, for about 10 years at that point. I felt I had sacrificed enough of my life. I wanted to start living for myself, do the things I wanted to do, not just what needed to be done. It has been said that *rich people have money, and wealthy people have time*. I had never had time before. All I had was some money. I never even genuinely enjoyed it. My mind was made up. Retirement it is!

Oddly enough, I didn't know how not to work, so, I needed to learn. The first few days were bizarre. I didn't know what to do with myself. I went to the gym and worked out for three hours the first day. I went to the grocery store immediately after and bought a shopping cart full of health food. Then I began thinking of all the things I had daydreamed about doing during work that I now, suddenly had time for. I could go to the beach, ride my bike, go bowling, play pool, go fishing, play catch with a friend, play tennis, and travel. The possibilities were endless. This was great. I began phoning friends. I asked just about all of them if they wanted to do any of these various activities with me. The responses were generally the same: "I'm working." I apparently was the only person I knew my age who wasn't working. I had no retired friends. Although I had all this newly found time on my hands, I didn't have anyone to spend it with. I did some activities alone but quickly lost interest in them. Without someone to share these experiences with, it just wasn't the same. It was a bummer.

Weeks, then months went by. I began going to the gym two times a day. I was eating extremely healthy and quickly got into the best shape of my life. When I was not exercising, I was studying the real estate market, making contacts, and asking realtors if they had any good deals, though almost everything was a good deal at that time. Banks were trying to offload dozens of properties that were in default, generally, through foreclosures or short sales. Since I had some cash, I bought a couple of apartments. Ridiculously cheap; about half of their market value. Under $30,000 each. I also bought a few houses. In some cases, for as little as $90,000. I cleaned them up and rented them out. On a few occasions, I immediately resold some for a quick gain. Real estate was by no means as profitable, exciting, or as fast-paced as running my propane business had been. It was boring in comparison, but I liked it. It gave me something to do, but not too much to do. It allowed me to keep and enjoy a great amount of leisure time, which was wonderful. I was at peace.

In search of hobbies, I could enjoy as a party of one, I bought a Harley-Davidson motorcycle. I drove it down to Key West. I had never felt so worry- free. My phone was off. I had the wind in my face, a gorgeous view of the ocean for most of the ride down, and nowhere else to be. I left the business world behind. I made several stops along the way, often finding a shady place to park my motorcycle and have a seat. I'd gaze out to the horizon, enjoy the gorgeous ocean views, and feel the priceless breeze. It felt so amazing to be alone out there. No one even knew where I was. There was something I really liked about that. It was just me and the ocean. I guess we had some catching up to do.

After enjoying the motorcycle for some time, I bought a small boat. I used it to take my friends out on the weekends. I started fishing more often, which I loved to do but never had time for. Not long after that, I took up scuba-diving lessons with some of my best friends. I was nervous at first, but once I overcame the fear, I had the time of my life diving and spearfishing. It's another world down there. I later took bowling lessons. I ordered a custom bowling ball and even bought bowling shoes. At one point, I even planted a small herb garden in my yard. I tried guitar lessons shortly after, which was harder than I thought. Heck, I even dabbled in archery. I loved everything I was doing. After experimenting in all those various activities, I finally felt I was genuinely enjoying my life. I decided to enroll in culinary school, which I had always dreamed of doing but never did. Now I had the time. It was no longer about getting a degree. I just wanted to enjoy the experience, and in some way, live out my dream, which is exactly what I did.

Over the course of the previous years, I had written down in a notebook some travel destinations that interested me, along with some life experiences I wished to have someday. There were just a few places on it. I guess you could say it was like a mini-bucket list. They had always seemed so unattainable for some reason. I just never thought I would ever have the time to visit these places or do the things on that list. I probably was right about that. If I was always at work and didn't make time for anything else, when would I ever have time to explore the world? Well, I wasn't working anymore, so what better time would I have than right now to live out my dreams?

Once my mind was made up, I began booking flights. To name a few, I traveled to: Georgia, Tennessee, New York, Colombia, Brazil, the Dominican Republic, and Montreal. I enjoyed every destination and made memories everywhere I went. I was finally living my life. But the most notable and impactful destination I traveled to was Israel. By chance or maybe even by fate, I had the opportunity to travel with a group of Christians to what is known to them as the Holy Land. I had the great honor of being baptized in the Jordan River by Pastor Benny Hinn, an Israeli televangelist best known for his miracle crusades. My life was never the same again after that. I can honestly say I felt the presence of God that day. I cried tears of joy when I came out of that ice-cold water.

Maybe all the pain and controversy I had been experiencing was a blessing in disguise. If it weren't for my differences with Danny, I never would have made the time to travel or have had any of these experiences. It all brought me here. It forced me to live. When would I ever have stopped working for months on end and booked flights all over the world? When would I have made time for all these activities? Never. I was now living a carefree, wonderful life.

I had a newly found appreciation for myself. Life was not all about work any longer. It was now about making myself happy. I was the priority. I was slowly learning how to treat myself better. Trying to live the life I felt I deserved, the life I had earned. Although I had a strong desire for betterment, some of the hardships I had encountered up to this point had taken their toll on me. I had years of distress under my belt, emotional baggage that wasn't serving me, and I needed to do away with. I knew this wasn't something I was going to be able to accomplish on my own; I needed help. The good news was, I had a strong desire to heal, and I was ready and willing to learn how to. And as the saying goes, "When the student is ready, the teacher will appear."

My aunt, who attended church regularly, introduced me to a Christian pastor who also happened to be a life coach, Pastor Milton. He, in turn, introduced me to the work of Tony Robbins. He suggested Tony's explanation of the *six human needs* could help me understand some of the underlying reasons for how I was feeling. Why I made some of the choices I was making now and had made in the past, all of which were impacting my entire life. He also mentioned that this understanding could give me some insight into the behavior of others as well. I was receptive. I began visiting the pastor once a week, for several weeks. As I learned, I applied. My understanding and implementation had a positive effect. After seeing how eager I was to learn, Pastor Milton suggested I attend one of Tony

Robbins' events someday. The thought of that intrigued me. He then mentioned the next event he would be attending was: The Leadership Academy in San Diego, which was designed to help sharpen your leadership skills. Although it was several months away, he invited me to join him. At that time, I felt I didn't really have any use for leadership skills; I was technically unemployed, but I figured I would go anyway. Besides, I had nothing else to do. I accepted his invitation and signed up for the event.

All that I learned from Pastor Milton and watching Tony Robbins' DVDs was starting to re-energize me. It led me down a new path. I became much more of a thinker. I began to study just about everything in greater detail. I felt great. I was growing, learning. It slowly aroused my desire to be in business again. I felt ready to get back to work. I had more to give. I wanted to earn more and do more. I wasn't done yet.

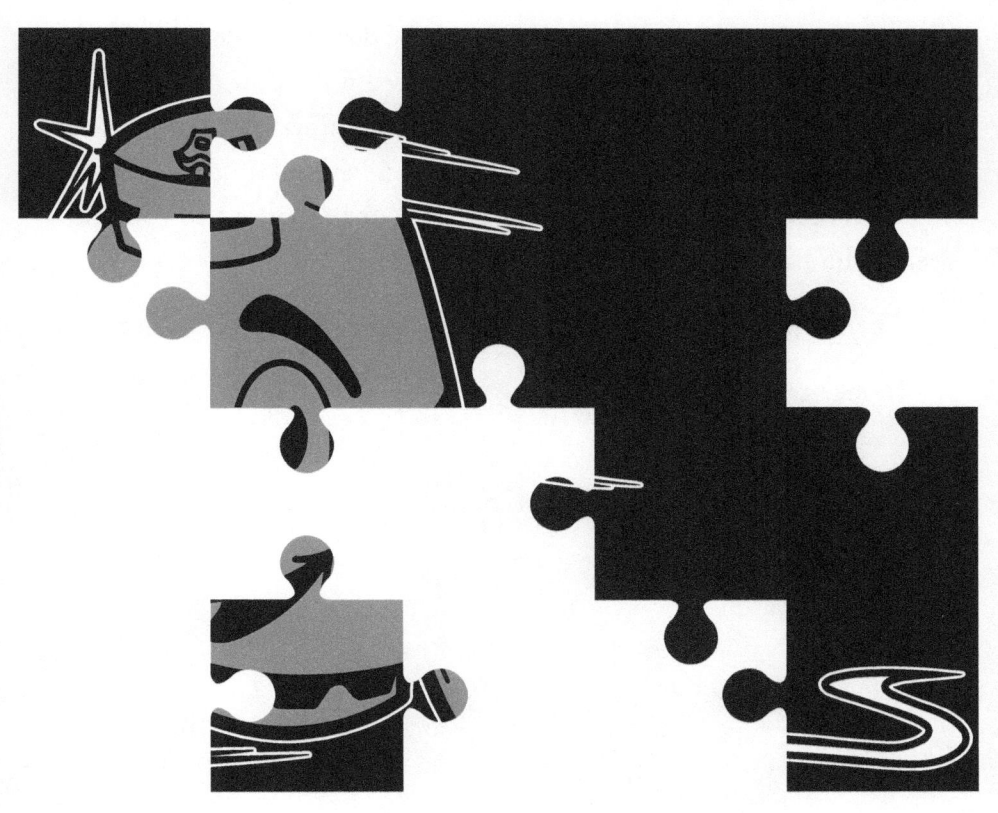

Reflection Point 21

Do something today that your future self will thank you for. My investments in real estate gave me the reassurance that I had a reliable source of income, regardless of whether I ever returned to work. My decision to live well beneath my means and be debt-free eased my mind. I was able to travel and do just about whatever I wanted, with not much money. I wasn't rich, but I had a wonderfully comfortable lifestyle. You can have all the money in the world, but if you have no time to enjoy it, what's the point? Take some time to enjoy your life, prioritize yourself, even if you have to schedule it in your calendar.

There's no greater feeling than experiencing peace within yourself.

Money cannot buy that.

What steps do you need to take to prove to yourself
that your fears are not real?

What brings you peace, and how could you do more of it?

Chapter 22:

Pay the Price

It had been several months since I threw my keys on my desk and walked out of the office. Throughout my entire absence, Danny and I had exchanged several text messages and emails, mainly about the future of our soured business relationship. In the beginning, I just didn't want to butt heads any longer. I was beyond flexible in finding a creative way out of this situation for both of us, and I had grown comfortable with the thought of never returning to work. In light of this, I told Danny that if he were interested in running the business permanently and made me any reasonable offer, I would sell to him. I mentioned I would be okay with monthly installments comparable to my salary, with zero percent interest, for a select number of years — in exchange for my ownership rights. The payments would be a little over $15,000 a month, which was far less than what I was collecting in salary, benefits, and distributions combined. So, the payment amount wouldn't affect him or the business in any way financially. I felt that offer was beyond reasonable, when considering Danny would be the sole owner, which would entitle him to my distributions, and 100% of the business profits going forward. In comparison to that amount, what I was settling for was pocket change. I was taking a loss, and, in my opinion, he was getting the deal of a lifetime. If he accepted, I may have regretted that decision, but the money wasn't that important to me. I just wanted a peaceful resolution.

As part of that deal, I had only one restriction: I wanted him to agree in writing not to sell Prestige Propane Exchange immediately afterward. Based on some of the comments Danny was making at that time, I thought he just wanted to sell Prestige Propane as soon as I transferred ownership to him. He proved me right when he declined my kindhearted offer. He said he would agree to my deal but with no holdback period, which made his intentions clear. He wanted to sell it soon afterward. I was a little hurt and disappointed by that but not surprised. I already knew through previous experience that he wasn't genuinely interested in either business. Now, why would I do him the favor of giving him a sweetheart deal, only to then see him auction off all my hard work to the highest bidder shortly after? Dismayed, I took that offer off the table.

We went back and forth, discussing different options for disentangling our unique partnership, but it never amounted to anything. We were gridlocked. Not long after, Danny hired a mediator to try to convince me to come back to work with him. It saddened me to decline, but I had to. I was steadfast in my decision not to re-enter into any form of a business union with him. I knew it would ultimately lead to more disagreements. It was either him or me; one of us had to go. The cycle continued; sometimes, I would offer to buy him out; other times, he would offer to buy me out. In either case, Danny wouldn't agree to any deal. Even his own deals. He made me an offer on more than one occasion, which I agreed to, and then he would back out. I didn't understand the reasoning behind his behavior. Did he just want to know what I would settle for? Maybe. But that wouldn't make much sense because I was quite flexible. Was he confused? Or perhaps it was just a fun game to play to push my buttons. I'm not sure what it was about, but I did know one thing: It was very odd and very frustrating.

After being kindhearted didn't work, I started to get aggravated. I had enough of the back and forth. I didn't want to be in this situation and wasn't interested in playing mind games. After much thought, I made a decision. I realized that what I truly wanted was my company back. I was genuinely happy before entering into this agreement, and even a good amount of time during it, when I wasn't at odds with Danny. My company wasn't the problem; our precarious partnership was. I just wanted what was mine, what I had worked for, and nothing more. Danny had decided also. He acknowledged that he didn't want to retain ownership in either company. Not surprising. However, Danny continued to make things difficult. We exchanged proposals. I generally suggested a version of the following two scenarios:

1) We split the companies back as they were before this agreement. Danny would retain 100% ownership of Local Propane. He could keep the land and equipment and do with it as he wished. I would then open a corporation for Prestige Propane, as I should have done years ago, and relocate on my own.

Or

2) He signs my company back over to me and even though I didn't want it, we'd have Local Propane appraised, and I would pay him for the entire value of what it was worth, which hovered around $1 million.

I believed it was only fair that we would each reap what we had sowed. Danny disagreed. He wanted me to pay him for half of the value of both Local Propane and Prestige Propane Exchange combined. I thought that was unfair. Why would I have to give him half the value of my company when he didn't do half of the work? Wasn't it courteous enough that I had been splitting profits with him the entire time? Those profits added up to a handsome amount of money, I assure you. I wasn't asking him for half the value of Local Propane. I just wanted what was mine. What's right is right. We tried it; it didn't work. Let's go our separate ways. That was my view. Had it been the other way around, I would've genuinely accepted that. I grew increasingly frustrated. If our mother was alive, I wouldn't have been stuck in this situation. Sadly, she wasn't. I was on my own. Yes, Danny was my brother, but he wasn't acting very brotherly about this. Or at least that's how I felt about it.

Throughout our debate, Danny kept citing that it didn't matter if I thought this was fair, because he was 51% owner of Local Propane and technically, Local Propane owned Prestige Propane Exchange. That's because it was registered as a DBA and not a standalone corporation. I was confused. *What the heck is he talking about?* I thought. Once I was educated on the matter, I was hit abruptly with a large dose of reality. I realized the magnitude of the mistake I had made.

When I had ignorantly agreed to test out this family deal and signed those documents, I had legally authorized Danny as president and majority shareholder of Local Propane, which owned the fictitious name *Speedy Tanks 2 You*; that was then later renamed Prestige Propane Exchange. I had no legal control of the business and no enforceable authority of my own company. I had never given myself a way out of this deal. I honestly never thought I needed to think of these things because I was dealing with my immediate family. But the truth is, business is business. Regardless of whom I was doing business with, I should've done more research and taken the time to know all the facts. My lack of awareness and education hindered me. I had given Danny irrevocable control of everything: Local Propane, and Prestige Propane Exchange. I was handcuffed. I had reached a dead end with no visible way out. My own brother had become my biggest adversary.

Against my wishes, Danny began to meet with several potential buyers and entertained offers to sell the businesses. The highest offer for both combined companies came in at $5 million. Based on that, Danny's 51% would entitle him to approximately $2.5 million if I agreed to sell. But I wasn't going to agree. Although I had, unfortunately, put myself in the position of not having control of my own business, I learned he'd still need my signature to sell it. I had lucked out. Our agreement didn't have a drag- along clause in it, which would've given him the power to force me into a sale. When the potential buyers would call me, hoping to hear that I would cooperate and sign over my ownership rights, they quickly learned we were gridlocked. There was no way I was going to sign it over. I wasn't selling. He couldn't force me into selling my business. When contacted, I suggested that the buyers buy Local Propane and leave me and Prestige Propane Exchange out of it. Which they were open to, but Danny didn't go for it. What happened next was beyond my imagination. I never thought that Danny could take it this far. Not like this.

After receiving several calls from various would-be investors Danny had instructed to contact me, I became upset. I was tired of being asked if I was selling my business. I wasn't. Impassioned, I drove to the office to speak to Danny in person. We got into an argument, as I could've expected. I yelled at him out of frustration. Unable to control my emotions, I punched a hole right through his office door. Regrettably, that little outburst and my lack of control gave him more ammo. Not long after that incident, Danny had a Certified Mail letter sent to my home; an attorney wrote it. The letter stated that, as a result of my outburst and public display of anger, an anonymous employee didn't feel safe with me in the office, and I was not allowed back on the premises; Danny had outsmarted me again. He used my flare-up to his advantage. What he did was tactful and intelligent. That is, of course, if what you're trying to do is pressure your partner into selling while establishing indisputable, unilateral control. What he did afterward, however, I felt was uncalled for, unthinkable even. It dramatically affected our personal relationship. Danny hired an armed security guard whose sole responsibility was to keep me off the premises. I couldn't set foot into my own office, in the company I had built from the ground up, with my bare hands. He then transferred all our company funds to another bank that I didn't have access to; stopped paying my weekly salary and canceled my health insurance, without warning. He also unsuccessfully tried to cancel my company credit cards. Shortly after, another letter found its way to my house via his attorney. This one stated that I was fired, and because I was a minority shareholder, he would provide me the details of the business on a need-to-know basis only. I couldn't believe it. This was by far the most malicious thing he'd ever done to me.

I didn't want to spend money on legal fees, but I felt Danny's actions left me no choice. The funny part, if you can call it funny, was that I was already paying for attorneys. Some of the payments made to the attorneys Danny had hired, and payments to the armed security guard were from our business account. Those were trying times.

While I tried to calmly navigate my way through the slew of uncomfortable situations, it was sometimes just more than I could handle, regardless of how much I tried to shrug off the wrongdoings. I never stopped feeling that I was being toyed with, and I couldn't stand it. I kept thinking to myself, *Why am I fighting this battle alone? Why isn't my father, who's partially responsible for this in the first place, stepping in and putting an end to all this nonsense?* Every time something happened, he was made aware of it, yet he did next to nothing to help. He would tell Danny at times what he was doing was wrong and suggest that we not argue, but that's all he did. But Danny ignored him, so his input made no difference.

Danny continued his wrath unchecked, and the saga continued. I don't remember which particular act it was, but what I do remember was feeling an overwhelming sense of injustice from yet another perpetual misdoing. I went to my father's house, one house over from me, to fill him in on the latest atrocity with hopes that he would finally do something about it, instead of just giving his opinion. After my stepmother let me in, I walked over to his bedroom where he was lying down watching TV. I began to brief him, "Guess what Danny did this time, Dad?..." Sadly, after filling him in, it was clear that he wasn't going to do anything, and he wasn't in the position to assist me in any way.

Even though he was Danny's father, Danny didn't have to listen to him; he was an adult with a controlling stake in our business and could essentially do whatever he pleased. As the conversation between my father and me progressed, I became more heartsick. His inability to help me, along with his lack of determination to find resolve, hurt my feelings. I yelled at him from across the room, "How could you let him do this to me, Dad? Do something about it!" I stated firmly. "What do you want me to do? He doesn't listen to me! I've tried," he replied as he threw his hands up. My eyes became watery, and I became emotional. He had no lifeline for me. As I began to respond, I could barely hold back the tears in my eyes. I began choking on my words as I gasped for air, "This is your fault! You put me in this position, and now you're not doing anything to help me get out of it!" I was devastated.

I'm sure if he could wave a magic wand and make everything better, he would've. But there was no magic wand and no one coming to my rescue. Quite frankly, he didn't know what to do or how to do it. Pleading my case to him was a waste of time. There was nothing left to say. Upset and heartbroken, I slammed the door to his bedroom as I left. I kicked a vase on the floor and knocked a picture frame off the wall out of frustration as I walked away. My father had always been my hero, and knowing he wasn't going to do anything to help me crushed me inside.

Defeated, I went home. I showered and got myself something to eat, then sat down on my recliner to watch some TV and relax. I received a call from my father saying he understood how I felt, and he was going to reach out to Danny again and try to help put an end to all of this. I apologized for my outburst and said I'd replace the vase and picture frame. He told me not to worry about it because he thought the vase was ugly anyway. After my conversation with him, I peacefully continued to watch TV.

A couple of hours had passed since I had left my father's house upset. As promised, my father reached out to Danny to try to settle things once and for all. But he didn't get the result he was after. In fact, the only person who gained from the conversation was Danny. As my father spoke to Danny in an effort to persuade him, he referenced my impassioned visit and how upset I had been. He mentioned that I broke the vase and knocked the picture frame off the wall. Although he did so innocently, to illustrate the game needed to come to an end, that was a mistake. He unknowingly gave Danny more ammunition.

As I watched TV calmly in my living room, I received another phone call from my father. I picked up. "Hello, Dad," I said. He began speaking hurriedly, "Maxie, I called Danny over to try and convince him to stop all of this, and when I mentioned you were so mad that you broke the vase and picture frame, he took it upon himself to call the cops. I'm sorry, Maxie. I didn't ask him to do that!" he said. "What? Are you serious? Why did he do that? What business is it of his? He wasn't even there," I replied. "I know, Maxie, it was my mistake; I didn't think he would do that. I'm very sorry. Please don't be upset with me," he said. I walked to the front door and saw two police cruisers outside of my gated driveway. With the phone still to my ear, I asked my father, "Well, what do they want?" "They said they just want to speak to you. I told them I had no complaint to file, so they're not going to arrest you. I guess they just want a statement," he replied. "A statement of what? I have nothing to say." I declared.

As I peeked through my blinds, I saw Danny speaking to the police officers. I didn't like the looks of it. I couldn't believe he had stooped this low. This was ridiculous. Assured that my father had no grievance with me, I went outside to address them. My father was present, and before I could even get a word out, reminded the officers that he had no complaint to file or charges to press. He reiterated that he didn't call them. Danny, who wasn't even present for my outburst, did. The officer asked a few silly questions and then instructed me to take a seat in the back of his patrol car. "No way! I said. "No officer, why?" My father added. "I thought you just wanted to ask him some questions?" The officer continued, "The gentlemen over there stated that you wanted to kill yourself, and because of that, we're going to have to detain you overnight to ensure you don't cause any harm to yourself, or anyone else." "WHAT?!" My father and I replied simultaneously. "I would never say that!" I said. "He wasn't even here; how could he hear him say that?" My father added. "Sir, I'm sorry, but if we get a report like that, we have to follow through and act upon it. You're going to have to spend the night at a mental health facility for observation," he said. As the officer forcefully lowered my head into his police car, I pleaded. "Dad, don't let them take me!" "No, son. Hang on. We're going to work this out," he replied. My father began arguing with the police officers and Danny, but unfortunately, he lost that argument.

The officer drove me away from my home and toward the psychiatric hospital for 24-hour observation. This was an all-time low, not just for Danny, but for my entire family. At a loss for words, I thought to myself, *Is this really happening? Am I on my way to a behavioral health clinic because my brother falsely accused me of wanting to kill myself? This is unbelievable!*

While he drove, I calmly began to assure the officer he was making a mistake. As I spoke, he kept his hands at 10 and 2 on the steering wheel. When I would make a point, he would nod, and his facial expressions would indicate understanding and reasoning. I honestly believe I had him convinced he was making an error. By the time we arrived at the mental ward, he was noticeably conflicted. But it was too late. We were in the parking lot of the mental health hospital. The officer leveled with me and basically told me to just take it on the chin. He explained that this didn't count as an arrest, and I would be out the next day. I had no choice but to hang in there.

Once I was inside, a staff member at the mental health unit prepared to psychologically evaluate me. As she summarized me with a scrutinizing gaze, she could tell that something was off. I wasn't her typical patient. She greeted me and then asked for my name and date of birth. But before she could ask any more questions, I insisted that she hear me out. I needed to confirm her suspicion. I didn't belong there, and she needed to know it. I gave her a brief description of what happened. I described the series of events that got me there; as I spoke, the woman sat there speechless. The more details I gave her, the more her jaw dropped. In disbelief, she even called another staff member into the room to listen in.

I asked if there was any way she could get me out of this mess. She was empathetic but assured me there wasn't a way out. Once I was in, I was in. Because of the complaint, they needed to complete an evaluation, and I had to spend the night. It was beyond her control. It was the law.

Beyond doubt, she was genuinely grieved by what I explained. She tried to cheer me up and offered some words of encouragement. She assured me that her evaluation would state that my admission was unjustified, and it was her opinion that I was wrongfully detained. She also gave me her word that I would be released the moment they were legally permitted to do so. I thanked her. Her kind words and display of compassion comforted me. For some reason, just knowing she knew I didn't belong there put me at ease. It made me feel a little better about being in this uncomfortable situation. After completing my evaluation, the staff member who listened in said she'd keep me out of the general population until it was time for everyone to go to bed.

She invited me to join her in the employee lounge to watch TV and even offered to share some of her Chinese food with me. That kind gesture gave me an overwhelming sense of relief. I cannot tell you how grateful I was for that. After a few hours of chatting with her and most of the staff, it was time for bed. She walked me to my holding cell, and I did my best to try to get some sleep. As I lay down and stared at the wall, I still couldn't believe where I was. It was all so bizarre.

When I awoke, it was time for breakfast. I was now mixed in with the rest of the population. Most of them were undeniably conflicted in some form or another. And although none of them seemed threatening in any way, I still felt uncomfortable.

In preparation for breakfast, we were asked to form a single-file-line. The patients had to take their pick from several simple items — cereal, yogurt, and fresh fruit. I wasn't hungry but was told to get in line anyway. There was a young man in front of me, likely in his mid-20s, who noticeably belonged. He began arguing with the server and raised his voice as he said, "I want it!" as he played tug of war with the lunch lady over a vanilla yogurt. He wanted two yogurts instead of just one, which wasn't allowed, for some reason. It seemed to me that he didn't understand why he couldn't have two, but the staff member assured me that he did. "He can have mine," I said as I handed him a yogurt from the table in front of us. The young man instantly became cheerful. As I sat down across from him at the breakfast table and drank a glass of water, he literally licked both yogurt containers clean. He was so happy. I'm not sure I've ever seen anyone so happy to eat yogurt in my life.

After breakfast, we were allowed to sit in a living room-style recreation area to read books or watch Television. They did their best to make the patients feel as if this were not a prison, but it was clear to me that it was.

There was no way out. I could see bars on the windows and high-security fences outside that prevented anyone from coming in or out. I couldn't help feeling a little anxious. I was trapped.

I sat on a green couch and began to watch TV with some of the patients. After a short while, the young man whom I offered my yogurt to came and sat directly next to me. He had a book in his hand; it was the Holy Bible. I was surprised to see him with a book in his hand, and even more surprised that it was the Bible. Something about him in that moment seemed different; he had a different energy about him. He began flipping through pages. He stopped on a page and ran his fingers over it. He then lifted the book, turned it toward me, and pointed at a verse with his index finger. "Read this," he said. "Sure, bud," I replied. I took the book from him and began to read:

"So do not fear, for I am with you;
do not be dismayed, for I am your God.
I will strengthen you and help you;
I will uphold you with my righteous right hand."

Isaiah 41:10

Goosebumps radiated up and down my arm, and my hairs stood on end. "That was for you," the young man said with a clear and confident smile. Then, in the flip of a switch, he grabbed his book, stood up, and walked away. It was surreal. I sat there in disbelief for a few minutes. I couldn't believe that had just happened. In that moment, I felt God was speaking directly to me. He was assuring me that everything was going to be alright. I felt a sense of sacred peace pour over me. I was instantly comforted and relieved. With my spirit now at ease, I nonchalantly looked through a few magazines and calmly watched some Jerry Springer with the rest of the patients. I only had a few hours for all of this to be over.

When the 24 hours had passed, and I was released, I had several family members and a good friend waiting for me in the lobby. It was comforting to see them there when I got out. They were all concerned and were as happy to see me as I was to see them. We all exchanged some hugs. My eldest aunt, who was also there, reaffirmed that this had gone way too far, and this foolishness with Danny needed to come to an end. She personally assured me that she'd do everything within her power to see this come to a resolution. They then drove me home to shower and get something to eat.

After much deliberation and many in-person meetings, my aunt kept true to her promise and helped facilitate a resolution between Danny and me. Danny delivered an ultimatum and I needed to decide what I wanted to do. I had one of two options:

Option A was to pay $4 million for Danny's 51% ownership in both businesses. I felt this option was unreasonable because the profit that Prestige Propane Exchange was generating independently gave it a value of around $4 million. On the other hand, Local Propane's profit only gave it a value of around $1 million. So, paying $4 million to purchase Danny's half was just about the entire value of both businesses combined. This meant with option A, I was essentially buying back my own company Prestige Propane Exchange, for exactly what it was worth. Even though I would be getting Local Propane with the deal, it's not what I had in mind. It's not as if I wanted Local Propane anyway. I felt the most Danny should have been entitled to was half the value of both businesses, which would have been around $2.5 million. Either way, he wouldn't budge. Danny was only willing to sign over his ownership rights for $4 million. Take it or leave it. In addition to the price, if I agreed to the terms of his deal, there was a deadline. I would need to produce a check for the entire amount, $4 million in cash, within six months of signing the agreement. If I couldn't come up with the money within that timeframe, both companies would be offered for sale to a third party for whatever price we could obtain at that point. I either needed to accept those terms, or it was...

Option B, we were going to go to court, where they would attempt to force me to sell. That would have most likely resulted in a court-appointed receivership. That is like having a court-appointed babysitter come in to take over your business until a conclusion is reached. The thought of that made me nauseous. If that happened, things were likely going to get even worse than they already were. This was hard to imagine at the time, but I imagined it. Word would get out that the company was unstable, and the courts had to take over. Which then meant there was no experienced operator in charge. Other companies would smell that blood in the water and begin to solicit our accounts aggressively. Employees most likely would quit because of the lack of certainty in their employment. Both companies then would begin to hemorrhage accounts to the competition. We would be the laughingstock of the propane industry, and when the dust would settle, there'd be nothing left to fight about. After playing out that highly likely scenario in my head, it didn't seem that I had much of a choice.

My aunt presented me a binding term sheet with the details spelled out on it. Danny had already signed. If I agreed to the terms, the attorneys would draft the official paperwork shortly afterward. I was scared to sign that paper. If I couldn't come up with the money, I'd be forced to sell my business, my baby, against my will. The thought of that left me feeling unsettled. After I whined about it for some time, I realized that whining wasn't going to get me anywhere. I needed to snap out of it and get out of this gridlock, so I signed. It wasn't ideal, but signing the agreement also gave me some form of power back. I now would have a formal contract with Danny. I could at least try to raise the money somehow and regain control of my business. Which was admittedly all I thought about. If I could miraculously pull it off somehow and come up with the money, Danny would have no choice but to sell it to me. He wouldn't be able to back out this time. I honestly didn't know if it was possible, but I applied faith. I just wanted to put this behind me. If God wanted me to have my company, it would be mine. If not, so be it. Now, where was I going to get $4 million? I obviously didn't have it.

At the signing of the purchase agreement, I figured I might appeal to Danny. I mentioned there was essentially no way I could come up with that amount of money. I needed him to give me a seller's note to purchase the companies back from him. Which meant he would finance the loan himself. I asked him for a five-year loan and offered to pay him a 5% interest rate. I would put my rental properties and the businesses up as collateral until he was paid in full. His reply to my proposition was, "That's not my problem. I'm not financing the deal. If you can't come up with the money in cash, I guess you'll be forced to sell in six months." It wasn't the reply I was hoping for, but it was worth a shot.

Note: A receivership is a court-appointed tool that may arise during a shareholder dispute to complete a project, liquidate assets, or sell a business, for example.

Before judgment, a court may appoint a receiver to protect a party that demonstrates a right, title, or interest in the real property if the property or its revenue-producing potential (1) is being subjected to or is in danger of waste, loss, substantial diminution in value, dissipation, or impairment; or has been or is about to be the subject of a voidable transaction.

A seller's note is an alternative form of business capital that is flexible but carries certain risks. The seller agrees to accept a portion of the purchase price in a series of deferred payments. This occurs when the business buyer does not have sufficient cash to cover the entire purchase price.

A drag-along right allows a majority shareholder (i.e., usually a shareholder holding more than 50% of shares in a company that have voting rights attached) of a company to force the remaining minority shareholders (i.e., usually a shareholder holding less than 50% of shares in a company that have voting rights attached) to accept an offer from a third party to purchase the whole company.

The majority shareholder who is "dragging" the other shareholders must offer the minority shareholders the same price, terms, and conditions that the majority shareholder has been offered. For example, a majority shareholder who holds 75% of the shares in the company who agrees to sell their shares in a share sale to a potential buyer must offer the same price for the shares to the minority shareholders if they want to "drag them along".

A drag-along clause will allow the majority shareholder to "drag" the remaining minority shareholders with them and require them to sell their shares to the potential buyer at the same price, in order to allow the buyer to purchase the entire company.

Certified mail with signature is a special USPS service that provides the person sending the mail piece with an official receipt showing proof the item was mailed. When the mail piece is delivered, the mail carrier requires a signature from the recipient. That signature is stored in the USPS database for a period of two years.

Reflection Point 22

You want to go into every situation with positivity, but it's a good idea to plan for the worst-case scenario. Had I done so, I wouldn't have been in this situation. My feeling that things should've been one way or another because I was dealing with family or because certain things were implied, meant nothing.

When put in an uncomfortable situation, don't give up. Marinating on the problem will not make it disappear; instead, focus on finding a solution. Don't let your ego step in and take over and get hung up on proving a point or needing to be right. Think of what you can do to protect yourself or get out of that situation. When I realized that Danny was unable to sell without my signature, I stood firm.

Stay calm despite circumstances. Whether you're right or wrong, the moment you act out, you lose. When I punched that wall, although I did so out of frustration, I not only made myself look blameworthy, but I gave Danny more leverage.

And most importantly, guidance can come in many forms, from just about anywhere. Even at your lowest point, you're not alone.

When has losing your cool made things worse?

What will you do differently next time?

Chapter 23:

Defying the Odds

I was eager to complete the transaction. I needed to find $4 million in cash to pay Danny and get my company back. With limited options, I concluded that my only hope was to get a bank loan. I began to network with as many lenders as I could and met with several bankers. I presented them all with what I was told was the necessary paperwork to secure the loan. Along with the documents, I routinely explained my situation. Every one of them was eager to earn my business at the onset, but inevitably, one by one, they all turned me down. I felt as if I had gone back in time and was reliving the seemingly impossible task of getting someone to insure *Speedy Tanks 2 You.*

There were two main factors that I knew were making this rather challenging. One, the financial climate at the time was sketchy. It was 2014, and many banks were hesitant to lend money. Two, our accounting wasn't in order. On the books, the companies didn't appear stable. The records were sloppy and vague. The existing accountant had done a poor job of maintaining our records. I didn't know whether it was the paperwork my accountant gave me, the economy, my lack of education, or some other sort of risk they perceived, but what I did know was, I wasn't meeting their criteria; hence, I wasn't getting the loan. I started to feel hopeless. I was running out of options, but I stayed persistent. I was used to hitting a wall and finding a way around it. There was always a loophole — a way to succeed. Although this time, things may have been different. The numbers were the numbers, and banks work off numbers, but something inside me told me not to let go. I needed to fight for what was mine.

Although it may have felt like it, meeting with the numerous bankers wasn't a waste of time. Every time I met with a new banker, he or she asked me questions I didn't have the answers to or paperwork I didn't have. As that would occur, I would take note and zero in on what they were looking for. Sometimes it was my net worth; other times it was the company's performance or specific metrics or ratio they wanted to see. I would get the answers to the questions and obtain the necessary paperwork needed to be more prepared for my next meeting with a banker. Each time, I gained an increased understanding of the way they worked and what was important to them. After meeting various bankers, I had answers and paperwork for just about anything I might have been asked; or, at the very least, an educated explanation for not having it. This allowed them to take me much more seriously and was a far better approach compared to "Um, I'm not sure. That's what my accountant gave me." Or even worse, "I don't know."

Several weeks into my search, I had a scheduled phone call with yet another banker. He was either the ninth or tenth banker I spoke to. His name was Carl Evans. During our call, Carl asked me a handful of questions about the business. This time, I was ready for them. They were all questions I had grown accustomed to being asked and could confidently answer. Pleased with my responses, Carl inquired about the whereabouts of the businesses and asked if I could give him a site tour. This wasn't an unusual request; other bankers had toured the site also. I agreed to meet him there the next day.

After the call, I jumped in the shower. I remember feeling drained. I began questioning myself and whether I should continue this crusade. *Am I heading in the wrong direction? Maybe God has other plans for me?* I wasn't sure what to do anymore. As the comforting warm water gently poured over my head, I rested my arm on the shower wall and pressed my forehead against it. I closed my eyes and started to pray aloud. I said, "Lord, if you want me to have this company, then I will have it. If you don't, then I'll move on, with no regrets. I'm going to have one more meeting with one more banker, and if it doesn't work out, then I will know it's not your will and it's not meant to be. Thank you, Lord. Amen."

After my shower, I had a pep in my step. I was reenergized. I began to prepare for the meeting. I figured it was going to be the last one, so I might as well give it my all. I had a list of all my rental properties. I made a case for why they were all worth more than the estimated values online. I printed documents that supported my positions and wrote a small summary of what I wanted to do with the business if I were able to take back control.

In preparation for the meeting, I dressed in slacks and a long-sleeved, button-down-collar shirt. I was there early and, of course, not allowed onsite because of the armed security guard at the entrance, whose sole purpose was to keep me from entering the building. The security guard was good-natured and appeared to be a nice guy, but he had his orders.

I had to call Danny's attorney beforehand to get permission to tour the premises, and by this point I felt he was noticeably annoyed. I couldn't blame him. Although I was relentless, I wasn't seeing any noticeable progress. When I called to get permission for the first few tours, my optimism was at peak levels. I thought I'd get the loan and it would be over quickly. But I was wrong. And having to ask permission to tour my own business time and time again irked me. It felt humiliating. I could picture him poking fun at my misfortune and wondering how many bankers I was going to have tour the business before I finally gave up. I'm sure that had something to do with the ever- decreasing time I was allotted. Permission to tour the business, which was once set at an hour, was now set for a not very confidence-inspiring 15 minutes.

When Carl Evans arrived, I was waiting outside in the parking lot. I didn't want to run the risk of them starting the clock on my 15 minutes early. Every second would count. I introduced myself to him and began first by giving him an outdoor tour of the facility. We began to slowly walk the premises together as the security guard respectfully trailed behind. The banker was gracious and seemed genuinely nice. He listened carefully to everything I had to say.

Once we completed a quick tour of the yard, we made our way inside. I no longer had an office, so we sat down at an empty desk, where I began to hand him my documents. I passed them over one at a time and explained in detail why the bank could rest assured this loan was a safe investment. I mentioned the reason for the loan was to end my controversy with Danny but didn't go into too much detail. I also made known that I had sold some of my rental properties in anticipation of getting a loan. If the bank were to agree to finance me, I would put up to $1 million as a down payment. As I spoke, Mr. Evans listened intently and nodded. I felt I had his full attention, but he asked very few questions. He hadn't even asked to look at the business's financial statements, probably the most relevant documents when issuing a business loan. That wasn't a good sign. By that point, I figured he was uninterested in issuing the loan and was being polite by hearing me out.

When I was done pleading my case, Mr. Evans pursed his lips, pushed his chair gently away from the desk, and slowly stood up. He then extended his arm to shake my hand. I guess I was right. He was done being polite and had heard enough. I couldn't blame him; he probably had somewhere else to be. I stood up as well, reached over and shook his hand. I asked, "So, I guess you guys will think about it and get back to me in a few days?" He shook his head, "No, there's no need for that," he replied. "I'm the SVP of the bank, and I don't need anyone else's approval. I'm going to give you the loan. You can tell your brother we can close in three weeks," he replied.

Holy mackerel! I couldn't believe it! First, I had no clue he was the SVP of the bank. Second, he just gave me the loan. Right there on the spot, without even looking at our financials. He hadn't even checked the financial health of the business but agreed to give me a $3 million loan based on our 15-minute conversation. He even stood up to secure his promise with an old-fashioned handshake, like a true gentleman. It was meant to be. I guess God wanted me to have it, after all.

I received a loan commitment letter from the bank the next day. Although I technically wasn't supposed to, I called Danny's attorney immediately. I was excited to finally get this over with. I still could hardly believe I was going to be able to close. I also may have wanted to rub it in, just a little bit. Once his secretary patched me through, I announced myself. "Hello Alvin, it's Max Lewis." I said. "Mr. Lewis, I already told you I cannot speak to you directly," he replied. Apparently, the American Bar Association enforced some type of code that prohibited him from communicating with me because I had legal representation; nevertheless, that didn't prevent me from calling him on more than one occasion to give him a piece of my mind.

"You can speak to me directly. You have my permission," I replied. "Listen, the reason for my call is, I have secured financing, and I wanted to schedule a closing date," I said. His response was priceless. "Uhm...wait... What did you just say?" He sounded confused. I responded slowly and with a hint of sarcasm. "What I said was, I have a loan commitment from a bank. They can close within three weeks, and I want to schedule a closing date," I replied. "Um...well...Can you send that over to me? You know...uh...I must make sure they are a serious bank...Uhm... I need to review it first." He was dumbstruck. "Absolutely. In fact, I already sent it over to you. Check your email. I'll wait. Oh, the title of the email is "Prepare for Closing," in case you're having trouble finding it," I said.

"Oh, I see it here. I'm going to need to get back to you," he said. After that conversation, I let my attorney handle the rest. I had no interest in speaking with Danny's attorney ever again.

As we approached the closing date, my patience was tested quite often. I felt as if Danny was trying to find ways to irritate me. I assumed it was done to either torment me or sabotage the deal, maybe both. It was strenuous, but I wasn't going to crack. There was no way I was going to allow Danny to wiggle out of this agreement, not after all I had been through. In preparation for closing, his attorneys wanted me to acknowledge that Danny's, put politely, questionable use of company money was done in good faith. They made a list of things Danny wasn't taking responsibility for. For example, he refused to issue a full credit, or even a partial credit, for the nearly $150,000 Danny spent on the needless security guard. He also refused to credit me for any of the company benefits I had been cut off from while I was banned from my own office, even though Danny continued to receive all his benefits during the entire time. Furthermore, he stopped paying my salary and doubled his own.

Since I no longer had access to the business bank accounts, there was nothing I could have done to stop him. Another item on that list was the roughly $80,000 Danny spent paying his attorneys. How was that a necessary business expense? They only represented Danny, not me. Those were personal expenses and decisions made exclusively by Danny; therefore, I felt he should have been 100% responsible for covering those costs. I felt it was unjust, but either way, I had to go along with it. They were not budging. If I continued to fight this, I would have further dragged out this agonizing ordeal. In the big picture, this was minutiae. And I wasn't about to get caught up in the minutiae.

The amusement continued up until the last minute. Consider one example of just how trivial it was: Around the time I received my loan commitment, a salesman at Prestige Propane had called me and mentioned he was having some grievance with Danny. The salesman had run out of business cards, and without those, he had nothing to hand out to prospective clients, which made it harder to do his job. When the salesman requested more cards from Danny, he refused to order them. When I heard this, I thought it was illogical. I told the salesman; that he should just order the cards if he needed them to do his job. He had my permission.

On May 8, 2014, the day before we were to close, Danny's attorney called my attorney so he could inform me they were going to delay or even cancel the closing. The reason was a $150 invoice for business cards (a legitimate company expense, mind you) that Danny had not approved. If I refused to take 100% responsibility and issue Danny a credit for 51% of the cost of those business cards, the transaction wouldn't take place, and he undoubtedly would cancel the deal.

Let me do that math for you:

Danny's 51% of $150 is $76.50. So even after I overlooked the fact that Danny paid the security guard with company money, to keep me off my own property; and I overlooked the fact that he paid his attorneys with company money, to strategized and negotiate against me, and he was about to receive a $4 million check from me; he still was willing to cancel the transaction if I didn't pay an additional 76 bucks? Was he serious? It was inconceivable.

I spoke my mind freely with my attorney: "So, let me get this right, Danny called his attorney, to call you; so you could call me, and inform me of Danny's decision to potentially walk away from a $4 million windfall, because of a $150 business card expense, of which I'm responsible for $76.50. Now, I need to make a decision. Then, you need to call back his attorney, so he can call Danny and inform him of my decision on whether I'm going to cancel the deal or pay an extra $76.50, when I already have agreed to pay $4 million, is that right?" "Yes," my lawyer chuckled. "He probably just racked up $400 in attorney's fees, trying to get another $76.50 out of me!" I laughed. "Yeah, I'm not going to cancel the deal. You can call Danny's attorney and let him know I'll give him an extra 76 bucks," I calmly stated, "Now, let's get this over with."

A series of nonsensical events like these previously would have made my blood boil, which would likely have caused me to lose my temper and do something foolish (like punch a wall). A younger, less experienced version of me would have fallen for them. That was no longer the case. Danny's crafty attempts to provoke me no longer worked. I had reached another level of awareness and maturity. I guess it was one last test I needed to pass. It was part of my lesson, I suppose. After this I knew he would have no more authority over me. There would be no more games to play. I would be free.

In preparation for the closing, I instructed my attorney to open two new corporations. I wanted to split the two companies formally and legally. Prestige Propane Exchange finally would have its independence; it was now its own corporation. I also renamed Local Propane to *Century Propane* and put that in a separate corporation.

There were two reasons I did this:

First, they were two different businesses with completely different business models and should be treated as such and run individually. After closing, I planned to build a dividing wall in the office, with approximately a 90/10 split, giving Prestige Propane the greater portion of the space. Instead of continuing to share resources and employees, as we had previously grown accustomed to doing, I then would give each company its own dedicated staff, uniforms, phone numbers, bank accounts, etc. This would allow me to measure productivity for each company separately and run a smoother operation on both sides.

Second, because I was obligated to purchase Local Propane and previously had no interest in it, I still wasn't sure if I wanted to keep it. By separating the two, if I decided to sell Local Propane and its assets, it would be much easier to part with, given that it would be a standalone business and not be comingled in any way.

Note: American Bar Association rule 4.2: Communication with person represented by counsel.

In representing a client, a lawyer shall not communicate about the subject of the representation with a person the lawyer knows to be represented by another lawyer in the matter, unless the lawyer has the consent of the other lawyer or is authorized to do so by law or a court order.

Reflection Point 23

My quarrel with Danny went on for a total of 14 months before coming to an end. Though arguing continually and being at odds with him for so long may not have been ideal, the most difficult times in our lives can bring about the greatest personal improvements. Although it was nearly impossible to view those events as good teachable moments at the time, those situations gave me a wealth of knowledge and references I would need in the future, which still hold value for me today. Life has its own unique way of teaching you patience and will test you as you continue to graduate to higher levels. There's good in every bad situation. It just depends on how you look at it.

Although I was upset with Danny throughout this period, it's important to note that I didn't know how he interpreted the events that took place. I only saw things from my perspective. I felt my pain, my hurt. I don't know what he was experiencing. I'm sure there were things I said and did that upset and hurt him as well; therefore, I chose to forgive and hope to be forgiven. In life, we all are going to be called upon to forgive someone sometime. What better way to show someone you love them? It's always the right choice. I'm eternally grateful for having had these experiences. They promoted growth and helped shape me into the person I am today. If I would have had it my way, things wouldn't have happened the way they did. I would have chosen differently, but the truth is, everything that transpired was supposed to — it was the way it needed to be. Danny was preparing me for the future, whether he did so knowingly or not, and who better than my own brother to teach me some of life's most valuable lessons? After all the hard times, Danny and I managed to mend our once-frayed relationship. Thank you, Danny, for helping shape me into the man I have become. I'm glad we were able to get through it all. I love you and appreciate you.

What is a strenuous experience you have had that ultimately
led to your personal growth?

Have you considered being thankful for it?
What about that experience helped shape you?

Chapter 24:

A Fresh Start

It was my first day back. I was now $3 million in debt to the bank and had an almost $40,000 monthly loan payment looming over me. The bank had given me a straight-line mortgage, and I needed to pay the entire amount back within seven years. To someone who had worked extremely hard to remain debt-free all his life, almost at all costs, facing this amount of debt at 32 years old was more than challenging. But at least finding the money to pay Danny was behind me. Now I was on to the next challenge, how to build a better business. Both companies were in a state of disarray, and I needed to straighten things out, immediately. It had been 14 months since I lost control of my business, and it showed. Everything was disorganized. The office was dirty and in need of a revamp. Some of the employees had developed extremely bad habits while I was gone. It had become a low-standard environment. Do the bare minimum seemed to be the norm now.

Throughout my sabbatical, I observed many things from the outside looking in that I felt could use some improvement. Some things that should have been implemented and others that needed to be eliminated and reinvented altogether. I began taking notes of them in a large notebook and later put them in order of importance. Some things on my list were small and could be done in a day; others were large and would take quite some time to complete. First on the list was split the companies, which I already had done legally at closing. Now I needed to do it physically. I just made my way down the list. I knew just about everything I needed to do for both businesses.

Everything was on the line, and I knew I had to be prepared for this task. On the first day, and almost every day afterward for the ensuing couple of weeks, I arrived at work around 7 a.m. and left the office around 11:30 p.m. I didn't stop working unless I needed to sleep.

I took this as an opportunity to study every aspect of the business with fresh eyes, almost as if I knew nothing about it beforehand. I questioned everyone and everything. I made the effort to meet with every employee individually. I spent time evaluating them, and even more time informing them of my expectations and standards for the business going forward. We were not going to run it the way they had grown accustomed to. Things would be kept clean and organized. We would all be wearing matching uniforms; shirts needed to be tucked in, and drivers would be required to wear steel- toed boots. I put a lot of emphasis on marketing. I refreshed every one of our trucks. I had all stickers removed from them, got them detailed, waxed, and then vinyl wrapped each truck with our branding. That alone made a dramatic improvement to our company image. They were beautiful. The wraps made those old trucks look brand new, which immediately gave the drivers a sense of pride. It increased their self-esteem as well as my own, and everyone else's in the company, for that matter. I redesigned and ordered new invoices with our logos on them. To get control of unnecessary expenses, I made it a point to cancel all automated recurring billing. In addition, I had my staff create purchase orders for my approval on any expense over $200. If I approved, I'd personally sign every check. I wanted stockrooms more organized and everything to be labeled. Bathrooms needed to be cleaned and restocked daily with toilet paper. Floors needed to be swept and mopped daily as well. The list went on and on.

Bit by bit, I went through the entire company, setting new standards and expectations across the board. I retrained everyone to the best of my ability. I took the time to examine new staffers I hadn't previously met while on my sabbatical. Some of them didn't like the things I was doing or changing, and even after I took the time to explain, I got resistance.

They wanted to do it their way. But it wasn't up to them, I was in charge. I had a clear vision for what I wanted, and we were going to change. When dealing with pushback, I'd often say, "Let's try it my way first. If it doesn't work out, we will try it your way." That worked with most people. If I felt they were just not going to cooperate or were underqualified, I took note. Without a doubt, there were some replacements that needed to be made. Some employees were good additions, although most weren't. And good enough employees weren't going to cut it. I wasn't willing to try my luck. Failure was not an option.

I repeatedly held meetings and emphasized to my staff that this was a *new* company, and employees needed to meet or exceed our new standards. This new company wasn't going to tolerate any of the bad habits they had developed. If they weren't on board with our new direction and willing to make the necessary adjustments in their performance, this wasn't the place for them to work. We were going to do everything the right way, regardless of the cost or effort required. We were going to work as a team, and we were going to grow. I shared my vision of the future with the staff, along with details on how the company's success ultimately would benefit them. All in all, it took me about two or three months to shift the company mindset and get them back on track. We got quite a bit done in a noticeably short time. My staff understood my expectations; they knew what was important to me and where I wanted the company to go.

I had long desired for Prestige Propane Exchange to function like a Fortune 500 company. That was my vision. This time around, I was going to do things differently. It needed to operate like a large corporation, not a comfortable mom and pop. It was time to get uncomfortable. I saw it clearly in my mind. I knew exactly what I wanted. I just didn't know how I was going to get there. I began to seek guidance from people I felt had the experience I needed. Little did I know, I had a blessing just around the corner. My Uncle Jake recently had retired as the CEO of a large, corporately run business. And luckily, Uncle Jake now was a business consultant for hire. I didn't know much about his past business experience or his career; I just knew him as Uncle Jake. I was curious to learn how he might be able to help me. He offered to stop by and take a look at what we had going on. After we had a short conversation, I knew he was exactly the man I needed. He had many of the answers I was looking for. Uncle Jake had the corporate mentality. I hired him to come in for a few hours twice a week and give his opinion on things. Although I did not apply every recommendation, having his input helped shape my vision.

To be more effective, we needed to improve our communication. And to improve communication, I needed everyone to be aware of what was occurring, in each department, at all times. We all needed to be on the same page. Uncle Jake suggested we begin hosting timed weekly management meetings with all my department heads. Each manager had 15 minutes to update the group on what they were doing and what they might need help with. Uncle Jake hosted the first few meetings and kept everyone in line. After we got into a routine, I took his place and hosted the meetings. He sat back and only listened. After awhile, he stopped attending the meetings altogether. I followed suit. After hosting the meetings for some time, I inevitably passed the responsibility of hosting to our general manager. I only sat and listened. Ultimately, I rarely needed to attend any of them. I just made sure they took place and received updates on what was going on.

I instantly applied what Uncle Jake taught me. Those meetings were extremely valuable. They kept us all on track, created accountability, and allowed people to get direct help from their coworkers. It was teamwork. We all were able to add value and help each other in one form or another. And with everyone working together to problem solve, we made smarter decisions.

As the organization grew larger, there were more and more decisions to be made. But not all of them were large or necessarily considered important. Many of them were rather small and, for the most part, seemingly insignificant. One of the most common issues was employees asking me personally to make some of those small decisions, and even sometimes, override their direct supervisors. That is something I never did. I gave each supervisor the respect they deserved, and never overstepped anyone's authority. Managers were free to make the decisions they wanted or needed to make. It also kept them accountable. After all, that's why I hired them. If I had to make all their decisions for them, I might as well have kept their salaries and done their jobs myself.

Here is an example of one of these interactions:

A driver approaches me and asks, "Hey Max, I'm scheduled to work on Saturday, but it's my best friend's birthday, and we are throwing a huge surprise party for him. Do you think I can take the day off?" I counter with, "I have no clue. I'm not your boss, so I can't make that call. Why don't you speak with Oliver about it? He's your supervisor." The driver continues, "But you're the owner. Can't you make any decisions you want?" "Well, yes, I'm the owner, but I don't work here, and I have no idea what Oliver has planned or what the schedules look like; that's his job to determine. And if I promise to give you the day off, then I'd be interfering with his job. And that's not how we do things. So, I'm not going to do that. I would recommend you speak with Oliver directly. I'm sure you guys can work something out."

After awhile, people stopped asking me to make exceptions for them. They knew I was going to defer to their direct supervisors; however, the supervisors didn't always make the right calls. Every so often, I would hear of some type of unjust or unfair treatment and recognize I needed to have a little pep talk with a member of my management staff. I always did this the same way. If I heard something I didn't like or necessarily agree with, I didn't side with the employees on the spot. Instead, I would assure my employees that they had been heard and say something like, "Okay, thanks for letting me know. I promise you I'm going to look into it, and we'll talk about this later." Then I would call the supervisor into my office and get his or her take on the situation. Once I had all the facts, I would then make recommendations to my management staff to encourage a better outcome in the future.

It was around this time that I attended my first Tony Robbins event with Pastor Milton in San Diego — The Leadership Academy. To say that I was happy that I went would be an understatement. Attending that event changed the course of my life. Tony Robbins wasn't in attendance, but he didn't need to be. It was still an incredible experience. I learned a great deal about human psychology, behavioral patterns, and how to lead. I became a more effective leader. At that event, I decided to sign up for every program Tony was having for the upcoming year. Considering how this one event made such a significant impact on my life, I could only imagine what an entire year could do for me. I steadily continued to improve my skills. It led me down a new path.

Although I hadn't fully developed my leadership skills, I noticed that I was doing a better job of communicating with people. I felt as if I almost always had the right words to say. It was like a muscle that had been developed and was there for me when I called on it.

To increase morale and unity, I began hosting monthly company meetings, to get everyone aligned, not just the management staff. I had never done that. The entire company would come together; we would play music, order pizza, and announce birthdays. Then, we would fill all the employees in on what was happening within the company — equipment we ordered, accounts we landed, goals we had. Everything was on the table. Afterward, we would play teamwork games for cash prizes. We would get to know one another and had a great time. We became a nucleus, a cohesive group. Over time, we grew close, almost like family.

I was several months into my return at Prestige Propane Exchange when I received a call from someone who worked at the Tony Robbins Organization. She mentioned that the "Date with Destiny" event I had signed up for in San Diego and was extremely looking forward to had already begun and was overflowing, with thousands of people in attendance. She was calling because they had been made aware of my absence and was wondering if I was merely running late or if I had decided not to attend. I was so caught up with improving Prestige Propane that I had completely forgotten about it. I communicated to her that it had slipped my mind and offered my sincerest apologies for my inexcusable absence. I mentioned that I felt it was now too short of a notice to make the necessary accommodations, and unfortunately, I wouldn't be able to take part. The young lady insisted that it was, in fact, not too late for me to attend. The event was being held not far from my office, and she reassured me that, if I made an effort, it would be worth my while. I asked if I could call her back to have a few minutes to think it through. She obliged.

After hanging up, I called my secretary Vivien into the room to get her take on it. After giving me a quick recap of everything we had going on for the week, Vivien pointed out that none of the action items required my presence. She then suggested that I go because there was no reason I shouldn't. She also added, "Better late than never." She was right. Everything was under control at the company, for the most part. The event was in Palm Beach, so it would only take me about an hour and a half to get there from Miami, and, the way I drive, I might even be able to shave 30 minutes off that time. The only hindrance wasn't having a place to stay. I asked Vivien to explore some options at nearby hotels to see if I could get a room. I presumed that the host hotel had likely booked up months in advance. As I contemplated in my office, I heard Vivien's voice come on over the intercom on my desk, "Guess what?" she said. I could hear the excitement in her voice. "What?" I replied. "There was a cancellation, and there is a room available at the host hotel. I put a hold on it," she said enthusiastically. I laughed in disbelief. I thought she was calling the neighboring hotels. I guess she figured it was worth a shot to give the host hotel a call, and it certainly was. It was a water-view room overlooking the marina. Costly, but available. It was decision time. I thought it over for a second, and I knew that this could help me. I also knew I could have made a million excuses for why I shouldn't go, but the truth was, there was no excuse. What was I waiting for? I jumped up out of my chair and affirmed aloud to myself, "I'm going." I didn't waste another second. I asked Vivien to book that room right away, reached for my car keys, and hurriedly made my way toward the door while I simultaneously called back the young lady from the Tony Robbins Organization on my cell phone. I informed her that I would undoubtedly be attending, and I was very much looking forward to it! I quickly drove home, grabbed a small bag to stuff some clothes into, and made my way directly to Palm Beach. I was sitting right in front of Tony Robbins within what felt like the blink of an eye. It was surreal.

The week I spent at that powerful event changed my life forever. I went in there as one person and came out another. I felt like a newborn child. It was as if I had gotten a second chance at life. I felt renewed, refreshed, and cleansed. I was truly alive for the first time in years. The previous, disheartened version of me had vanished. I had done away with everything that was bogging me down, much of which I wasn't even consciously aware of. There was depression I was harboring after my mother's passing. Anger, and resentment I had been feeling toward Danny. Along with unwarranted stress and inexplicable fears I had been feeling;

it was all gone. I was healed, freed from my past. I saw life through a different lens. Attending that program was probably the absolute best decision I've ever made. Although, given the series of events leading up to it, I felt as though life decided for me. I was guided to it. I have no doubts about that.

The day after the event, I stayed in my hotel room for almost the entire day. I didn't watch TV. I didn't make any calls on my cell and kept my ringer off. I had downloaded so much and gone through such a transformational experience that I needed time to sit with myself and absorb it. I guess you could say I was recalibrating. It was a special day, a spirit filled day. I couldn't allow anything or anyone to taint it. After some time, I ordered room service and sat out on the balcony, quietly taking the time to appreciate the world around me. I felt an overwhelming sense of gratitude for all I was experiencing. I closed my eyes to take in the surrounding sounds and drew a big breath of fresh, crisp air. The sun's nurturing glow ever so gently warmed my entire body. I heard birds chirping softly in the distance. Every so often, a cool breeze would rustle the leaves on the nearby trees, and the branches would gently creak as they rocked back and forth. It was a beautiful moment; I was recharging.

I calmly and carefully reviewed my notes throughout the day, rewriting them and organizing them as I often do. I reflected on everything I had learned throughout this experience, the man I now had become and the man I was going to be. Everything had changed. I knew the minute I walked out that door, my new life would begin. It was all going to be vastly different. I took all the time I needed, and then some. Once I felt ready, I gathered my things, my thoughts, and my newly found aspirations and made my way back home.

Tony, I am eternally thankful for you!

Reflection Point 24

Breathe life into people. When I passed the responsibility of hosting the weekly and monthly meetings to my team, it freed up my time for other things and gave my team the opportunity to learn and grow. We were all in it together. We all grew together.

Follow the chain of command. Even if you're the boss, you shouldn't bend the rules for convenience sake; it ultimately will cause more problems. Lead by example. Let your team make their own decisions and help them learn from their mistakes. You don't need to control everything.

If life is guiding you in a new direction, don't be afraid to take a leap of faith. After attending Tony's event, I finally was able to face and heal wounds that were subconsciously affecting my life. Confronting my emotions gave me a chance to write a new story and design a brighter future for myself. I decided my past could no longer dictate my future; I left it behind. I buried it!

What is a time-consuming activity you can hand-off to someone else after providing them with the proper training?

In what ways will accomplishing this benefit you?

What is a life-changing decision you can make today that can help release you from your past?

Chapter 25:

Laying the Foundation

On my first day back at work, I was extremely energized and in high spirits. I felt different, and I knew I had changed, but my team didn't. I needed to bring them up to speed. Once in the lobby, and before even setting foot into my office, I called for a meeting with my management team. As soon as everyone gathered, I politely greeted them all and asked for their undivided attention. I began to describe to them some of the life-changing experiences I had at the event. I followed that by expressing my heartfelt gratitude for every one of them and took the time to point out each person's admirable qualities. Then I praised them for their commitment to our company. I guaranteed growth and prosperity for everyone and promised to do whatever it took to create such a future. Whether it required changes to the business or even my own behavior, I wouldn't relent until we were successful.

My team seemed captivated. I had everyone's undivided attention. It was a special moment for us all. They saw a light in my eyes that hadn't been there. I was a new man. I knew that things were going to be different. Now, they knew it too. I had always appreciated them but never actually expressed it. Not like this. Now, they felt it. I was grateful for them. Those 10-15 minutes made a significant impact on everyone present. There were ear-to-ear smiles and rosy, bashful cheeks across the room. As my words came to a close, you could feel that the energy in the room had shifted. It was powerful and impressionable. This heartfelt demonstration brought us closer together, I'm certain. After exchanging some high fives and even a few hugs, we concluded our meeting. I then retreated to my office for some alone time.

While at the Tony Robbins' event, I had set a considerably large goal for myself, a goal that scared me, but also made me feel alive. My goal was to ultimately sell Prestige Propane for $25 million. It was a rather ambitious intention for me and the business, but I had my mind set on it, and I planned to do anything and everything I needed to accomplish it. In light of that, I then had to determine what the challenges were, what needed to change, whom I needed to become to make this happen: *What did a $25 million company even look like? How many customers did I need to have? How many tanks would I need to exchange each year? How much money would I have to be making for Prestige Propane to be worth $25 million?* These were all specifically good questions I didn't have any answers to. So, I set out to get them.

I began by calling people in the propane industry who I felt could give me some insight toward answering questions I had. I spoke to business owners, former owners, and people who worked in the business-development division of some other larger propane companies. I asked them all the same, simple, straightforward question, *What do I need to do to make my company worth $25 million?* It was perhaps naive, but I was unashamed to ask it. And I'm glad the first person I asked wasn't the last. He was a man I admired. When I asked my question, he didn't offer any insight. Instead, he took the opportunity to discourage me. His response to my question was: "There's nothing you can do to make your company that valuable. It's not possible." It was disappointing to hear, especially at such an impressionable stage in my journey, and, even more so, hearing it from him, whom I looked up to. But I knew better. I brushed his comment off and decided immediately that I wasn't going to ask him for any more advice. I knew too well that words alone have great power, and I wasn't going to accept anything negative, from anyone.

The other people I asked were much more helpful. Most of them were surprised by the boldness of that question. I got a few giggles here and there, often followed by a pause to consider the question. Then they'd slowly repeat it back to me: "How can you make your company worth $25 million? Hmm..." Almost everyone was willing to help and volunteered valuable pieces of information. It was encouraging. With every conversation, I had more conviction. Every time I received a quality suggestion for what might help me get closer to achieving my company outcome, I wrote it down, and I made it a mandatory action to be taken. I later put all of them in list form and began researching and implementing them, one by one.

This was the list I wrote in my notebook:

<u>Things I need to get done to be able to sell for $25 million:</u>

1) **Don't run any personal expenses through the business. Take distributions instead. This gives clarity on the actual profit of the business.**

2) **Deposit all money and pay tax on all income. Every penny needs to be accounted for. Don't take any cash home.**

3) **Have audited or reviewed financial statements from now on. Everything needs to be transparent.**

4) **Sell more gallons of propane. It will give the company a greater value.**

5) **Increase and maintain a profit margin of 30%. That's a healthy amount.**

6) **No single account can be more than 10% of our sales. Avoid any customer concentration risk. Buyers don't like that.**

7) **Grow sales revenue year over year. Buyers DO like that.**

8) **Create the necessary systems and structure to have the company run itself. I do need to be involved, but I shouldn't have to be here.**

9) Open two more branches of the company: one in Central Florida, second in North Florida. This will give us a larger presence and the ability to service large corporate accounts statewide.

After creating that list, I bought two 6-foot by 4-foot, dry-erase whiteboards. I had one hung in my office, directly behind my desk. On that one I wrote down all my short-term and long-term company goals. I organized them into a checklist of things in order of importance and natural progression; along with the things and people I needed to accomplish them. I had it all mapped out right behind me. Anyone who walked into my office knew exactly what my goals were, what I was looking for and what was important to me. No mystery, no surprise. Look at the board. This is what I'm working toward, and this is what we're working on as a company. If an activity we're performing brings us closer to our goal, we continue to do it. If it doesn't, it's not relevant to me or to our company.

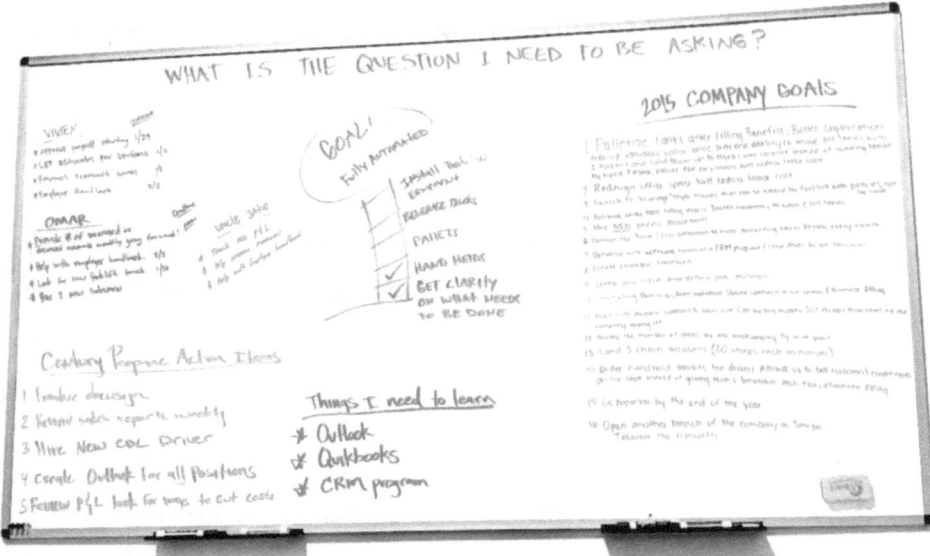

This was the list:

<u>2015 Company Goals</u>

1) Palletize propane tanks after filling. This provides better organization, frees up valuable space once stacked, and gives us the ability to move and load all tanks with one forklift instead of doing it by hand. It's faster, easier, and safer for employees and will reduce labor costs.

2) Redesign our office space. This will create better work-flow and efficiency.

3) Switch to beverage-style trucks that can be loaded by a forklift with pallets, instead of by hand.

4) Automate the tank-filling process. Install machinery to wash and fill tanks.

5) Hire a new, highly skilled accountant.

6) Common size profit and loss statement to make accounting easier to understand and review monthly.

7) Optimize with software. Implement a CRM program to track all leads and issue iPads to all salesmen. This will help us land more accounts.

8) Create an employee handbook.

9) Create and teach mandatory safety protocols to all employees.

10) Start using DocuSign; it's faster and easier. We can upload contracts into our system and eliminate filing.

11) **Meet with propane suppliers to lower costs. Maybe we can buy propane 20% cheaper than we're paying now?**

12) **Double the number of tanks we're exchanging by next year.**

13) **Land three large chain accounts. (20 stores each minimum.)**

14) **Order handheld tablets for drivers. This will allow us to bill customers credit cards on the spot instead of giving them terms. Which will improve cash flow and eliminate filing.**

15) **Go paperless by the end of this year.**

16) **Open another branch of the company in Tampa and take over the market!**

The other 6-foot by 4-foot whiteboard was hung in my bedroom at home, right next to my bed. It looked massive in that tiny room. I loved it. I wrote empowering quotes and reminders on it, along with all my personal goals, fitness goals, relationship goals, affirmations, motivational quotes, and an example of the person I needed to be to make these things happen. I would update them often, keeping it fresh. I read the board every morning when I woke up, and each night before I went to sleep. On that whiteboard I also wrote the goal of selling Prestige Propane for $25 Million. I didn't have that objective on the whiteboard at work because I didn't want the employees to see that and get discouraged. In addition, I set a date. I wanted to achieve this by May 9th, 2019. That would give me 5 years from the day I regained control of my business to accomplish it. I even took the time to write myself a check and taped it to my wall. "To: Max Lewis. Amount: $25,000,000. Note: Sale of Company." I felt a little silly doing it but, at the same time, it was exciting.

In addition to everything on the board, I wrote out a statement of how and when I would receive my money and taped it above my headboard. I read that statement aloud every day when I woke up and every night before bed. *I'm going to receive $25 million no later than May 9th, 2019. I'm going to do so by putting all my energy and focus into creating an exceptional business that has enormous value, which I will then sell.* I then would close my eyes to visualize it all manifesting and take the time to feel what it'd be like to have all that money and the nearly countless things I would do with it. Although I sometimes felt childish reciting it, especially if I had company over, I pushed through and fought back against any non-empowering thoughts. I did my absolute best to apply every effort and believe it would happen. Just being there in my mind was rewarding in itself. It felt great, so great that I would often end my visualization with a shout from how excited I got! "Woohoo! Yeah, baby!"

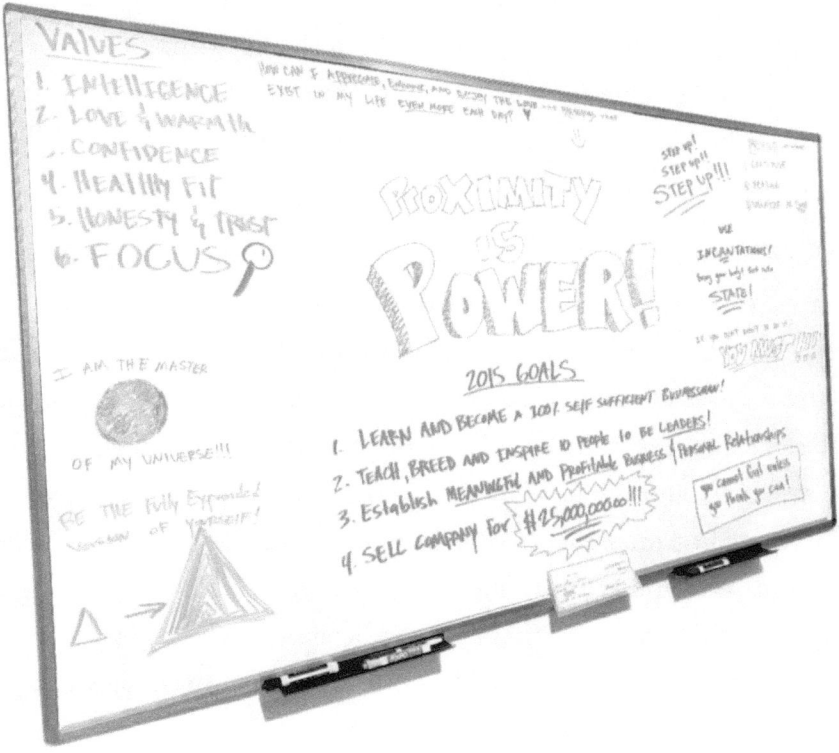

It was scary to set the bar that high, but that's exactly why I had to do it. I wanted to test my limits. It made me excited just thinking of accomplishing something so monumental, so colossal. It was a worthy goal — one worth pursuing.

As we began documenting everything properly and running the company correctly, our accounting became much more accurate. Numbers started to change. Things started to add up and make a little more sense. I didn't really know how to read a P&L or a balance sheet, but with some help from Uncle Jake, I was able to get a better feel for exactly where I was in this process and what I might need to do to get to where I wanted to go. But there was also a flip side to that. Along with the proper reporting of gallons of propane sold, tanks sold, and cash deposits came an increase in liabilities. One of those liabilities, for example, would be taxes. If you're going to be depositing every penny earned, you're undoubtedly going to pay taxes on every penny, especially if you're running the company in a less-tax-efficient manner to show as much profit as possible, as I was.

The first time I heard my accountant say how much I needed to pay in taxes, I almost fell off my chair. I finally understood why so many small business owners preferred to deposit the money they made under their mattresses instead of into their bank accounts. It was quite the eye-opener. The same goes for insurance. The more business you're doing, products you're selling, and vehicles you add to your policy, the more money the insurance companies charge you. That's because it's an increase in their exposure. Which means, it's more likely for you to file a claim at some point, which would cost them money. It almost felt as if I was being punished for being successful. The better I did, the more they charged me.

As a result of this understanding, I didn't like seeing our insurance agent, ever. He visited often, and I knew every time he walked through the door, it was going to cost me money. I assure you that I resisted the urge to strangle him on more than one occasion. But I channeled my better self and resisted the impulse. For the most part, I remained composed and took the rate increases graciously. After all, without insurance, I wouldn't be able to do business. It was all part of the growing process.

From the many calls I placed trying to discern what a $25 million business in the propane industry looked like, I learned two things. First, generally, company values were based on a multiple of net profit. And smaller companies were assigned a smaller multiple. For example, a small propane company that was profiting around $300,000 a year might sell for only a multiple of three to five times its earnings, giving a company that size a potential value of anywhere between $900,000 and $1.5 million.

Second, if the business was larger, the multiple might be higher. The larger the business, the larger the multiple. A few reasons for this might be because larger companies are perceived as less risky. They generate higher revenue and profits, and they have a more diverse customer base.

As an example, let's say a larger company was making upward of $1 million a year, which would be more than three times greater than the smaller company's earnings of $300,000 a year. The owner of that company might expect his business to be valued at a multiple of five to seven times the yearly net profit instead of just three to five times. In this scenario, the larger company might be worth up to $5 million to $7 million: Applying this information, I concluded that to reach my goal of selling my company for $25 million, I essentially would need to be making $3.5 million in profit each year.

However, a multiple is just a tool to gauge value. A business is only worth what someone is willing to pay for it. In many cases, businesses have been sold for much more than they profit annually, and in other cases, people have sold their businesses for far less than what the potential value may have been. There even have been some cases in which companies that actually lose money sell for large amounts. It's all relative to the viewpoint of the buyer or seller. Every deal is uniquely different. So, my challenge at this point was to add BIG value, quickly.

Reflection Point 25

Set a high goal for yourself, then determine exactly what you need to do to accomplish it. You know yourself better than anyone else; create a system that works for you. The ridiculously large whiteboards kept the outcomes I wanted front and center whether I was at home or at work. Having my goals spelled out on the wall, day and night, helped me stay on track.

When seeking direction, I would suggest that you ask the most skilled and experienced people you can think of with information on the subject. Try to keep your questions relevant to your source. Don't ask the janitor for expert advice on accounting, and don't ask your accountant for expert advice on mopping a floor.

And keep in mind, not everyone you seek advice from is going to be helpful. If someone tries to dim your light by putting you or your dreams down, don't share your aspirations with them any longer, even if that person is a close friend or family member. Protect your dreams!

Go to page 415 now for your own manifestation check.
Remember to dream BIG!

How do you organize your thoughts? How can you improve
your strategy?

Whose guidance should you seek to help shine a light
on your chosen path?

Chapter 26:

Squeaky Clean

We began working our way down my new checklist. Many of the items on the list required significant time and energy to carry out, but the first one was easy. We needed to find a better system for transporting BBQ tanks around our facility, that would eliminate the need to move them around by hand. Finding a solution for this would afford us more time and energy. When we attempted to stack our BBQ tanks on standard wooden shipping pallets, it was difficult to secure them. Although the traditional wooden platform works very well for shipping boxes and other types of freight, we couldn't get it to work for transporting BBQ tanks. The tanks became unstable because the features of wooden pallets didn't accommodate the tanks' unique shape.

The planks of wood were spaced out in a way that created a gap every few inches, which caused the tanks to slant. We needed a flat, smooth surface that would be more suitable for the tanks to sit on, or at least that's what we thought. Even when we found pallets made out of aluminum that had a smooth surface, the BBQ tanks stacked on them in quantities of around 18 slid right off and onto the floor. Which sent the tanks rolling in every direction. This not only damaged the tanks, it also was potentially dangerous and just as inefficient as the wooden pallets; therefore, neither wooden pallets nor aluminum pallets were usable. We needed a better option and needed to continue to find better ways to be more efficient.

After doing a little research, we discovered a company that invented a solution. It was far better than just having a flat surface for the BBQ tanks to sit on. In fact, they invented a custom-molded pallet for the sole purpose of transporting BBQ tanks. It was genius. These pallets were manufactured in an injection mold and were built around the design of a BBQ tank. They had a concave design that kept the tanks deeply seated into the mold cavity, securing the tanks for any form of transport. They were just what we needed. Other large companies had already been using these specialized, plastic molded pallets for years. We were just not aware of it. The extraordinary pallets' unique design enabled us to secure 12 BBQ tanks on each platform. We now had the ability to stack each pallet, one on top of the other, for up to four layers, safely and comfortably. We stacked them into clusters of 48 tanks. This enabled us to move large quantities of organized BBQ tanks around our yard with a single forklift, in a matter of seconds, without the fear of them falling. This made it much easier to get an accurate inventory count, with much less manpower.

For so long, we typically had the production manager, accompanied by two other employees, count an abundance of heavy BBQ tanks by hand, twice daily, to try and arrive at an accurate inventory number. Now, just one person could look at a cluster of tanks on a pallet and intuitively know that it contained 48 tanks. Implementing this palletized system made our lives much easier. It effectually improved our workflow. We became more organized; it made production easier and freed up valuable space in our yard. This promoted better use of our time and manpower. One down.

Now that we had the pallet system, we could replace our semi-customized, flatbed-style trucks, which could be loaded only by hand, with industry- standard, beverage-style trucks that could be loaded with a forklift. These trucks had four or six compartments on either side, each with its own dedicated roll-down door. This made it possible for us to pick up an entire pallet of 48 tanks and load it directly into each separate truck compartment with a forklift. With this new system, an entire truck could be loaded by a single employee in about five minutes; light years faster than the four men who would take around 20 minutes to load each of our flatbed delivery trucks by hand.

After successfully introducing the palletized system to our operation and committing to upgrade most of our delivery vehicles to beverage-style trucks, we continued to make our way down the list. It was time to do some work on the inside. Our office space had a poorly designed workflow because it had never been properly arranged. We were working with what we had. We continually adapted to the pre-existing state of things. That's what we knew how to do; it's the way we always did things.

This approach reminds me of the *Ham Story* I once heard:

There was a husband who won a prized country ham in a sales contest. When he got home, he handed the beautiful ham to his wife, who immediately cut the ham's ends off and placed it in a baking pan.

The husband asked his wife, "Why did you cut the ends off my prized ham?"

"Well, that's how you bake them," she responded. "That's how my Mama cooked a ham."

"Why did she do it that way?" he asked.

"I'm not sure," she said. "Let's call Mama and ask her."

So, the husband and his wife called Mama. Her reply was... "Well, my mama always did it that way."

The husband and his wife then called her Granny to get her reasoning behind cutting the ends off the ham.

"Granny," the wife asked, "Why do you always cut the ends off the ham? My husband says I shouldn't do it that way, and Mama says she cut the ends

because you always cut the ends. And I did it because she did it! Nobody knows why we do this. So why did you cut the ends off the ham?"

"Well," Granny responded, "I don't know why you two do it, but I did it because my oven pan was too small!"

The moral of the story is, you shouldn't do things because "that's the way they have always been done."

Now that we had resources and smart people on board, it was time to start thinking of things in a better way, from scratch. Instead of just doing things "the way they had always been done," we had the opportunity to reinvent ourselves, and that is exactly what we were going to do.

We needed to rebuild the entire space and make it work for us. Uncle Jake found a company that could assist us in redesigning the layout. They suggested custom cubicles. At first, I was a bit put off by the idea. I thought it was cheesy. But once I learned more about the cubicles and what they could do for the space, I quickly saw the value. The cubicle company suggested they might give us some guidance in maximizing the space we had to work with, while still considering every element of our workflow. They had someone from their company come out to take some measurements of our workspace. They mentioned that I should be on the lookout for an email from them with their recommendation for an optimal layout.

After looking over the email with the sketch of their proposed design and price quote, I knew it was a no brainer. We decided to go for it. We tore everything down and rebuilt the entire office from scratch. The office was now custom-built to suit our needs. We weren't just using what we had; we created what we needed. It was all done purposefully. We made the highest and best use out of the space we had to work with. With just a little over $8,000, we transformed the entire office space and created a much more effective and efficient environment for everyone. Two down.

Next up on the checklist was automated filling equipment. I was curious about what it might cost to have some of this equipment installed. I knew it was important for the future of my business if I planned to continue growing. Since the inception of my tank-exchange business, we had not only been loading the trucks by hand, but we also had been hand washing, hand painting, manually refilling, and hand placing our branded sleeves over each tank. Automated machinery was long overdue. We had made some minor improvements over time, adding industrial-strength pressure cleaners to help remove grease from dirty BBQ tanks. We also had installed a small spray booth a few years back, with an older conveyor system to aid in the painting of the tanks, but, for the most part, our system was primitive. As a result, we were overstaffed in the production department.

Technology had come a long way, and it was time to make a change. By installing automated production equipment, I figured we would be able to triple our production numbers in the same amount of time. In addition, we would be able to run a much safer operation with fewer employees, which would save me a great deal of money. This was an essential piece of the puzzle. The first quote I received for a fully automated production line was $1.5 million, way too high. That quote included state-of-the-art machinery that would paint, wash, refill, and check the BBQ tanks for leaks before getting approval to hit the road. After passing the leak test, the tanks would be dressed in an informative plastic sleeve that had our brand's marketing material and listed all the important product information as well as safety information. It would've been nice, but I didn't have the money.

Instead of giving up on the idea altogether, Uncle Jake and I decided to look at this challenge from a different perspective. We studied the builders' design of production equipment and began to pick apart the quote. After brainstorming for a bit, we realized that, if we had just a few of the key components, we could drastically improve the efficiency of the operation and, at the same time, not spend $1.5 million. We basically cherry-picked what we felt could have the biggest impact on production and what we felt was necessary to improve the operation overall. Simply put, everything we needed and nothing we didn't. After making our list, we asked the production company to re-issue a new quote.

Here are the items we selected:

1. Automated tank-washing machine. This could wash BBQ tanks nonstop and reduce the need for six employees down to just two, while producing about five times as many clean tanks. It also could do a better job of cleaning the tanks than our employees could, which would give us a better product and improve our quality-control process. It was fast and easy to use.

2. Gravity-fed rollers. We wanted a few lengths of gravity-fed rollers to interconnect our workstations and help create constant workflow. Another added benefit with this system was that, once our employees had completed the work at their designated workspace, they would no longer need to pick up tanks and carry them to the next station. By our calculations, adding the rollers would reduce the need for manual labor by around 80%; and undoubtedly make our employees happier. With less manual labor, the likelihood of back injuries and other workload-related injuries also would decrease.

3. Five semi-automated tank-refilling stations. With the addition of this setup, one employee could replace the need for five. In addition to that, we'd fill about three times as many tanks. The machine was programmable and filled the tanks by weight. This ensured the tanks never would be overfilled. There was close to no chance of human error.

4. One leak-detector device. Instead of dunking a tank underwater or spraying it with a soapy liquid to identify a leak, this machine measured CO_2 levels near the valve of each tank as it made its way down the gravity-fed rollers. It was faster, safer, and again, almost eliminated the possibility of human error.

The cherry-picked items Uncle Jake and I selected only came out to $252,000 installed. That was a phenomenal price. I couldn't believe how much we were able to shave off the original price quote, more than 80%. Even more encouraging than that was the fact that the production company liked our custom-tailored design and assured us it would not only work, but also drastically improve our operations. Unfortunately, I still didn't have the money to buy it.

As we shared some ideas, Uncle Jake suggested that our bank might be willing to give me a line of credit when they saw how much this could improve our operations. The thought of more debt made my stomach turn, but I needed this if I were going to make my company worth $25 million. It wasn't an option. After presenting this to the bank and filling out some paperwork, the bank did, indeed, approve a line of credit for the entire amount. We ordered the machinery as soon as the funds were made available and requested that the manufacturer install the equipment without delay. They did just that. This changed my entire business and what a difference! It was a godsend. The cherry- picked version of the production equipment was extremely effective. It enhanced the operation spectacularly. We went from producing tanks five days a week to only needing to produce tanks two days a week, leaving the already-reduced production staff twiddling their thumbs. We were generating tanks at lightning speed with less effort while achieving greater quality control. We went from never having enough full BBQ tanks ready for distribution, to *always* having BBQ tanks ready for distribution! The machinery completely transformed our business and took us to the next level. It was one of the best financial decisions I'd ever made, worth every penny and then some.

Here's the gist of it:

Our dedicated forklift driver would unload the dirty BBQ tanks that came off our trucks and set the pallet of dirty, empty tanks next to the tank- washing machine. The tanks then were loaded by hand onto a conveyor that led toward the washing machine. Dirty tanks went in on one end and came out clean on the other end. An employee would be waiting on the clean end to visually inspect each washed tank to ensure it met our standards. Then, a small strip of gravity-fed conveyor would roll the tanks to the semi-automated tank-filling machinery, where one man now could fill up to five tanks at a time by doing little more than pushing a button. When the tanks arrived at this station, they were waist high. There was no need to bend down and pick up the tank to place it on a scale. The employee at that station would pull the tank onto a weight scale, present a fill nozzle to the tank's valve, and the automated machinery would automatically latch on to it. The employee then would press the fill button, and the machinery would automatically begin refilling the tank to its preset weight capacity. Because it didn't require his supervision, the employee would repeat the process at the four other refill stations that were all within about 10 feet of one another.

Once the tanks reached their filling level, the automated attachment would disconnect itself automatically from the tank. The employee then would put the tank back on the gravity-fed conveyor. The tank then would continue making its way to the automated leak-detection device, where each tank was tested for leaks. The automated machine would deploy a housing that covered the tank's valve and began measuring for CO_2 levels in the air around the valve. If the machinery detected a leak, it would push the tank off the line into a small holding pen. Those tanks would be reinspected. If the tank had a leak, it would be removed from the production line to be repaired or destroyed if repairing it wasn't viable. The tanks that didn't have leaks would proceed down the line to get dressed in their branded sleeve. After being sleeved, those gleaming, show-stopping tanks would again be placed on a pallet. Once they were on pallets, our forklift operator would relocate the tanks. They would be set aside until it was time to load them onto the delivery trucks.

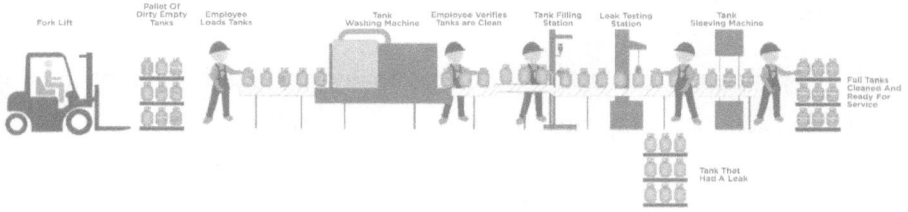

The production system was exactly what we needed. Once it was firmly integrated into our operations, we continued making our way through the checklist and attacked the remaining items as quickly and efficiently as possible. Day by day, we became better and better, refining the business and redefining who we were as a company.

Reflection Point 26

When faced with a daunting task, you may find it less overwhelming if you break it down into smaller pieces. There's power in taking several small steps to accomplish a big goal. Automating our facility was done by evaluating and implementing minor changes, one at a time. Those small changes eventually led to a monumental outcome.

When you're actively looking at things from a curious perspective, you find answers that will not only surprise you but also surprise those around you. When we took time to analyze the quote from the automated tank-filling equipment company, we were able to create a custom-tailored design that worked specifically for us, saving me a lot of money. The cherry-picked design was something the company hadn't thought of or offered; however, they were impressed by our creative vision and helped it come to life.

To conclude, seek understanding on why you're doing things the way you do them, and stay curious to find better options.

Are your dreams really YOUR dreams?

Are you designing your own future or have you been *influenced* to pursue something else?

What do you want at your core?

Chapter 27:

The Golden Ticket

I remained committed to the idea of growing my company. I embodied the right attitude and seldomly got off track or lost focus. However, while on my quest, I realized I was missing some fundamental skills to become the sort of man I wanted to be, skills I didn't possess but needed to learn, skills I should already have acquired by this point, specifically, skills you acquire with a formal education. I had to do a better job of educating myself. I had always been resourceful and managed to learn a great deal from online sources such as YouTube, but there was some knowledge that I just didn't possess. This made me feel uncomfortable and vulnerable. I felt I knew a good amount about business at the level I had been operating at, but I wasn't sure what everyone else knew at the level I aspired to.

Simply put, I didn't know what I didn't know. What I did know was that I was committed to the journey, and I had to do something about it. Now, what would that be?

I continued my routine and steadily progressed when I got a little nudge in the right direction. I was at a holistic wellness center having acupuncture performed for a pain in my wrist. While I was being worked on by the therapist, we exchanged some small talk. She was an overly sweet, older woman who spoke softly and assuredly. Being in her presence put me at ease. During our conversation, she asked how I injured my wrist. I told her I injured it at the gym lifting weights. She then asked me to lie down and get comfortable to begin a procedure on my wrist. Carrying on with the small talk, she then asked what I did for a living. As I lay there relaxing in the cozy, dimly lit room, I calmly gave her a detailed explanation of my company and filled her in on some of the big plans I had for the future. As time passed, we continued our dialogue. I openly spoke my mind. For much of the conversation, I kept my eyes closed and just relaxed. I felt safe, with an overwhelming sense of tranquility. While dribbling out my thoughts, I casually mentioned that I lacked understanding of some accounting terminology I had overheard. After listening to my dilemma, she offered me a piece of advice that influenced me. It was almost an obvious observation, as the best advice often is. What she said was: "You need to become a 100% self-sufficient businessman. You need to learn all the things you don't know about business so you can understand what other professionals are talking about, and no one will ever be able to have an edge on you." It was random but genuinely great advice. I believe that short, casual conversation, altered the course of my life. I had to educate myself. I needed to know what I did not know. It was that simple. Figuratively speaking, I needed to get out of this comfort zone and go learn some things.

The most difficult challenge I then faced was accounting. I knew nothing about it. The meetings I was having with my accountant were about as close to useless as they could have been. I would start off by driving 30 minutes to her office every month. Once I arrived, the accountant would present documents to me, which might as well have been written in Japanese, and then go into several short-winded dissertations on each page, all the while using such obscure terms as debits, credits, depreciation, appreciation, accrual, revenues, variable expenses, assets, liabilities, income statement, balance sheet, statement of cash flows, along with several other confusing terms and theories, which apparently all had to be in balance or something like that. It was totally foreign to me.

While I sat there listening to this useless information, the accountant would frequently ask me to turn to the next page. I would religiously exhibit a blank stare, waiting for a pause so I might ask my question.

Which was: "So… is that good or bad?" That felt like the only question I ever asked in those meetings. I was clueless. In my world, adding, subtracting, dividing, and multiplying were just about all I needed. I had rarely heard most of these terms and phrases being thrown around. I never felt the need to learn any of it. At that time, I thought that was the point of paying an accountant. On the few occasions I was curious enough to ask, what the accountant explained to me made zero sense; however, I would often nod as if I did understand. I was embarrassed to admit my ignorance. My accountant was one of the many people who naturally assumed that I had attended college or had a general understanding of what we discussed.

I had to start somewhere, so I decided to sign up for an evening accounting course at the local community college. Jessica and I had long since split up, and my girlfriend at the time agreed to keep me company and take the class with me. As we took our seats on the first day of class, I remember thinking that the teacher was quite young, but I wasn't going to hold that against her, I was young too. Shortly after beginning the class, she started discussing the theory of general financial terms and principles. I can't recall now what it was exactly, but she said something that didn't resonate well with my real-world experience. I raised my hand and asked, "What's your experience with that?" "With that, I personally have no firsthand experience, but I recently graduated with an accounting degree, and that's what they taught us," she replied. "So, you've never worked for a company in the accounting department?" I asked. "No, not personally," she admitted. I knew nothing about accounting, but I knew that I needed to get out of that classroom if I knew anything. I wanted to learn from an expert — someone who had firsthand, real-world experience, not from someone who had only earned a degree. I leaned over to my girlfriend and whispered, "We've got to get out of here. I need to learn from someone with more experience." She nodded her head and agreed, "Okay." We politely got up, thanked the teacher for her time, and left.

It wasn't long until I was having lunch at a sushi restaurant in Miami Beach with six friends I had met through the Tony Robbins Organization. Because we were all on a similar wavelength, we got together from time to time and offered support and quality advice to one another. Our gatherings were encouraging and served as a community backbone. We often leaned on each other to overcome challenges.

During our lunch, I humbly implied to the group that I lacked some understanding in the accounting department. One of the women looked at me and said, "Well, you need Keith Cunningham's accounting course, honey, and you'd better hurry because I think it starts next week." Everyone else chimed in with a bunch of "yeahs", "uh-huhs", and head nods, as if it were completely obvious. Apparently, I was the only person in the group who hadn't heard of Keith Cunningham. Here all these people were, friends of mine; all six of them, who were all in possession of a solution for my handicap. I had just never mentioned that accounting was a challenge for me, so they never suggested this helpful advice. I wish I had spoken up sooner. That moment of vulnerability was another reminder that I wasn't alone in my lack of expertise. We all face similar challenges. No one is born knowing it all.

"Who? Who's Keith Cunningham?" I asked. "He teaches a course called The 4-Day MBA; you'll learn everything you need to know about accounting in just four days. All of us here have taken his course already," she replied. "Really? How do I sign up? Where do I get his information?" I asked desperately. I knew this was exactly what I needed. This could help me overcome my lack of understanding and education. "Easy, you can look him up online and then call to sign up," she replied. I thanked her, eagerly finished my lunch, and headed back to work.

Once I was back at my office. I began to research The 4-Day MBA online. It was in Texas. My friends never mentioned that minor detail. There was another surprise, also. The course wasn't starting the following week; it was starting the following day. After reading those two facts, I muttered to myself, "Well, I guess I'm not going. I'll just go to the next one." Of course, I was taking the easy way out. Somewhat discouraged, I decided I might as well call anyway and get some information for the next event, which was months away. I called the number on their website.

The young lady who picked up the phone filled me in on how much the course cost and other important details. I jokingly told her about my lunch with my friends in Miami Beach and how they failed to mention the course was in Texas. When I verbalized that I wouldn't be able to make it because I was in Miami, more than 1,000 miles away, and it was short notice, she asked, "Well why not? Just book a flight and come on over. We have two seats left, and we'd love to have you sitting in one of them." I hadn't thought about it that way. Her question stuck with me: *Yeah, why not? It worked out when I dropped everything at a moment's notice to attend the Tony Robbins Date with Destiny event. Why not take the chance again? What is more important than this right now? Nothing. I need to learn this. It's holding me back. I can hop on a plane tonight, be there by morning and take the class.* I quickly made up my mind. I asked the young lady to charge my credit card, booked the flight, and I was off.

While on the plane, I couldn't help thinking how strange this all was. I laughed to myself while looking out the window as the plane taxied down the runway, preparing for takeoff. The speed at which things were unfolding was surreal. First was the Tony Robbins Date with Destiny event that I hadn't planned to attend, which completely changed my life, and now this. When I woke up that morning, I had no intention of going anywhere, yet here I was, on a plane, headed to Texas, in the middle of the night, with only a few hours' notice. It was so bizarre, but it felt right. I was right where I needed to be. I felt I was being guided to the right path.

I was completely wrong about the 4-Day MBA. It wasn't just an accounting course that I needed to take; it was far more valuable than that. This was heaven-sent. In only four days, Keith Cunningham and his method of teaching opened another portal in my mind. He simplified the scary world of accounting, and it wasn't intimidating anymore. It became fun. In addition to that priceless education, Keith taught us the importance of developing a strong culture in our businesses, better ways to treat and value employees, and innumerable other principles and philosophies, along with thought- provoking questions and insights. These insights hadn't only assisted in his success but, in a countless number of others, he has enlightened along the way. It was by far the most valuable business education I had ever received. I think I learned more in those four days than I did in all four years of high school. Keith Cunningham always will hold a special place in my heart. He's one of the most kindhearted and distinct individuals I have ever had the pleasure of meeting.

I forever will feel grateful for what he has taught me and the impact he has had on my life. I thank you, Keith.

Reflection Point 27

When we're vulnerable with ourselves and others, we leave a door open for people to offer their guidance. When I candidly admitted to the acupuncture therapist that I lacked financial knowledge, she gave me great advice that shed light on the importance of educating myself. That valuable insight motivated me to be more proactive in finding a solution. When I casually mentioned my predicament to my like-minded friends, I was rewarded with a quick fix. When I was later encouraged to drop everything at a moment's notice and fly to Texas, initially it felt like a tough decision, but it also felt right. I needed to get out of my comfort zone and take a chance. If you make a move, God will make a way.

I strongly believe that the people we spend our time with will have the greatest impact on our lives. It's probably the most effective method of changing your life, and the good news is, it's probably the easiest as well. All you need to do is spend time with the people who are getting the results you're after. If you spend time with bankers all day, you eventually will learn something about banking. If you spend time with people who do drugs all day, you eventually are going to try drugs. If I left you on a remote island for six months where the only language being spoken was Chinese, you'd be speaking Chinese by the time I picked you up. Get the point?

Are you spending your time with the right crowd?

What is something you wish you could have learned by now?

Without making excuses, what's stopping you?

Chapter 28:

The Power of Vending Machines

I returned home with a pile of notes and a new and improved agenda. This was the third time I felt a need to take extreme action. With each level of increased competence came more opportunities to improve, better ways to do things, better ideas. The more I was able to continually absorb, the more I could incorporate into the business and, more importantly, into the people. I stacked on the lessons I learned brick by brick, layer by layer. With each new addition, the business gradually strengthened.

During my sabbatical and before getting my business back, I had made independent observations of things I felt needed improvement. I wrote them in my notebook and did my best to implement those changes from day one.

After my transformational experience with Tony's Date with Destiny course, I became cognizant of a psychological component to consider while running my business. I needed to become a better communicator, and I did. I declared my commitment to do so when I addressed my staff on my first day back and made the necessary adjustments from that day forward.

After taking Keith's course, I had a much greater understanding of how business was done on the level I was striving toward. I gained an even greater understanding of what I needed to do to improve my business. My approach to incorporate what I learned would be no different from how I approached everything else: I was going to take immediate action. In addition to accounting, I acquired skills I didn't even know I needed, skills that would help to enhance our company's dynamic, which I realized was just as important, if not more important, than the accounting. Establishing a strong company culture could get me much farther down the road than just about anything. After all, it was the employees who were doing all the work. They represented our company and me. Shouldn't I want them to be as happy as possible? It made sense. If they were happier, it would show in their work and attitudes. Which likely would increase employee retention; their cheerful behavior would rub off on the customers and, in turn, help me keep and attract more business. Now, it was time to get to work on it.

While in Texas, I had made a list of several key insights, things I needed to pay closer attention to, and things I needed to look for; the right questions to ask myself, my customers, and my employees, as well as how to ask them. I also wrote what I envisioned our company culture could become if I were to successfully implement what I learned from Keith. First, I was determined to adopt the custom of asking many more questions to all our employees, but not casual questions for the sake of small talk. Going forward, I would ask specific, detailed questions that would lead to some improvement to our organization, whether it was functional or nothing more than employee satisfaction. I was going to ask quality questions, to just about everyone, regarding just about everything — from the janitors to the office staff. I would become passionately inquisitive with a purpose. I was determined to make this a better place to work, the best place to work. I would become the staff's biggest advocate. I would put all their needs first, above all else. I wanted them to be as happy as possible.

I began with: *Snacks*

On my first day back from Texas, I immediately got to work on what Keith had taught me. I held a 15-minute water cooler meeting with the entire staff. Once I had everyone's attention, I addressed them and asked,

"Hey guys, I'm only going to take a few minutes of your time. I just want to know some of the things you all feel we can improve on as a company. I have a question for all of you: What do you think would make this a better place to work?" There was no response. They were dead silent, either thinking about the question or, maybe, they were a little caught off guard and curious as to why I might have been asking that question in the first place. Perhaps it was both, but I assumed the latter. "Guys, it's not a setup," I chuckled. "Honestly, l want to know what you all think would make things better around here. You can just shout out your answers, let's hear it!" The suggestions began peppering in as the employees started to participate. It started as a distant murmur of voices, then turned into a minor uproar. I heard a few of the requests that were yelled out, but one came in much more frequently and at a much higher octave than the rest. Surprisingly, that request was for vending machines. I learned that the employees desperately wanted vending machines to buy sodas and snacks during their break without having to leave the property. This was news to me. I never had known they wanted vending machines because, well, I had never asked. It was a simple request to fill. Without hesitation, I replied, "Okay, you've got it. Vending machines, it is." I assigned the task of finding a company to install a vending machine to my general manager right then. The employees were pleased.

A couple of weeks after the vending machines had been installed, I received a check for $143 from the vending machines company. I wasn't sure what it was for. Upon inquiring, the vending machine company informed me it was my percentage of the profit they made from selling soda and snacks to the employees. I wasn't aware that I would be getting a commission split from the vending machine sales. I informed the vending company that I wasn't interested in making money off my team. Instead, I insisted that they pass those savings along to my staff by lowering all the prices in the vending machines, effectively charging them half of what they already had been paying. It was one of the smallest and seemingly most insignificant gestures I could've done for them, yet the reaction I got from the employees was magnificent.

Before the prices had been lowered on the machines, I announced at the next company meeting that the price change would be taking place. You should have seen the reactions of the 40 employees in the room. Most of them shouted, clapped, and cheered. They were overjoyed. It caught me by surprise, honestly. Their genuine response made me smile and laugh. You can't buy that kind of excitement. They were celebrating together, over half-priced snacks in a vending machine. Although I'd like to think they were really celebrating that someone finally was listening. Maybe even for the first time. They were being heard and appreciated. We were all bound just a little tighter that day. Even though it was pint-sized progress, it was another step toward earning their trust and loyalty. It was an eye-opening example of the power of asking the right questions. An example of the impact you can have when you listen to people and show them you care about them. That thoughtful little gesture led me to have this wonderful experience. It was a great lesson for me and a phenomenal tool. I was learning to listen, even to the little things. After all, it's the little things that make people happy, isn't it? I knew small changes like these would become instrumental in forming our culture. We were becoming a company that cared about our employees first and addressed everything else soon after.

Next up was: Uniforms

Almost right after that, I got another opportunity to flex some of the muscles Keith helped me develop. I had given my younger cousin Mack Varela, who was interning for an office job, several arbitrary tasks to complete as an opportunity to prove his worth to our company. If he proved worthy, I would offer permanent employment. One of the tasks was to place an order for some new company T-shirts for our drivers and production employees who were working out in the sun all day. The shirts were supposed to be collared, button-down short-sleeved shirts. They were from a particular brand, made from a heavy material that held up to being laundered repeatedly and then ironed, without tearing or fading. Somehow, and I mean, I have no idea how, Mack completely screwed up the order. The shirts we received weren't the brand that could be repeatedly cleaned by our uniform-washing company's commercial machine. The shirts were thin, very thin. They were long-sleeved shirts, and our logo was on the back of the shirt instead of the front, in a different color, with the wrong phone number on them and, maybe the worst part of all, he ordered 300 of them! What was I going to do with 300 of these things? Even if I could see past all the mistakes and how ghastly they were, how could I give long-sleeved shirts to people who work in the sun all day? Even worse, the shirts cost me $3,000, and as part of a custom order, the cost was nonrefundable. Great.

When I questioned Mack about this mix-up in my office, he said it undoubtedly was the printing company's fault. That wasn't what he ordered, and he would never have approved of it. Taking that into account, I instructed Mack to call the printing company and demand a full refund or have them reprint the entire order correctly. I then sent him on his way so I could get some work done. About 30 minutes later, Mack was back knocking on my office door. With my head down, buried in paperwork, I granted him permission to enter. "Come in," I said. When I finally looked up from my desk to give him my full attention, I found Mack standing there, with a flushed red face, and tiny beads of perspiration on his neck and forehead. It looked as though he had gotten rather worked up. In visible distress, Mack began to vaguely describe the difficulty he was having with the printing company. As he gave me his full account of the conversation he had just had with them, he waved his hands to and fro. He gasped for air several times between sentences, huffing and puffing his way through the story. Mack explained that the printing company, although at complete fault, was unjustly giving him an extremely hard time and was refusing to issue our company a refund. I thought that was strange. I had never had an issue with the printing company until now. Sensing Mack was getting a little out of his depth, I assigned him to another menial task, and I handed this potentially problematic situation to my general manager Omar so he could handle it. I knew there had to be some sort of mix-up.

To my surprise, Omar informed me that he too was having a difficult time with the printing company, but he had a new piece of information. Omar said the printing company was claiming to have an email confirmation of this order by an authorized representative of Prestige Propane Exchange. They also said the proofs for that design had been approved, as well as the 300-shirt quantity; therefore, they need not refund our money. When Omar asked if a Mack Varela had approved the order, the man he spoke with said he didn't recall that name but assured us they had an email confirmation and would get back to us with the proof. Well, if not Mack, who was it? I had Omar call my secretary Vivien, my office manager Justin, my dispatch manager Oliver, and production supervisor Ben, to my office for a quick meeting. I wanted to make sure we weren't having a miscommunication somewhere. Among the five of us, we made most of the decisions for the company. But there was no mix-up. No one had any knowledge of the order. We were all confused. Who could have ordered these shirts? Who would have approved this? None of our management staff, that's for sure. We all knew better. I had

Omar call back and request that the printing company send whatever proof they had directly to my email for review. Omar said I would have it by day's end.

I was sitting at my desk hours later when the email from the printing company arrived. They forwarded me the emailed confirmation they had. The mystery was about to be solved. The email confirmation was written in all caps, and it read: "I MACK VARELA, OF PRESTIGE PROPANE EXCHANGE IN MIAMI FLORIDA, HEREBY APPROVE THE ORDER OF 300 LONG-SLEEVED T-SHIRTS." Directly below this was a sample image of the awkward shirts. I slapped my hand down on my desk and began to laugh hysterically. They had him dead to rights. He couldn't have made us more liable if he wanted to. I called in my management team, kept a straight face, and told them in a serious tone, "Guys, this is a lot more serious than I thought. I was able to solve the mystery, but you're not going to believe who was behind all of this." I invited them all to walk around my desk and read the email that was displayed on my monitor screen. The four of them walked behind my desk and began to read aloud. Shortly after, the room erupted in laughter. It was Mack! That little rascal had the entire management team in complete disarray. Probably because he was just too scared and embarrassed to admit his mistake. Losing the $3,000 wasn't ideal, but at least we all got a good laugh out of it. We told a few jokes and then decided to get back to work.

Shortly after, I had Mack brought back to my office. When he arrived, I kept a straight face and gave him a very stern talking to. I explained the importance of telling the truth and how we all make mistakes, which we can work around, but deciding to lie to us was no mistake. I forgave him and asked that he apologize to the management staff as well as promise that he never would lie to us again. I also made him aware of how lucky he was to be my cousin; if he were not, he would've been paying for those shirts. In addition, I communicated that we would unfortunately be throwing the shirts away. In my opinion, they weren't going to be useful for our staff, and due to the misinformation printed on them and unattractive design, I didn't want them to be given out to family and friends either. It was an improper representation of our company; therefore, they could never be worn in public.

Once Mack had left my office, I called our production supervisor, Ben, into the room. When he arrived, I pointed at the shirts and asked that he have some of our employees toss all the boxes in a dumpster outside. Ben glanced over at the pile of boxes in the corner of my office. He then walked over and pulled out one of the shirts. He took a moment to carefully examine it, front and back. "It would be a shame to throw these away, they're brand new!" he said. "We can't do anything with them. The information is incorrect; they can't be washed by our laundering company, and they are all long- sleeved," I replied. Ben thought for a second while my head remained down as I rifled through some paperwork. "Well, I can give them out only to our production staff, and they can choose whether they want to wear them or not. If they choose to use them, I can instruct them to only wear them onsite. At least that way, we can get some use out of them," he continued. "We can also use them on days when it's cold; it could help keep the employees working outside warm, or maybe, we can use them on days we get really dirty, like when we change the oil in the trucks. Or we can just use them as rags, but in either case, anything would be better than just throwing them away," he concluded. His points made sense. I rolled my eyes, took in a deep breath, and exhaled sharply. "Fine," I said as I reluctantly agreed. "But I better not see those shirts anywhere other than our production facility. They're embarrassing," I said. "Yeah, they're pretty bad," Ben smiled and agreed. He then began removing the boxes from my office.

About a week later, after arriving at work, I walked the property and inspected our production facility. I did this often. I liked to be in touch with everything going on. During my rounds, I noticed most of the production staff were wearing the infamous shirts. One of my older employees, Alfred, who was also wearing one, walked right by me. I stopped to shake his hand and say hello. After exchanging a few polite words, I said, "I'll bet you're loving that shirt, aren't you?" as I smirked and expressed amusement. To my surprise, Alfred's response was, "Oh, yes. I love them! We all love them." He didn't appear to be joking. "It's the worst shirt on Earth, Alfred. What are you talking about?" I asked. "Well, they're much thinner than our regular uniforms, so we don't sweat that much. And the long sleeves are great because they protect us from the sun, so we don't get sunburned from our elbows to our wrist anymore," he said excitingly, smiling. He continued… "And most of the guys like the fact that we can take them home and wash them ourselves. Sometimes the uniform company we use misplaces our regular uniforms or forgets to deliver them, and we don't have clean ones to wear." I couldn't believe my ears. Did he really just say all of that? I walked directly over to the production manager and asked him to halt production for a five-minute meeting. I wanted some insight immediately.

Once all were gathered, I asked the group of about 15–20 guys, "By a show of hands, who likes the new long-sleeved shirts more than the short- sleeved, button-down uniform?" Every one of them raised their hands. I was shocked, but I continued, "Alfred mentioned that some of you haven't been getting your uniforms returned from the uniform company on time. How many of you have had that experience?" About two-thirds of them raised their hands. "Okay, last question. If I cancel the uniform-washing company and give you guys these long-sleeved shirts instead, which of you would prefer that option?" They all raised their hands again. The meeting was over. I thanked them all and politely dismissed them.

I went back to my office and asked Vivien to provide me the most recent monthly invoice from the uniform-washing company. After doing some quick math, I discovered that I was paying more money to wash our short-sleeved, button-down uniforms each month than it would cost me to re-issue the entire staff a newly celebrated long-sleeved shirt, very single month, which wasn't likely. I was sure the shirts would last more than a month; they might even last a year. Granted, I would need to redesign them to get them up to our standards so they could be worn in public, but that was the easy part. This was a much cheaper option but, more important, it made the staff happy.

I held another meeting, this time with the entire company, it had become customary for me to keep everyone involved in the decisions we were making. I also wanted to get all their valuable feedback. As we began, I gave a censored version of Mack's contribution to this shirt's existence and discovery. I then jokingly gave him full credit for the current design. I thanked Ben and Alfred for their assistance. I then applauded the production team for their ability to see past the shirt's superficial flaws and praised them for focusing on ways to extract value instead of creating waste. I then mentioned that the shirts would be redesigned and issued to our production staff and our drivers. I passed a few of the shirts around so the rest of the employees could see them. As the shirts made their way through the crowd, several people tried them on. To my amazement, numerous office staff and sales team members were quite fond of the shirts as well. They were speaking among themselves, but I still could make out some of what they were saying. I started hearing people say they preferred them to our existing office uniforms. I also heard a few people say they felt cozy and comfortable in them.

Then one of the salesmen yelled out, "Can the office staff and sales team wear the new shirts to work once they are redesigned?" "If you want to, sure, I don't see why not," I replied. I heard some celebrating going on among the office staff and sales team. "Awesome!" "Yes!" "This is great!" and some high fives followed. "Okay, wait a sec. What's going on with the sales team and office uniforms? You guys don't like your uniforms either?" I asked. One of our account managers, Steven, stood up to answer. "Boss, the problem is, it's too hot outside. The guys on the sales team spend most of their day out in the sun, and it gets uncomfortable to be in slacks with a button-down shirt tucked into your pants. I usually have to bring two spare shirts to work every day to change into because of how sweaty I get." "Hey, Steven! Do you change your sweaty underwear too?" One of the other account managers exclaimed as he teased. We all laughed. "Okay guys, seriously, is this true for everyone?" I asked. The sales team affirmed that just about all of them had the same opinion; the uniforms made them sweaty and were not comfortable. "How about the office staff? What's wrong with your uniforms?" I asked. "They're starchy and don't fit that well," our call attendant blurted out. "Boss, I think we'd all be more comfortable in some athletic wear, like Nike polos or Under Armour," Steven added. "Okay, well, do you guys think you could get just as many accounts if you wore sportier clothes?" I asked. "Yes, we will probably get more!" Steven shouted. The rest of the team confirmed it.

"Okay everyone, here's what we're going to do. I'm going to make some much better shirts to hand out to everyone; they'll be sportier and loose- fitting. But for now, and from this day going forward, you can wear whatever you want to work, whatever makes you comfortable. You guys can bring in whatever articles of clothing you want to wear, and if you want your clothes branded with the company logo, I'll pay for the branding and the clothes, just bring me your receipts. If you don't want your clothes branded, that's fine also. But I'm not going to pay for your clothes. (I chuckled) We're going to base our opinions simply off results. Uniforms are no longer mandatory." Everyone cheered with excitement.

This was unbelievable, yet another development. These Q & A interactions with my team were eye-opening. I learned something every time we got together. Listening to what my employees had to say made my job much easier. I was just going with the flow. Before we ended the meeting, we poked a little more fun at Mack, and all shared some laughs. We all then publicly thanked Mack and clapped it up for him. He got multiple pats on the back and even a friendly head noogie.

As a team, we turned an unsightly error into another huge win. Everyone was now benefiting from Mack's mistake. After the meeting, I went to my office, redesigned the shirts, placed another order, and canceled our uniform contract. By being observant and open-minded, I not only was able to make just about everyone much happier, but I also was able to save the company a great deal in laundry expenses. Thanks again, Mack.

In the next few weeks, people showed up to work in their activewear. They all looked much more comfortable. For the most part, they still dressed presentably, but they were happier. It allowed them to be who they were and feel confident. I embraced the change also. I avoided my suits and ties and started wearing almost exclusively Lululemon gear; it's how I felt most comfortable — Lululemon T-shirt and Lululemon sweatpants. They're still my daily choice to this day, and I've never been happier.

Soon after it was: The Drivers

Throughout all the years I had been running my business, we consistently had a problem retaining delivery drivers. For the most part, we relied heavily on a few dependable legacy employees, who had been with us for several years. Those core employees were reliable and kept us moving forward. Many of them were like part of the family and obviously loved working at the company.

But, for some reason, we never could make newly hired drivers happy. Once they learned how physically demanding the work was, they rarely got past their first two or three weeks of employment. Those who managed to get past the first few weeks often asked for more compensation immediately after completing their probationary period. Of course, getting a raise after just a few weeks of work wasn't likely, especially when considering that the new drivers often wanted to receive similar or greater compensation than we gave to our current employees.

This always puzzled me. Drivers' quitting or threatening to quit was stressful, but it also was one of the most time-consuming, ongoing, melodramatic problems I had. We would hire a promising driver and, just a few weeks later, he would demand a raise. When I would deny the raise, the driver often would quit or, even worse, stay and be disgruntled — spreading dissatisfaction throughout our organization, attempting to turn our content employees against the company. I'd eventually hear of this behavior and confront the disgruntled employee, and the end result was rarely good.

For years, I couldn't understand why it was so challenging to find drivers who were willing to do the job for the pay I was offering, but it should've been obvious. I wasn't putting myself in their position or recognizing how physically demanding the job was, and, I wasn't offering competitive wages, either. In fact, I was paying the bare minimum I could get away with. If a prospective employee wanted $15 an hour, I would offer $13 an hour. If he wanted $10 an hour, I would offer $8 or $9. That's what I was taught — don't pay more than you must; pay just enough. Unfortunately, that was poor advice. It was a complete lack of empathy. And looking at it from the employee's perspective, I'm sure that approach wasn't very encouraging or reassuring. I probably wouldn't have wanted to work for me either.

The truth is, I never gave this issue much thought. I got so used to its being a nagging problem, I never thought there could possibly be a solution. The ironic part was that the entirety of the business relied on having delivery drivers. Without drivers, who'd deliver the propane? By low-balling them and trying to save as much money as possible on wages, I not only was causing a recurring problem for myself, but additionally, gambling with our reputation. If we couldn't make our deliveries on time, we wouldn't be dependable. And if we weren't dependable, we'd lose business. Not smart.

In the past, even after the company was considerably large, on several occasions I would have to get on a truck to make deliveries because we didn't have anyone to do the job. I didn't mind filling in, but the reality was, my time could've been much better spent elsewhere. I needed to be working on the business, not in it. I just didn't know any better. The way to approach and solve this problem only became clear to me after returning from Texas.

After overhearing dispatch manager, Oliver, say we had lost yet another quality driver, I decided to address the issue on the spot. It was going to end today. Thankfully, I was better equipped to address this challenge now. I went straight to my office and sat down with a pen and notepad as I began to think of why we continued to have this issue. I wrote down a simple question: *Why are the drivers leaving?* I then began answering my own question. *They complain about pay. They complain about benefits. They complain about using the minutes on their cell phones to communicate with our dispatcher. Then, they get better job offers elsewhere.* I wrote down another question. *What do I need to change to never have to deal with this again?* Before answering that, I wrote another question:

What can I do to turn this completely around and have the drivers value their jobs and the opportunity they have to work here? I found that question more appealing, so I began writing an answer to it. *Make this a better place to work than the competition in the employees' eyes, not mine.* Then I wrote, *How? What do they want?* I began to brainstorm on all the issues I had heard them gripe about and even came up with some new benefits I thought they might find attractive. I wrote, *Give them all a raise, pay more than the competition, if possible; give them all a company cell phone, give them medical benefits, give them all a weekly fuel allowance for their personal vehicles, maybe $40 worth of gasoline a week; give them an opportunity to earn a commission when referring new customers to our business. Pay them a percentage for every tank they exchange or sell out in the field. Even though it's part of their job, that might even incentivize them to get more deliveries done and, at the same time, give them a sense of ownership.* I continued to load several pages of my notepad with ideas.

When I was done brainstorming on driver benefits, I asked myself: *How much money is this going to cost me across the board?* The simple answer was, *a lot.* I didn't even bother to do the math. The next question I wrote was, *Is it going to be worth it?* My answer was, *yes.* Like many small business owners, I wasn't too thrilled about increasing my expenses, but I knew it was the right move. There was no doubt that the added cost would be substantial, but the time and energy we were putting in to continually train and hire new drivers was far worse than this added expense. Keeping that in mind, this was more like an investment. If we didn't have to worry about hiring people all the time, we could get much more work done. This ongoing issue was more of a disruption in our workflow than anything else. Not to mention, I was certain our legacy employees were going to be euphoric about these newly added benefits. If any employees were deserving of these perks, it was them. Their unwavering devotion to our company was proof of that.

I paged Vivien and asked her to call all our competitors and other similar companies to find out what they were paying their delivery drivers. Once I had the competitors' average salary and benefit information, I began to design a new package for our drivers. Our entry-level driver positions previously were paying $11 an hour. No benefits. Our highest-paid, legacy employee at the time was making $14 an hour and had a company cell phone. Everyone else landed somewhere between the $11–$14 hourly range. Based on the information my secretary gave me, other companies were paying around $14–$16 to entry-level drivers who were similarly skilled.

Once I completed designing our new salary and benefits program, I informed the dispatch manager, Oliver, to arrange a meeting with every driver that day after work. New hires, legacy drivers, even the forklift driver, everyone who touched a steering wheel. I also wanted both managers, Omar and Oliver, in attendance. After concluding the business day, Oliver crammed everyone into our tiny conference room to host the meeting. From my office, I could hear laughter and what sounded like joyful conversations blaring. Because it was after hours, they joked and laughed a little louder than usual. And because they were all being packed into the conference room like pickles into a jar, I'm sure they all found some humor in that; nevertheless, Oliver managed to accommodate everyone into the confined space. Under normal circumstances, the conference room only sat eight people, and I'd say there were about 20 people in there. It had become a standing-room-only setting. Oliver summoned me once he had everyone present. As I walked in, I greeted everyone and made my way to the far end of the room. Everyone was so cheerful. There was great energy in the atmosphere. At that moment, I decided I was going to have a little fun with them, just for laughs.

As the chatter lessened, I began to get their attention. Before the room was completely quiet, I started speaking. "Guys, listen up… thanks for coming to this after-hours meeting on such short notice. You all know I wouldn't keep you after work if it wasn't important. I have some good news, but before we get into that, I have some really, really bad news." I paused. I bowed my head for a moment and let out a huge sigh. I then slowly began to raise my head; with my lips now pursed, I gently nodded, as if to express grave disappointment. Now, the room was pin-drop quiet. I had their full attention. Everyone in the room was motionless and nervously awaiting the bad news. They didn't know what was coming, but they knew it was coming. And whatever it was, it wasn't good. I began gradually panning the room, making eye contact with each person, one by one, displaying my unyielding disappointment. As the suspense rose, I showed a look of despair. I then took a deep breath and declared, "Guys... I'm really sorry to tell you, but you all have been fired." I then paused for dramatic effect. On the receiving end of that news, there were 20 expressionless, thousand-yard stares. They were utterly speechless. They looked like a group of breathless mannequins.

I then continued, "Okay, so that's the bad news. Now, the good news is, I'm rehiring all of you starting tomorrow for $17 an hour — plus benefits. That goes for everyone! As of tomorrow, you're all going to be making $17 an hour." I heard them gasp as they began to breathe again. Sighs of relief and some cheering ensued. "Wait…wait…wait…guys, listen up, there's more. Starting next week, you all will receive a free company cell phone; you'll receive a company credit card to be used for up to $40 worth of gasoline every week for your personal vehicles. You'll receive a commission for any customers you refer to the business, and we're going to pay you a commission for every tank you sell on your routes. So, it's much more than $17 an hour," I rapidly said. It was a lot for them to take in, and it just kept getting better and better.

The looks I saw around the room were priceless. Those guys looked like they just won the lottery. Truthfully, it filled me up to see how happy they were. At that moment, I couldn't have cared less about how much my increased expenses were. This was so much more important than making a few more dollars at the end of the month. It was about them. For many of them, it quite literally changed their lives. After commissions, for most of the employees, it was about a 50% raise or greater. They were able to provide much more for themselves and their families, and, once again, I found a way to connect with my employees and make them feel appreciated. They had a tremendous value, and adequately compensating them for their efforts was the very least I could do. Knowing that we could have such a powerful effect on people, overflowed my heart with joy.

The consequential payoff was nothing short of exceptional. After that day, we no longer struggled to retain drivers. Instead, we had a waiting list of people eager to join our team. Even past employees who had heard of our new salary and benefits program began calling and asking if they could get their old jobs back. It was wild. Our problem had been turned on its head. Nothing like what we had ever experienced. This was a vital enhancement, a major turning point for our organization and a contributing factor to our success. I was becoming a better person, a better coworker, a better business owner, and a better leader. We took another huge leap in our commitment to excellence.

As a side note, this increase in pay and benefits didn't affect us monetarily. We were able to hire and retain quality employees, and the commission program did, in actuality, increase productivity. As a whole, the drivers began making more deliveries and exchanging more tanks. In fact, the very next month we set a new company record for the number of tanks sold. This sent our sales figures through the roof. The money we paid out in commissions was trivial compared to the increase in profits and productivity. In addition, several drivers also made it a habit to solicit new business for our company and made hundreds, and often thousands, of extra dollars a month while doing so.

Reflection Point 28

Success in your life and business is ultimately dependent on your involvement. You need to participate in your own rescue. This isn't a job that can be pawned off on someone else.

Try not to take mishaps too seriously. As illustrated with Mack, presumed mistakes often turn out to be good fortune. When faced with a recurring challenge, analyze problems in depth and get to the root of the issue. Don't surface solve. Sometimes we need to start over completely from scratch.

Make it a habit to ask people for their opinions. Creating opportunities for an open dialogue may not only enlighten you, but it will also exhibit a meaningful sense of appreciation. This will go a long way in contributing to your success.

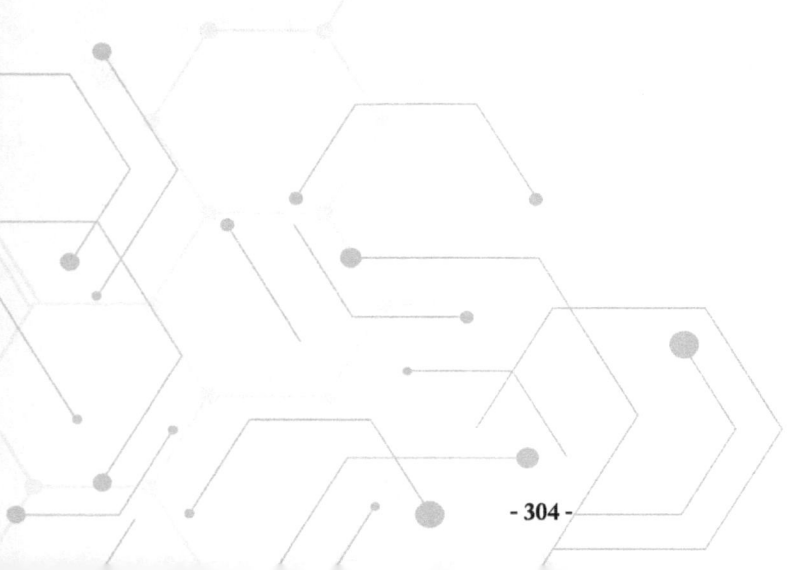

How do you honestly respond to feedback?

How could you improve your response?

What is an existing challenge in your life that might be solved by implementing a unique approach?

What could be the solution?

Chapter 29:

Questions and Thinking Time

If there were two things that influenced me most after studying with Keith Cunningham, those things were *Questions and Thinking Time*. Taking enough time to ask yourself the most thought-provoking questions and allocating the appropriate time to answer them is a highly underrated exercise. Unfortunately, few people ever do it.

Most people would assume they have thoroughly thought through the important decisions they make, primarily because they have had the topic circulating through their minds for an entire day or some other extended period. I'd say it's quite easy to have something fixated at the forefront of your mind, especially if that something is important to you. I'm sure we all have experienced moments when we can't get something out of our heads, even when we try. Experts say we have between 50,000 and 80,000 thoughts running through our brains every day. We're always thinking, day and night. But having something on your mind is not the same as thinking, and not all thinking is created equal. There are many different ways and forms of thinking. How we go about it and the amount of time we invest in the process are what make the biggest difference. This will vary and is unique from person to person. But, as it is true for just about everything else, the more you invest in something, the more you'll gain from it. Thinking is no different. The more you invest in perfecting your technique, the more you'll gain from it.

Many people claim to do some of their best thinking and develop their finest ideas in the shower. I have experienced this myself. This is because they are in a warm, comfortable, and safe space with a constant white noise that creates a relaxed environment with little to no distractions. A relaxed state of mind is important to be creative. By letting your mind detach, you allow new ideas to flow in. This kind of environment primes your mind to think creatively. So, if we know this, why not purposely create an environment where you can intentionally channel your creativity and document your quality thoughts without wasting all that hot water? That's what thinking time is. It's a simple concept but also genius.

When I've questioned my friends about how they think, I've found that most of them start by asking themselves a basic question. They seldom ever write it down, and then, without giving their undeveloped question very much thought, grab one of the earliest ideas that come flashing into their mind and assume they've solved their problem. But the reality is, they have barely scratched the surface and have missed out on the *gold*. Those seemingly obvious, easily thought of answers rarely produce the desired outcome.

Keith emphasized that, when faced with an important decision to make, **we take the time to sit in a quiet room to eliminate any auditory or visual distractions. In fact, you need to remove even the *possibility* of any potential distractions. You need to be in a controlled environment. Once you have that established, get yourself a blank notebook or notepad and something to write with. Now, most important, start with a quality question to work on. Then think, really think. Do not get distracted and do not get up. The true art of thinking time lies in the ability to sit in silence, and let your mind take off. Channel all your concentration and use the power of your combined thoughts to help find the answers you're looking for. Begin by answering your initial question. As you're performing this exercise, write everything down, everything you think of, all the answers, new questions, and ideas that come passing through your mind. Write them down!**

Then, continue to be inquisitive. Ask yourself a different variation of your initial question or a different question altogether. Those variant questions will take you down a new path, hopefully, several paths. When you have the appropriate amount of thinking time, it probably will lead to a superior answer and evident course of action. Remember, the better the questions you have, the better your answers will be. The recommended time period is one hour, but the most important thing is that you get started. Commit to the process and see where your thoughts take you.

I feel that doing this type of exercise regularly and adequately can be one of your greatest assets in life, if not the single greatest asset. Nearly everything in your life requires a decision, and your decisions are a direct result of the things you think about. It's probably my favorite thing to do, think. It gives me clarity and helps me make much better decisions. By thinking things thoroughly through, and analyzing a variety of potential outcomes, you give yourself the greatest possible chance at success, in all you do. Can you even put a price tag on that? I believe the person who thinks things through thoroughly will ultimately win — at anything. Thinking time will change your life; it changed mine.

Reflection Point 29

Exercise your brain. If you haven't already, I strongly encourage you to go back and answer the questions at the end of each chapter. Be sure to allocate enough time to thoroughly reflect on each one. It is one of the most valuable parts of this book. Make the time for self-discovery.

What thought-provoking questions should you be asking yourself
before making an important decision?
*(e.g. Will this drain me? Whose opinion should I get on this? How could
this impact me down the road?)*

Starting NOW, what will you do differently going forward?

Chapter 30:

For the Best

With my newly found financial understanding came the desire to make more changes. Ironically, after meeting with my accountant immediately after my completion of Keith's course, I realized that she didn't have the bandwidth to provide the service I now required. The tables had turned. I needed better financial reporting, with more detail and clarity. I also wanted someone who was solely focused on my business at all times. Besides not fully understanding everything I was requesting or having the experience in providing such detail, she could not give the personal attention I needed; therefore, she couldn't satisfy my request. I wasn't going to settle for whatever financial guidance she was capable of offering. I was going to get what I needed, simple as that. My mind was made up. It was time to make a change. I wanted to hire an in- house accountant to replace my off-site accountant the moment I found a suitable substitute. But who was going to be that replacement?

I had a friend named Arthur, whom I greatly admired. He was an extremely intelligent young man, a great friend, and a phenomenal sounding board. He also happened to own a midsize, well-run business. Arthur and I would get together from time to time to have lunch and enjoy each other's company. At our lunch meetings, we would solicit advice from each other. I always found our conversations meaningful and valuable. I'm sure he did, too. During one of our lunch conversations, Arthur filled me in on his current projects and some of the challenges he was facing. As it was customary for us, I asked questions and offered my observations throughout our discourse. After we had worked through all he had going on, I would disclose what was bugging me at the time. "I've been a little stressed out, man, I'm having a tough time finding the right accountant. That and finding the right employees for important roles within my company. I guess good employees are hard to find, right?" I said. "Not if you know exactly what you're looking for," he responded. "Have you ever read the book *WHO* by Geoff Smart?" he asked. "No, I haven't," I replied. "Buy the book today. Don't do anything or hire anyone else until you've finished reading it. He has all the answers you're looking for. You can thank me later," he added smiling.

When I got home that evening, I purchased the book on Amazon and began to read it on my girlfriend's Kindle fire. I instantly saw the value. Arthur was right. The book appeared to contain every answer I was looking for. It wasn't just a nice read; it taught me a skill — what to look for and how to look for it; how to create a job description for the roles I was trying to fill; how to conduct interviews, and how to grade each candidate's interview to ultimately hire the right person for the job. Instead of hiring whoever was available and working around their capabilities, as I'd been doing my entire career. I've never read a book so quickly. I feverishly took notes and developed requirement criteria and interview questions for my new accountant and for every position in my company. Every role was unique, so each required a different set of skills.

Reading that book and applying the techniques it taught me were monumental. I had clarity on exactly the kind of people I needed to fill each role, and along with it, the ability to sift out the great candidates from the timewasters. Because my standards were now set so high, it took me much longer to find a suitable candidate to fill the in-house accounting role. After a while, I grew a little frustrated with the amount of interviews I had to conduct. I went several months interviewing potential candidates, which meant I went that entire time without the details I needed to run the business properly. At one point, I was tempted to just hire any accountant; it was better than having none. But I never settled. Through persistence I found the perfect fit. It was worth the wait. If you ever need to hire someone, buy that book.

Once I completed the process of hiring my new accountant, I had a new awareness of how to differentiate a quality employee from a poor fit in my organization. My skills had been sharpened, and I was extremely glad that I took the time to educate myself, although this newfound skill and knowledge didn't come without a burdensome task. It forced me to finally come to terms with a very touchy subject, one I had been avoiding, almost from the very moment I regained control of my business. But it was time to face the music. I had an extremely tough decision to make, a decision I felt I honestly could not make. I needed to fire Justin, my office manager.

This was particularly difficult for me because Justin was my very first employee. He started as a helper and had worked his way up through the ranks. Justin had been with the company on and off for about 10 years. He was one of my friends from school. I loved him; he was almost family. But unfortunately, that alone didn't qualify him as the right candidate for the job. The position had since outgrown him, and the glaring truth was, he was the wrong person for the assignment. Uncle Jake had previously brought that to my attention on more than one occasion, but I didn't want to hear it. How was I going to fire my first employee? My friend? I assumed Uncle Jake was far removed from the personal aspect and didn't understand my dilemma. But the reality was, Uncle Jake understood quite well. This had nothing to do with friendships; it was about having the right person in the right role. Uncle Jake saw clearly, and it was I whose judgment was skewed because of my personal relationship.

When it came to Justin, I was conflicted. After my first few days back with the company, I wasn't sure if it was my standards that had drastically changed, or if it was Justin's disposition that had changed. But after only a few days, I realized that it was both. As we pushed forward and began to raise our company standards, it became more and more evident that Justin had become half-hearted about the business. He frequently opposed innovation.

He was aware of everything we had going on and what our objectives were, but he was largely uninterested in participating. His lack of enthusiasm made that clear to just about everyone. Justin would arrive at work late each morning and was the first to leave each afternoon. He rarely made himself available to help our team with anything. There was always an excuse. His most frequent reply to just about any request was, "I'll get to that later." In our weekly company meetings, he was unenthusiastic and rarely smiled. When it was his turn to speak, he often provided us with incomplete information. When confronted about it, he would make excuses for his negligence and downplay the importance of what we were relying on him for. He would say such things as, "Is it really that important?" or, "I don't see why any of this matters." His dismissive attitude was very frustrating and discouraging for the rest of the team. It seemed he was unconcerned with keeping pace with the rest of us. It felt as if we were running with a parachute strapped to our backs. Unfortunately, he had become a picture-perfect example of the sort of employee we had to remove to keep our progress and culture intact.

While still turning a blind eye, I tried everything to get him on track. I had several heart-to-heart conversations with him and expressed my concern for his conduct. When that didn't work, I tried motivating him. I frequently reminded him of our mission and the bright future that was ahead for all of us. That had no effect either. Exploring other options, I later proposed he might consider a different role within the company; I thought that could've been a solution. He was uninterested in that option as well. He was altogether unchangeable. I didn't know what else to do. I certainly couldn't increase his salary; he was making more money than anyone else in the company at the time. I had run out of options. I grew tired of trying to cheer him up every day. I lost my desire to convince him to cooperate, and there was only one thing left to do. It was time to let him go. It was an outcome that I felt he almost longed for, in a weird way. Knowing that this was an extremely tough decision for me, Uncle Jake volunteered to step in and relieve Justin from his duties. I couldn't even be in the room for it. It was too personal. Although, the way I saw it, with Justin's unwillingness to participate, he essentially fired himself.

Once Justin gathered his things and left, I decided to call him on his cell phone to explain our decision. I was apprehensive about placing the call because I wasn't sure what his reaction was going to be. I thought it over before dialing. *Is he going to be saddened by the news of his termination and overcome with emotion? What if he's terribly upset? Actually, he might not even care. Let me just call him. We need to have a conversation, either way. He at least deserves that much from me.* Justin picked up on the second ring. He spoke calmly and softly. I was relieved to hear him this way. I was even more relieved when he mentioned he wasn't surprised that he'd been fired. In fact, he said that he knew this was coming; he was aware that he had been pushing his luck and giving the company a lackluster version of himself. The truth was, it wasn't that he was incapable of filling the role; it was just that his heart wasn't in it any longer. He wasn't happy. I guess we both were just barely holding on and delaying the inevitable. Had it not been for Uncle Jake, who knows how long we would've remained in that mutually unfavorable position together. But regardless of how we arrived at this point, it was clear that cutting ties was best for both of us. We both were now free to pursue our own interests. Having that brief conversation with Justin reassured me that I had made the right decision.

We issued Justin a very generous severance package and wished him the best. With Justin no longer occupying a role he had no interest in growing into, we were able to hire a more qualified and experienced replacement who already had the skills we were looking for, truly the right person for the job. Once we had that role filled, things instantly began to run much more smoothly. We had made the tough decision and pulled the breakaway handle; the parachute was now gone. Full speed ahead.

By the end of 2014, I'd been back in control for roughly six months. After it was all said and done, the company had made an annualized profit of around $950,000. But that isn't what we had in the bank. Most of what I made in the second half of the year went right back into the business. But this was good news. I had a much clearer view of where we were and where we needed to be. I knew right where I was standing. I needed to more than triple the amount of profit we were making. There was still much to be done.

Reflection Point 30

Even if you may feel you know all there is to know on a topic, there's always more to learn. There's always room for improvement.

The disenchantment of someone whose heart isn't in it can trickle down onto those in close proximity and affect your entire culture. Hiring highly qualified people may cost you more money at first but will save you more time and anguish in the long run. If you're going to pay anyway, you might as well pay a little more and get your money's worth.

What is a tough decision you've been putting off?

Does it have the potential to set you or someone else free?

How good would it feel to be finally free from it?
What would be different?

Chapter 31:

Fun and Games

With more of the right people on board and fewer obstacles in the way, our company environment continued to take shape. Our office had changed. I no longer felt I had to micromanage anyone. My team was composed of all-stars who didn't require repeated reminders on what they needed to do. On the contrary, they tackled and solved challenges before I was ever even aware that an obstacle existed. You could feel the positive energy circulating around you the moment you walked through the entrance doors of our building. The air smelled different. It was clean, crisp air. The employees smiled and laughed often; they loved being there. It became an inviting place for all; friends of mine, as well as friends of our staff, began to stop in more often and spend some of their leisure time at our company, which we encouraged. We wanted happy, positive people around and for everyone within those doors to feel right at home. We had a *Let's get it done* attitude; we were serious about getting to work but still made time to be personable and enjoy ourselves.

I wanted to reward my team and, also, add a little excitement to our office. To display my trust in them, I decided to give them more freedom. I began to fill our lobby with entertaining games and merrymaking equipment. I announced that anyone wanting to blow off some steam, settle a score, or just take a little break and have fun with a coworker had the freedom to use the equipment at their own discretion. No permission was necessary.

The moment you walked into our business, you saw a double Shoot Out, a two-player arcade basketball game with an LED electronic scorekeeper, timer, and buzzer. It was a charming addition to our lobby. Just walk right up, pick up one of the basketballs, and shoot. The timer would start as soon as you made the first basket. Besides pure entertainment, we would often use it to settle silly disputes with a quick round of head-to- head competition. Oftentimes, almost customarily, at one point, employees held miniature tournaments to find out who was paying for lunch on a daily basis with this game. A pool of contestants would join in and try their luck at getting the high score in less than 60 seconds. Loser's pay for lunch; the ultimate winner eats free.

I'd regularly hear employees casually teasing each other about the match they just had or the one they were going to have later on: "Whatever you say, Alex. Just remember, I'm the grandmaster at basketball. I can't be beaten." Or something like, "Oh yeah, well if I beat you in Shoot Out, I'm riding shotgun, and you're paying for lunch!" This game got loads of action and was by far the most popular addition in the office.

Not too far from the basketball game was a small trampoline, commonly referred to as a rebounder, placed directly in front of our call attendant's cubicle. When people would walk by and notice it on the floor, they'd ask our call attendant why it was there. She would then explain and encourage them to hop on and bounce up and down for a minute or two and feel what it was like to be a kid again. It became so popular with the staff, and visitors alike, that I bought another one later on. I placed it right next to the first one. Now two people could bounce up and down together, or one person could jump from one trampoline to the other and vice-versa. Our employees, traveling salesmen, vendors, and even the mailman could be caught jumping up and down on those things regularly throughout the day. Apart from the health benefits, it was a great way to let loose, have some fun, and quickly put a smile on your face. Just watching people laugh and giggle as they jumped up and down was reward enough for having them there. It was hilarious.

On the adjacent wall, we installed a Power Plate, which we also used purely for amusement. It would shake the daylights out of you. Employees and visitors were welcome to hop on board and try to hold on as one of our team members would crank that thing up to the max, all while laughing hysterically as the person standing on it held on for dear life.

In the center of our lobby, we had a string fastened to the ceiling. The other end of it was secured with a simple knot to a silver loop about the size of a half-dollar. It was used to play *Bimini Ring Toss*. The object of the game is to attempt to swing the silver ring across the room and try to have it land directly onto a hook mounted on an adjoining wall. It's kind of like trying to hit a bullseye but with a relaxed, sweeping motion. It may not sound like it, but this game is highly competitive and very addicting. If you're easily entertained, it'll completely captivate you.

We had a full-sized Pac-Man arcade game not far from that, and, at one point, we even had Duck Hunt. These little games added smiles and fun to our days that ordinarily wouldn't have been there otherwise. And it wasn't just for the people playing the games or using the equipment. Onlookers would briefly gather in amusement, share a smile, and cheer on whomever they were rooting for. It was a community thing.

These small changes helped shape our working environment and enhanced our welcoming ambience. The best part of all was, no one abused their freedom. Employees would play their games and have fun for a few minutes, then get back to work. I honestly think allowing them to have that freedom made them even more productive. These simple things added intangible energy to our atmosphere. It increased the joy we experienced daily and helped shape our fun-filled environment. This was part of our culture. It was who we were. We wanted to have fun, so we did. Who said work shouldn't be fun, anyway?

I then introduced: Role-Playing

As part of our orientation and a continuing education exercise for our sales team, I began to host interactive, role-playing workshops. They say salesman are born, not made. I happen to agree, but that doesn't mean good salesmen can't improve, and that was the objective. I wanted them to have the best possible chance of success, so I invested time into them. Role- playing was an appealing alternative to instructing them how to sell or merely telling them what I expected and then hoping for the best outcome. Worse, would be having to physically go out in the field and take note of their individual performances. That would've taken a lifetime. My preferred method of learning has always been to observe, watch, and implement on the spot. Just as small children pick up their parents' habits, simple and effective. I found role-playing to be a fun and easy way to teach and learn, so I figured my staff would enjoy it as well. I was right. This was a surprisingly valuable teaching exercise.

These meetings were held about once a month, for several hours each. During these meetings, my account managers would take their turns trying to win me over as I pretended to be a difficult and witty prospect, with no time for nonsense. Many times, roles would be reversed, and I often would play the sales rep and show them how I thought it should be done. These lessons were not only highly entertaining but also very valuable. Watching them react and respond in this controlled environment gave me clarity on some of the responses and behaviors that had been ingrained in them. I learned things that they might have said or done when they were put in stressful situations. Some of their responses impressed me, and others, at times, left me in complete shock. Some people just shut down and couldn't take the pressure. But that was okay. If you were going to make a mistake, this was the place to make it, in a safe, supportive environment. When I saw or heard something I wasn't fond of, I would take the time and opportunity to teach them better ways to react and respond. That way, they were better equipped for the next time they were put into a challenging situation. It gave them familiarity with the type of scenarios that I most certainly knew they would experience out in the field.

During these exhibitions, I would teach all I had learned from my many years of experience on the road as a door-to-door salesman. I would point out minor details and do my best to give them the skills I felt they would need to succeed. Our sales representatives, who we called *account managers*, couldn't represent our company without first having run through the gauntlet. We needed to see what you were made of. If you passed the test, you got our seal of approval and could set out on the road as a trainee with one of our seasoned salesmen to get your feet wet. The meetings would be held in our conference room. We kept the door closed. We would rearrange the room to replicate some of the environments we commonly found ourselves in out in the field. We played music before starting each meeting to set the tone of the environment, which was supposed to be educational but also fun. We moved chairs, brought in propane tanks and other items as props. Sometimes even such silly things as wigs, fake mustaches, hats, and goofy sunglasses found their way into the room. It was like a movie set. All the salesmen would be in attendance, and oftentimes, other staff members would request to sit in and watch the show; however, all audience members had strict instructions to remain totally silent.

Once our little stage was set, I would get into character and pretend to be a version of the customer they were trying to win over. But the catch was, they never knew whom they were getting. Throughout the day, I would continually change my character. I would deploy a variety of accents, mannerisms, attitudes, and tonalities — some of which I encountered over the years, and others I made up. At times, some of my accents were so exaggerated it was difficult to keep a straight face, which would result in the room bursting out in laughter. I would then need to take a moment to compose myself and get back into character. It was all in the spirit of fun. They never knew what to expect. Sometimes I was cooperative and eager to do business with them; other times, it would be nearly impossible for them to win me over — unless, of course, they had given me an iron-clad sales pitch that I could not resist. I often chose the weakest members of our team to participate first. I wanted to help sharpen their skills.

Once selected, the salesman would have to exit the room first, knock on the door, and wait for a reply. They were only allowed to enter the room once I granted permission. Sometimes I would let them in right away; other times, I made them sweat it out for a few seconds. Once inside, the salesman had to be in character also, but he was playing himself. Obligatory for every scene, each participant needed to walk into the room, close the door behind him and then introduce himself. If he missed any part of that, he failed, was kicked out immediately, and would need to start over. After successfully entering, the salesman would likely find me seated in a chair at the head of our conference table on the opposite side of the room. Once he completed the first obligatory requirement, the stage was set. He then needed to pretend he was out on the field, trying to earn my business and begin his own, unique sales pitch.

It would go a little something like this:

A rookie salesman enters and closes the door behind him. He then walks up to me with an outstretched arm to shake my hand and begins his quick- fire presentation, "Hello, sir, my name is Mario, and I'm a sales rep from Prestige Propane Exchange; how would you like to save some money on propane gas today?" Sealed with an awkward smile. To which my character then would respond with something like, "I wouldn't like to save any money on propane today. I don't know who you are and I'm busy. So please, get out of my office." Then the entire audience of staff members would erupt in laughter. Following each scene, I would stand up and give my detailed observations on each performance. I would explain all the points where I felt the salesman could've used some improvement. After that, I would ask the rest of the audience if they felt I had missed something or had anything to add. We would then clap it up for the salesman and start a new scene, or repeat a scene, if necessary.

Here's my take on Mario's:

"Okay, before we start, thanks for going first and breaking the ice. Guys, let's give Mario a round of applause, please. Now, who here felt that Mario rushed through his sales pitch? Can I see a show of hands? Okay, Mario, from the looks of it, almost everyone agrees your sales pitch felt a little rushed. Let's break it down. First, you didn't need to immediately mention what company you were from; you could've just given your name. It wasn't necessary for you to volunteer that information so early on. Second, calling yourself a salesman typically sets off an alarm in the prospect's mind, and it's a great way to get the door slammed in your face. That's why we prefer to use the term account manager instead. In the future, if you have a chance to paint a better picture of yourself, do it. Every little thing counts. Third, you came in guns blazing and immediately talked yourself right into a corner with that cheesy, irritable question: "How would you like to save some money today?" That was an easy question for the prospective customer to say no to. By framing the question that way, you're almost begging him to say no right away, and honestly, who could blame him? The guy has never seen you in his life and probably couldn't care less about his propane bill in that instance. The last thing he wants is to be pestered by a door-to-door salesman."

"I know that might seem like the obvious way to sell, but for a moment, I want us all to put ourselves in the customer's place. Think about what we'd say if a stranger walked into this room, right now, and asked us if we wanted to save some money on our landscaping bill? We'd collectively ask that guy to take a hike, wouldn't we? Then altogether laugh about his random intrusion afterward. Who here wants to talk about their landscaping bill, am I right? So, why did we ask him to leave? It's because we are all busy in here learning how to become better salesmen, aren't we? We don't have time for him or whatever he's trying to sell. Now, if the same guy popped his head in and said, 'Hey guys, I'm sorry to interrupt. The receptionist told me you were in here hosting a sales training exercise. I'd love to sit in and join you if that's okay? I'm a salesman also but in the lawn care industry. I just want to learn something. I promise I'll be quiet.' Chances are, we'd all let him sit in.

Let's say, after our meeting, he personally thanked me for letting him sit in and learn. If he then said, as a thank you, he wanted to repay the favor by saving us a ton of money on our landscaping bill, chances are I'd at least hear him out, and quite possibly, even invite him to my office to compare his rates, which would likely result in his landing our account. Think about that for a second. In the second scenario, he didn't make us feel like he was trying to sell us anything. He came in with a different angle, a much more personable approach— he wasn't antagonistic in any way. He expressed a heartfelt appreciation and used that to further his own agenda. As a result, he not only got to sit in and learn something, but he also earned our business."

"I have had success with that type of approach — it's more personable, gives you an opportunity to form some kind of relationship, and you don't come off sounding like a salesman. In the future, you might want to try asking a nonthreatening question first. Perhaps you can ask about his business or something you have observed based on your surroundings. Throw out a compliment or even display a mutual interest in something you think he might like. For example, if the prospect has a framed basketball jersey in his office, and you like basketball, compliment him on it before revealing why you're even there in the first place. It'll throw him off guard and get him talking about what he likes to talk about, which is himself, his main interest. That's what we all like to talk about, ourselves. Once he's engaged, ask him another question. Keep him talking. Get him to like you. You're trying to build rapport. Regardless of what his answers are, you're looking to start a conversation.

Throughout the interaction, keep the conversation flowing in a positive direction. It will likely get him thinking of you in a friendly manner. If you do your job correctly, he should be talking as much or more than you are. You might even get him to laugh or smile. Once his guard is down, that's when you ease your way into the subject, calmly and confidently. That's the right time. At that point, ask a better-worded question, and your result should be much different. You gave a good effort, Mario, but be a little more relaxed and a little more creative in the future. The fact that you got a big fat no doesn't mean you failed; you just have more to learn. You need to ask the right questions, at the right time, to the right person. Take some notes on the next few scenes and prepare for your next time up. Does anyone have anything to add? If not, let's clap it up for Mario. Who wants to go next?" I ask as the clapping begins to fade.

"I'll tell you what, I'm going to go next. Omar has the most experience, so I'll ask him to come up and play the role of the potential customer. Omar, can you do us the honor, please? Guys, clap it up for Omar. Now remember, use your imagination; we're going to pretend there are certain things in the room that aren't there. Just go along with it.

Omar, don't forget to invent a name for your character," I say as I'm exiting the room.

I knock, wait for permission to enter, and then walk into the room, mindfully closing the door behind me. Hey, good afternoon. My name is Max. Nice to meet you!" I say as I make my way to greet him. "Hi Max, my name is Chris; nice to meet you as well." Chris stands up to shake my hand. "Wow! Is that an autographed Lebron James Miami Heat basketball jersey you have on the wall? That's awesome!" I say. "Yes, it is! My wife bought it for me as an anniversary gift two years ago," Chris replies. "You're one lucky man. Is he your favorite player?" I ask. "Well, actually, Jordan was my favorite, but he's a close second. Nobody was better than Jordan," Chris insists. "Yeah, I loved Jordan also. I watched him all throughout my childhood. You have great taste, Chris," I compliment. "Thanks man, I appreciate that," Chris responds.

"Anyway, I don't want to take up too much of your time, Chris; I was driving by, and I noticed your old forklift tanks outside. I'm actually one of the account managers at Prestige Propane, and I wanted to show you something." I begin to pull my cell phone from my pocket while I continue to talk. "You guys have incredibly old, very rusty, and very heavy steel propane tanks. That's a thing of the past, Chris. Check this out;" I turn my phone to show Chris a few pictures of some gleaming aluminum forklift tanks. "These are aluminum forklift tanks; they don't rust, they're about 20 lbs. lighter than the steel ones you have, which will be much easier on your employees, and the best part is, I guarantee you we're charging way less for propane than your current provider," I conclude. "Wow, you're right. Those are a lot nicer- looking than our tanks," Chris responds. I then reiterate, "Yeah, and as I said, they'll never rust, so for the most part, they're always going to look clean and presentable. And remember, they're lighter, easier, and safer to carry around. Your employees are going to love them." Without giving him a chance to respond, I push forward, "Do you know how much you're paying for each tank right now?" I question. "Um, I'm not sure. Let me pull up my last invoice," Chris replies then turns around and pretends to look for his invoice in an imaginary filing cabinet. "Sounds good. I guarantee I'm going to save you enough money to buy a few extra Heat tickets each month," I jokingly state. Chris chuckles, and says, "That'd be great; oh, here it is." As he turns around, Chris hands me the imaginary invoice, "$27 for each tank exchange, wow! You're paying a lot more than I thought, Chris, and you're exchanging 10 tanks a week; so, you're a good customer. I'm surprised you're paying this much!" I replied, dramatizing whatever price was on his invoice. "Really? Well, what price can your company give me?" Chris asks. I then quote a much lower price, instantaneously making me a hero. "$19 a tank. That means you're going to save $8 a tank! Which is $80 a week. Multiply that by four weeks in the month, and you're saving $320 a month! Didn't I guarantee you were going to have some extra money for Heat tickets?" I smile and point at Chris. "You did! When can you sign me up?" Chris asks. End scene.

"Thank you, Omar, great job! Please have a seat. Guys, clap it up for Omar! Now, that's an example. Chris could've been more difficult, and maybe his prices could've been more competitive, but as you all know, that wouldn't have prevented me from doing my absolute best to earn his business. You experienced guys know, not all accounts are easy to land. Sometimes you get them on the first visit; other times you might have to visit them 10 times and try several different approaches to make some progress. Either way, I guarantee you can land any account you set your mind to getting. I personally have landed every single account I've ever set my sights on, but it wasn't easy. I had a list of all the accounts I wanted to get when I started this business, written on a sheet of paper in a notebook. I kept that list with me the entire time I was doing sales. I wrote down the dates I visited them, the prices they were paying, the reasons they gave me for not wanting to do business with me, and the things they were and weren't interested in; anything I thought might help me win them over the next time I swung by. I would study those notes just before getting out of my car each time I revisited them. It gave me an edge. I never stopped until I got every account on that list. They all presented their own unique set of challenges. One of those accounts even took me four years to land, but I got it," I explained.

This method of teaching proved to be highly effective. After I hosted several of these role-playing seminars, their skills improved. As the account managers got better, I began to throw everything I had at them, making it harder and harder to convince me to do business with them. As a result, they became more skilled than they needed to be. It became more challenging to find flaws in their sales pitches. Once I felt they had a firm understanding of how to conduct this exercise, I had Omar begin to host the theatrics to keep them sharp-witted. Just like the transition of our weekly management meetings, I sat in for the first few and only interjected on occasion to provide some guidance and feedback. Once I felt he could handle it on his own, and my presence was no longer necessary, it became his show to run.

To catch everyone off guard, even Omar, I would pop in un-announced, and make cameo appearances at random. I wanted them to know I could show up at any moment. It kept them mindful and for the most part, in line with my expectations. I would casually enter the room, sit down, and listen in for a few minutes, careful not to interfere with the curriculum that was being taught. If all seemed in order, I would exit quietly. But if I heard something that didn't sit well with me, I would discretely ask Omar for a word outside and realign him with my expectations. I remained steadfast in not correcting my managers in front of other employees. I utilized this "pop-in" strategy in every aspect of my business. I didn't have a set work schedule; therefore, employees never knew when I might show up but, I still wanted to keep an eye on things. It reminds me of a Spanish saying my father used to quote, "*El ojo del amo engorda el ganado.*" Which roughly translated means, "The watchful eye of the shepherd fattens the cow." I guess if I were to describe it in business terms I'd say, "The watchful eye of the owner will result in a strong and healthy business."

Reflection Point 31

Don't take life too seriously. Have a little fun along the way. Create a pleasant atmosphere for yourself, regardless of where you are.

I prioritized creating an environment that my team and I wanted to be in, whether we were working or not. That decision helped improve our culture and, as a result, our productivity. I treated my staff the way I would have liked to be treated. I didn't want them to respect me merely because I was the owner; I earned it. That's how I chose to lead. I rarely referred to myself as anyone's boss; I preferred to say: We work together. There was no ego involved. We were all on the same team, and we all had a role to play. Every person was as important as the next, regardless of job titles. Collectively, we were the company. It wasn't a logo, what we sold, or the industry we were in. It was the people.

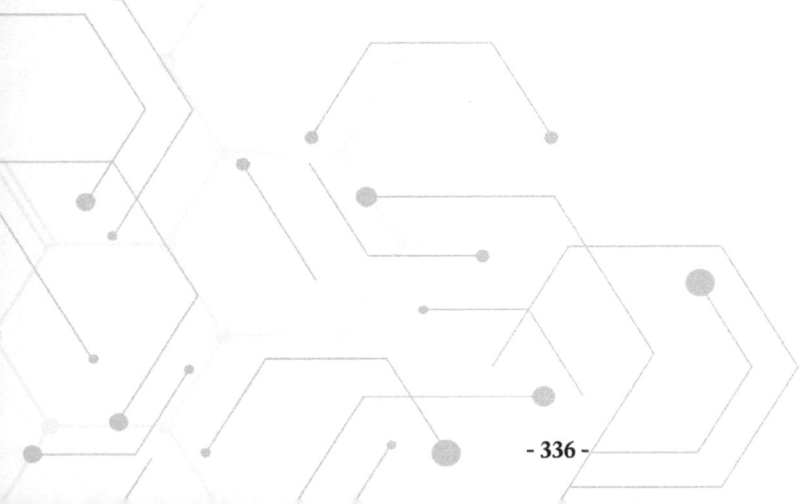

In your opinion, what is the difference between a boss and a leader?

What kind of environment would you like to create
for yourself and others?

How can you incorporate more FUN into your life on a daily basis?

Chapter 32:

Expanding Our Horizons

Our organization had become a machine, or maybe I should say, more like a weapon, overpowering anything we aimed it at. Once we had our sights set on getting a new account, it was all but guaranteed to come to fruition. It honestly felt as though other companies stepped out of our way. We were a driving force that did anything and everything to gain new business, and, as a result, we scooped up customers rapidly.

With this kind of momentum snowballing, it appeared that my long-term plan of opening a second location was going to become a reality much sooner than I had anticipated. My account managers, whom we now playfully referred to as *The Wolf Pack*, continually pushed me to go into newer markets. But I refused to, primarily because I wanted to avoid *stepping over dollars, to pick up dimes*, as the saying goes. Which to me was the equivalent of traveling longer distances to acquire new business in other markets when there was still local business to be had. The way I saw it, if I could get the majority of the local market to do business with us, I would be a very wealthy man. I wanted to keep my company lean and mean for as long as possible. My main objective was to grow our profits, not our footprint. As Keith would say, "The goal is not to get big; the goal is to get rich."

In gaining as much local business as possible, it was only a matter of time until the pickings got slim, and the account managers began to feel that the companies they repeatedly called on with no success were unattainable. But what they saw as a roadblock, I viewed as an opportunity to get crafty. In an effort to get every account we could out of our region, I came up with high- paying contests designed to stimulate their creativity. I had them swap prospects and territories with one another to get fresh eyes on every potential account. This strategy provided us insights that may have been overlooked. I set target dates to obtain the accounts and offered large bounties for any individuals or teams who landed them. The added strategy was effective, and once acquired, the additional local business helped further streamline and improve our routes. This proved to much of my team that their limits were self-imposed and got them realigned.

After a while, the customers we were getting began to stretch the limits of our boundaries. We already had expanded as far south as possible and covered the lower part of the state, from coast to coast. Our trucks already were traveling so far north to make deliveries it had become impractical to service some of the accounts we were landing. At times, I even rejected new business brought to me by the account managers because it didn't make sense to service them. Logistically, we needed to be in closer proximity to supply their needs. If we were going to acquire that new business, we needed to make a move, and there was only one way to go: up. I had put it off long enough. Although I did not personally look forward to traveling up north, I knew that every time I did something I didn't want to do, it propelled me to a level I never had been to before.

Making the move north would allow me to take the leash off and let The Wolf Pack do what they do best, and it would give us the opportunity to gain new market share in unexplored territories. They needed to get out into the wild to stalk some fresh prey and see some new faces.

We needed to position ourselves in a location that would give us the best chance to replicate the success we already had achieved in South Florida. The two most predominant cities in Central Florida are Tampa and Orlando. If we were going to make a move, it would make the most sense to choose one of these two large markets. Which one was it going to be? From Tampa, we could service Orlando and vice-versa, but which would give us a greater local presence? I needed to choose the city with the largest consumer population to gather as much of the local business as possible. Tampa was on the Midwest coast of Florida, and Orlando was on the East Coast. I began to research important details to support my decision-making; population, density, and local competition, to name a few. One of my main considerations was the fact that Tampa had a pro football team. This naturally led me to assume there would be tailgating and home BBQs when the locals got together to watch the games. If there were to be tailgating and casual get-togethers on the weekends, I figured I'd probably sell more propane. Conversely, Orlando lacked a pro football team, which to me suggested the residents would consume less propane, hence fewer sales for my business. Another drawback was Orlando seemed to be more transient by nature. Many people visit Orlando for the theme parks then they leave. With that in mind, I figured people who came into town for the weekend were less likely to be using BBQ grills during their vacations; it was more likely they would be stepping out to eat. Tampa, however, had a larger population of year-round residents. Based on those two key factors, my decision was made. I had my target: Tampa.

Once I had my new market area set, I had to begin to learn about it. I had an enormous number of questions running through my mind. *I wonder what the people are like? Who the strongest competitor is? What's the best area to set up shop?* I did extensive research online to try to gain some perspective but ultimately decided to drive over there and check it out in person. I figured I would spend about a week studying the area. I knew that nothing I read online was going to beat having firsthand experience, so, I packed a bag and headed up I-75.

On the day of my trip, I got in my car and calmly made my way north. Oddly enough, I don't even think I broke the speed limit that day, which was rather unusual. I took time to enjoy the ride and even made a couple of stops to appreciate some of the beautiful sights. I was in no rush whatsoever. But once I arrived in the Tampa area, it was time to get to work. The lollygagging was put aside. I began to painstakingly study the surroundings. I curiously observed the people, the roads, and the traffic. I took notes on the distances between industrial and residential areas — the good and bad parts of town. I visited important landmarks and took several photographs to refresh my memory later. I made it a point to interact with the locals whenever possible. I initiated conversations with just about anyone I sat close to in restaurants.

Throughout my exploration, whenever I saw a competitor's propane display cage at a gas station or supermarket, I immediately would pull over to analyze it. I then would enter the establishment and ask to speak to the owner or manager. After giving my name and then mentioning I was visiting from out of town, I casually introduced myself as an account manager for Prestige Propane Exchange who was just curious to understand the local market. I asked how they felt about their current service providers and the prices they were paying, and then listened. My radar was trying to pick up anything that sounded like a complaint. I wanted to know if the local competition was dropping the ball anywhere and, if they were, where exactly. If I discovered the recurring pains the customers were having, I then knew precisely what to offer them the next time I came back to earn their business. The right medicine to cure their ailments, so to speak.

I then would explain the benefits our company provided compared to what they were receiving, being sure to highlight any of the areas I felt were important to the customer, along with the improved pricing we could offer. I then would ask if they were interested in a service like ours. In essence, I was performing a survey. I needed to take Tampa's temperature to make sure I wasn't making a very costly mistake. I was trying to gain as much information as possible before committing to this move. To my satisfaction, almost every one of the retailers I spoke to seemed interested. In some cases, they were even desperate. After I pitched them, many of the retailers I spoke to asked if I could begin servicing them immediately. That was an exceptionally good sign. The market seemed ripe for the picking. I wrote down every piece of information I received — names of people I spoke to, addresses, and the prices they were paying.

With every delightful insight, I was encouraged to dig deeper. I drove by all the local competitors' establishments to get a feel for what they were doing, the equipment they had, and how large their businesses were. None of them intimidated me. For the most part, the marketing, equipment, and trucks I saw looked antiquated. If there was pride of ownership, it surely wasn't evident. To me, that was a clear sign that the establishments subscribed to the long-lasting tradition of carelessness when it came to their appearance. This was frequently associated with having ancient management in place, which indicated in my experience that they were less likely to be concerned about losing their customers. To them, propane trucks didn't need to look flashy or, dare I say, even sexy. After all, they were selling propane. So, who cares, right? Well, in my opinion, that was a big no-no. We had to look good, always. Our professional self-esteem stood alone. We didn't need to tell you we were the right choice; it was self-evident. That's the type of company I like to do business with — the best in the industry. The competition had been conducting business in Tampa longer than I had, but I was determined to do it better.

After completing my due diligence on Tampa, I knew without a doubt that it was our next move. It was a clear opportunity that could be greatly profited from. Now that I had my mind made up, I needed to decide what equipment would be necessary, which led me to ask myself an intriguing question: *How can I open a second branch without spending the same amount of money I have invested into our company headquarters?* That was a question worth taking the time to answer properly. It would make my life much easier and save me a lot of money in the process.

While working on that question, I realized that although I wanted a second location based in Tampa, I didn't technically need another production facility. If I could procure a bigger flatbed truck that could transport a larger quantity of BBQ tanks, I could ship my already processed and filled tanks from my facility in Miami straight to Tampa. That would do away with the necessity for any costly production equipment and eliminate the overhead of a large production staff. My investment in the second branch would be zero. All I would need is a place to store everything.

With this strategy in mind, I continued to work on this question by making a list of all the things I thought I needed to have a fully operational second branch, if I could, in effect, have the full tanks transported to Tampa. First, I needed a location that met the state's requirements to store propane. That in itself was slightly challenging. I then would need insurance and the licenses required to operate that facility, at least two trucks to make the local deliveries, a healthy amount of full propane tanks, and display cage inventory. I also would need a forklift to load and unload my trucks, some fire extinguishers to give to the retailers, and only one driver to start. That's what I needed. Honestly, that wasn't too bad.

But where could I find a staging facility, one that wasn't only large enough but met all the specifications and requirements I would need to store propane tanks, while not spending a modest fortune? I called a few commercial realtors in the area to search the MLS for properties that met my criteria. To no surprise, there were very few properties that matched that description, and the few that did were rather expensive. None of them interested me, but I didn't rule them out altogether. If I needed to spend the money, I would've, but I wasn't yet ready to decide. I needed to think about it some more.

Then came the lightning strike, ZAP!

Why don't I call a local propane supplier in the area and ask if they'd be willing to rent me some space? Anyone operating an existing propane business already meets the prerequisites. That way, I can avoid making a significantly large investment into either buying or renting a suitable property. All I would have to do is pay rent. If successful, I would essentially be able to try my luck in this new market, almost risk-free. All of the other things I need to purchase to start the business are assets. If, for some reason, this expansion into Tampa doesn't work out, I could just repurpose the assets in Miami and use them there. This is genius, I thought.

I phoned a few of the local propane businesses in the Tampa area, and let's just say I wasn't pleasantly received. Our company had a fierce reputation, and the thought of letting us into the local market probably was the last thing any of them wanted to take credit for. But, as usual, persistence paid off once again. After a few tries, I eventually spoke with a company that wasn't put off by the idea, so I set up a meeting with them.

In our meeting, I explained that Prestige Propane was undoubtedly coming into the Tampa market and only needed a staging area to comply with local and state regulations. If they would be so kind as to rent us some land, I'd do my best not to compete with them. Considering our aggressive reputation, I would say this chance at immunity for a small, local competitor was quite valuable. I asked several questions about what they might be willing to help us with and expressed that I wanted to come to terms with them right away. We negotiated a little and quickly came to an agreement on a one-year lease with an option to renew. Along with the lease, we were guaranteed the ability to purchase propane directly from them if needed, for pennies above cost. We also got permission to use their forklift to load and unload our company trucks. This was a jackpot. Here's the best, most insane part, I got all of that in exchange for only $500 a month. I couldn't believe it. It was virtually free. This arrangement put us in compliance and gave me the staging area I needed. Apart from saving valuable time, I avoided investing an extraordinary amount of money. Re-creating what we had in Miami potentially could have cost me up to $2 million. Thankfully, I was able to create an equivalent with just about $250,000, most of which was spent on assets. I was all set. I had essentially created a risk-free attempt at opening a second operation. With our Tampa company location now secured, I needed to turn my attention to company infrastructure, especially staffing.

Instead of hiring a receptionist and opening a local company phone line, I decided to add a 1-800 number to our Miami location. That way, when Tampa accounts would call, our experienced team at company headquarters could field the calls and then dispatch them to the driver in Tampa. All I would need to do is buy the Tampa driver a cell phone. For the time being, we had no routes; so consequently, he wasn't going to be terribly busy. That was a simple fix. We had a qualified driver hired within a couple of days.

I also started thinking about having a place to stay. I wasn't moving to Tampa, but I knew I would be in town often. I made several appointments with realtors to look at housing in various parts of town. I toured several homes and got a feel for what kind of property I might need and where it should be strategically situated — close to the airport and expressway, not too far from the action. I wanted something spacious, with the capacity to accommodate several people. I did the math and realized it would be much more convenient and far less of an expense to rent a house than it would be to rent a hotel room every time I flew into town, especially if I came up for several weeks. Besides, we needed a base. We had the staging area for our equipment secured, but we still needed a place to get organized, have meetings, and even relax and unwind. I rented a 3/2 on a large lot with a two- car garage. It was only $1,300 a month, which I felt was a bargain.

With the home rented and the staging area in place, I began to have my staff transport anything I felt we needed to start running our satellite operation up to Tampa — two trucks, hundreds of full BBQ tanks, new display cages, and signage. Once the infrastructure was set and we were well equipped to take on a large amount of new business, all that was left was to get that business. But how was I going to do that with no staff?

Here's how:

I decided we were going to run a recurring blitz. Instead of slowly growing our business over time, I had a better concept. The idea was to have all of our salesmen come into town, gather as many accounts as they could in about a week's time, and then head back to Miami. That would give our delivery driver enough leeway to begin setting up our display cages for our newly acquired accounts throughout the area. Once the driver was finished, we would send the account managers back to round up some more business. This strategy gave me the benefit of having our experts in the field developing this market and gave them some well-deserved paydays.

When we furnished the house, we designed it to accommodate up to 15 people at a time. It wasn't always necessary, but I wanted the ability to house the entire Wolf Pack, my general manager Omar, and myself, if needed. At maximum capacity, it turned into a sleepover-style arrangement. They may not have been the most comforting accommodations, but we made it fun. We had regular beds, a couple of bunkbeds, a sleeper, and some air mattresses on the floor.

Before our first blitz in Tampa, we got the Wolf Pack riled up. We held several meetings and discussed all the lucrative accounts we wanted. We then structured an attractive, in-house competition among all of our sales team for each blitz. There were different tiers based on performance and different bonuses based on the number of accounts they could land. We also rewarded them on the size and the price they were able to land them for. The winners of each category would be compensated with large bonuses and had several opportunities to win prizes.

Once we arrived in Tampa, we got together for a family-style dinner and settled in. At first light it was boots on the ground. The sales team set off in different directions to try to earn their share of the local business. This strategy proved to be remarkably effective. By the end of the first week, our sales team had dozens upon dozens of new accounts signed up. At week's end, we returned to our headquarters in Miami. We held meetings to recap and congratulate the account managers, then tallied up the winners and issued bonus checks for those who earned them.

Our regional delivery driver began delivering our equipment to all the new retailers. The account managers made sure their customers' needs were well taken care of. It was the perfect strategy. While our team was back in Miami, it gave our local Tampa driver enough time to deliver all our display cages. Three weeks later, we were back at it. We deployed this strategy repeatedly. The team would come in, clean house, and our driver would arrive shortly after to install our display cages. It was extremely efficient and effective. If our retailers needed unscheduled service or needed to contact us, they could either phone their account manager or call our 1-800 number. Our dispatcher then would communicate with our Tampa employee on his company cell phone.

We grew that local market from $0.00 to almost $1 million in recurring sales in a little over 12 months.

Reflection Point 32

"If you don't want to do it, you must." That is the exact quote I read off my whiteboard in my bedroom while deliberating whether I should expand to Tampa. I did not want to do all the extra work required, but I knew staying in my comfort zone would have gotten me nowhere.

When embarking on a new endeavor, take time to discover what you need to accomplish your outcomes, and make a plan.

If it crosses your mind, don't be afraid to reach out to perceived adversaries and ask questions. They might be friendlier than you think.

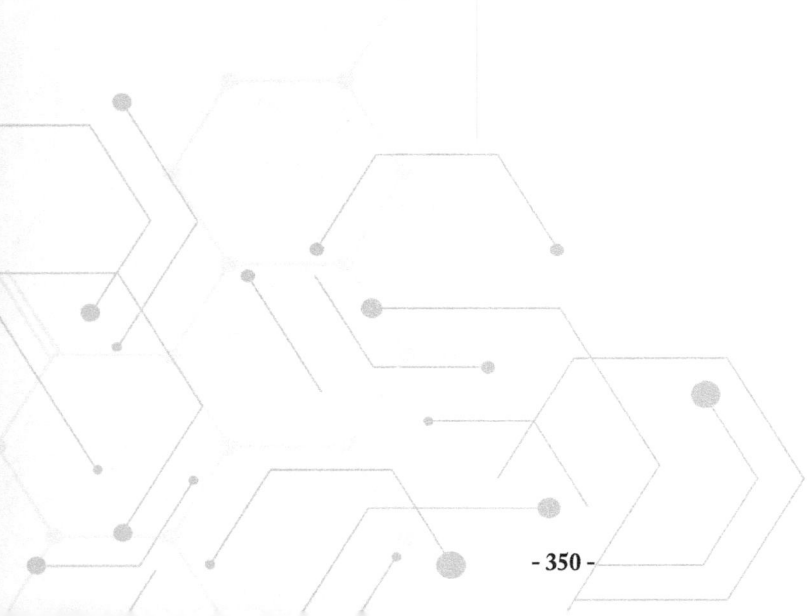

Who do you view as an enemy who also has the potential
to be your greatest ally?

How can you change the dynamic?

Chapter 33:

Manifesting

On a red, hardcover notebook I had at home, I upgraded my mini-bucket list to a *100 things to do before I die* list. It contained some of the most amazing, awe-inspiring things I could think of. I had been actualizing on impulse, almost from the moment I began creating it. I wasn't just hoping to do some of these things someday, I was actively in pursuit of them and checked items off as I achieved them. I was seeing my dreams through. On that list of 100 things, #39 was, *Have a really GREAT article written about me.* I don't remember the inspiration behind it or what I even wanted the article to say. All I know is that the thought of it brought a smile to my face. I wanted it to come true. It excited me to think that, one day, someone might take the time to say something nice and acknowledge me in public. Whether it was in a newspaper or on a blog, or anywhere else, that didn't matter.

On the business end, everything was thriving. Our swift expansion into Central Florida sent many shockwaves throughout the propane industry. We were a force to be reckoned with. Our rapid growth and unique approach to propane garnered a lot of attention, not only to our company but to me personally.

Not long after, I went to the annual propane convention in Tennessee to network and meet with potential vendors. While I was casually speaking in a group setting amongst peers, a man I was unfamiliar with spoke to me. I assumed he was a fellow business owner. "Hey Max, my name is Mark. I heard about the success you guys have been having. I was wondering if I could ask you a few questions?" he inquired. "Sure, what's up?" I replied. "Is it true that you took a leave of absence and, after returning, increased sales by over 40 percent each year for the past two consecutive years?" Mark asked. "Yes, that's true, but we have done quite a bit of work to accomplish that. So if you're looking for some quick tips, it isn't going to be that easy," I jokingly replied. "Wow. That's incredible. You don't hear about something like that in the propane industry every day," he said. "Well, thank you. I appreciate the compliment," I replied. "Hey, um, if you wouldn't mind getting together over a coffee later, I'd love to pick your brain and ask you some more questions. I'd really like to hear more about what you've done to grow your business, and maybe you can provide some more color on some of the challenges you've overcome. And if you're up for it, I can write a piece about you in the upcoming issue of Propane Magazine USA." I was stunned for a second and then eagerly agreed. "Yeah, that would be great; thank you!" I replied. After the conference, Mark and I met over coffee. He was a nice guy. I joyfully answered all the questions he had. He had done his homework. I was surprised by how much he knew about me. After the interview, I paid for our coffees, thanked him for the opportunity, and wished him well. The interview was short and fun. The coffee and the company weren't bad either.

The next month, the article was published nationally in Propane Magazine USA. I received a copy in the mail and a pat on the back from my staff for being featured. A few days later, I was scrolling through my company emails when I noticed an interesting one. The subject line read, *Propane Magazine.* I opened the email; it was from an owner of another propane gas company up North. The first sentence of his email read, *Hey Max, I just read that really GREAT article they wrote about you in Propane Magazine USA, congratulations!*

I can't tell you how big a smile that brought to my face. I hooted with laughter; I was giddy. Having the article written was a dream come true, but having the man verbatim quote what I had on my improved bucket list was surreal. Hair-raising even. I got exactly what I wanted. When I showed my girlfriend, she was left speechless. When she finally spoke, she uttered, "I can't believe that. It's exactly what you have written on your bucket list in your red book. It's practically the same sentence. Great is even written in all caps," she pointed out. She was as taken aback as I was. "It's like you're predicting the future," she said. "I'm not predicting the future; I'm creating it! I specifically asked for this. I put that energy out into the world and here it is, coming to reality. It's proof of the power of intent," I replied excitingly. I smiled, grabbed my red notebook, and checked it off my list. It was a very memorable moment for me, and another beautiful part of the journey that I'll never forget.

After that article was published, people began to call. For the most part, they were from other, much larger propane companies who worked in business development departments. Their main interest was to identify and acquire well-run businesses to increase the size of their own companies. With the spotlight on us after the article came out, we had popped up on their radars. In fact, we looked like the ideal candidate for acquisition, a well-run, thriving business. In addition to the larger propane companies, we also caught the attention of several private equity firms, investors who sought to acquire equity ownership in the company.

As the calls came in, I eagerly began to entertain them. I have to say, fielding the first few calls was very exciting. It was an experience I hadn't had before. There were several people from different backgrounds clamoring for my attention, all at once, every one of them desperate to speak to me and offer me some money for my business, in some form or another. What's not to like? But after a short while, the conversations started to sound the same. The big propane companies all expressed interest in buying my business outright. They then asked a handful of important, qualifying questions and carefully listened to my responses to ensure that I was indeed a suitable candidate. Once satisfied with my replies, they would suggest we take the next step. In the hopes to receive my sensitive financial information, they would volunteer to sign a non-disclosure agreement, commonly referred to as an NDA, to symbolize they weren't going to share my company information with anyone else.

The private equity guys had a similar approach, only far less appealing. The average offer went a little something like this:

If we did come to an agreement and I chose to sell to them, they wanted me to retain some ownership in the company, typically around 30%. They portrayed this as something that would be beneficial to me because, as the company continued to grow, my 30% would be worth much more in the future. That would give me a *second bite at the apple* down the line when the private equity firm inevitably resold the business for even more money. They generally offered to give me some money upfront and, on every occasion, wanted to finance the transaction, with me as the lender. The money owed to me was consistently offered as an earnout, a contractual provision that the seller of a business is to obtain future compensation only if the business achieves certain financial goals. And the last stipulation was the cherry on top; I needed to stay on board to run the company.

So, let me get this straight: I give them a controlling stake of my business for little money upfront. I have to keep 30% of a company I'm trying to sell, and then I have to work for them. If for any reason it doesn't go so well, because of the earnout provision, I don't get paid the rest of the money owed to me. Why on Earth would I do that? No, thanks!

I did the dance and played along for the first few suitors, but it was a waste of time, not to mention exhausting. The truth was, I wanted to sell, but I wasn't ready to. None of the offers I received were even close to $25 million, and they shouldn't have been. I still wasn't earning enough to make the company worth that amount of money. In addition to the income I needed to increase the value, other important elements needed to be in place before I offered my business for sale, things I knew would help me get top dollar. One was audited or reviewed financial statements for at least two years, which would ensure the accuracy of my financial reporting to any potential buyer. I was skipping over important steps. There was still work to do and growth to be had. If I were going to sell, it would be on my terms. I needed to be in the driver's seat. I wasn't ready for this yet. I was underprepared. You don't take a cake out of the oven when it's only halfway done baking, do you? No, so why was I negotiating with a half-baked business as a bargaining chip?

After entertaining more than a dozen calls from potential investors, I decided to put an end to it. I didn't have time to play on the phone all day. The thought that someone might offer me more money for my company than it was actually worth was a fantasy. My numbers were just not there yet. There was still more work to be done, and I needed to do it. Period. All this talking was just a huge distraction. Once I made that distinction, I told every interested party, regardless of where we were in the discussion, that I was no longer willing to sell my business. I insisted that I would need no less than a year before resuming any negotiations. I then assured them they would be first to know if and when the business would be for sale. But for now, it was back to work.

Note: A non-disclosure agreement, commonly referred to as an NDA, is a legally binding contract that establishes a confidential relationship.

The party or parties signing the agreement agree that sensitive information they may obtain will not be made available to any others. An NDA also may be referred to as a confidentiality agreement.

Review & Audited financial statement: A review provides limited assurance rather than a reasonable amount of assurance; so, in simple terms, a review reports on the plausibility of the financial statements. An audit provides a reasonable level of assurance in the form of a positive statement such as "presents fairly" or "presents a true and fair view".

Reflection Point 33

Daily affirmations and visualizing your desired end results have great power. When you visualize, you materialize.

Stay laser focused on your goals and be aware of time wasters. Don't let giant *squirrels* distract you from your big picture. Run your life and your business on your terms. Setting terms, goals, and boundaries is essential for growth.

What proactive approach do you take to manifesting your goals?

_____

_____

_____

What are some of the things that would be on your bucket list?

_____

_____

_____

_____

What is a time waster you could eliminate to improve your life?
Why not try it for a week?

_____

_____

_____

Chapter 34:

Thirty-Seven

With our operations steadily growing and almost 100% of our profits going back into the business, I began to take a closer look at my main expenses, and the things that significantly affected our bottom line. In this case, I was examining BBQ tanks. At the rate we were growing, we were frequently purchasing thousands of tanks at a time, and they weren't cheap. The desire to solve this issue was even more pressing every time I opened invoices from the supplier. They were dreadful. The amounts we owed for each shipment were equal to the price of a nice new car. Sometimes, a few cars. With our increasing need for them, every new invoice was pricier than the preceding one. There had to be a way to buy the tanks for less. I just needed to find out how.

I had our now in-house accountant call just about every supplier in the United States trying to get better pricing on them. With the quantities we were purchasing, we received discount offers, but they never were enough to provide the substantial cost savings I wanted.

One afternoon while brainstorming with my management staff, I asked our production manager Ben to sift through at least 200 tanks in our yard. I requested that he put aside one tank from each manufacturer. I wanted to see if there was someone we were overlooking. I knew there were several across the globe, but not all were approved to do business in the USA. Generally, their information was in small print and not that obvious at first glance. I knew it would take some time, but after a few hours, Ben brought a handful of tanks to my office. To our disappointment, there was no oversight, no discovery. It appeared that we already knew all the manufacturers that were approved to do business in America.

A few weeks later, while reviewing a new shipment of tanks from one of our suppliers, my general manager Omar mentioned that he had discovered something. The BBQ tanks we were buying from California were actually being shipped to us from China. He identified a very small "Made in China" notice on them. Frankly, we were shocked. We all had assumed that the tanks we had been purchasing were all made in the USA. After the shock subsided, a glaring opportunity set in. If we could buy directly from the Chinese manufacturer, we could cut out the middleman we had unknowingly been dealing with in California and likely save a large amount of money.

We began to study the tanks in finer detail. We looked at all the imprints trying to discover who exactly was making them. After some scrutiny, we found what appeared to be the company's name, but we were not quite sure. None of us were familiar with the markings. We plugged the curious markings into a Google search bar on my desktop and there it was. We got an email address and phone number to the manufacturer. The only catch was, they mainly spoke Chinese. The early communications were strange, to say the least, but we managed to get our point across using as few words as possible to avoid confusion. It went a little something like this: "We buy many BBQ tanks in the USA. Can you sell directly to us?" Their reply: "Yes, my friends, we are professional company. I have best products will interest you."

After a little back-and-forth, the manufacturer in China put us in touch with a liaison in St. Louis. That made things much easier because he spoke English rather well. We called the intermediary and told him how many tanks we were purchasing regularly. He seemed impressed by the amount and mentioned that they would definitely be able to ship to us directly at the quantities we were purchasing. This gave us the ability to buy directly from the manufacturer by the container load. We negotiated a little and agreed on a price. By ordering the tanks directly from China, we were able to cut out the middleman and shave 35% off the cost of each tank. That was huge, especially when considering it was the same tank we already were buying thousands of. The only adjustment we had to make was in placing our orders. Because the tanks were being shipped overseas on container ships, they required a three-month lead time. From that point on, we forecast our needs and ordered well in advance, often procuring more than we thought we might need to fill our demand. All in all, it didn't require much effort on our part. It was a simple adaptation. The extra profit went straight to the bottom line, increasing our earnings, which in turn increased my company's value.

After filing my taxes for the previous year, 2015, my second year in business with full control, I managed to make more than $2 million in profit. Granted, I didn't have that amount of money in my possession, because I had reinvested most of it back into assets to grow the business, but that's what the company had made on paper. The business profits had just about doubled within one year. This created another nauseating tax bill, but it still was extremely exciting. The sizeable earnings gave a significant value to the business. I was making tremendous progress. My dream's coming to fruition was right on the horizon. If I used a seven-times-earnings multiplier, my company would now be worth approximately $14 million.

Around the same time as this brewing excitement, something else significant happened. I was at home on a weekend when a friend in the industry called to fill me in on some fascinating news he had heard. The word on the street was a regional propane company sold their business at a 10-times-earnings multiple instead of the more common seven-times-earnings multiple. This was out of the ordinary. At first, I wasn't sure if it had been sold for that much because of a specific, unique reason or if the industry had just raised the market price for such businesses. That particular company had command over a specific market, which may have been why they were able to sell for that amount, but, either way, it didn't matter to me. It still happened. It was news, and everyone was going to hear about it. And I knew that, if they could do it, so could I. I just needed to find the right angle and make my business as uniquely valuable as theirs was, if not more.

Applying this multiplier suggested that my company was worth much more money; to be exact, $7 million more. And if I could obtain the same multiplier, my company just might be worth a whopping $21 million, giving it a quantum leap in value. That is, of course, if somebody would be willing to pay a 10-times multiple for my business. Either way, it was cause for celebration. This was a phenomenal sign. It was extremely encouraging for me.

After hanging up with my friend, I walked into my bedroom and closed the door behind me for some privacy. I needed to verify this information and speak to someone who was in the know. I scrolled through my phone in search of just the right person to call. His name was Frank. I had met him at a propane conference about a year before. Frank was in the business development department of a large corporation and had experience purchasing other propane companies. I wasn't sure if he'd answer my call, but I didn't care. I had to call someone, and he was the best person I could think of. To my relief, he picked up. After quickly greeting and thanking him for taking my call on the weekend, I asked if he had heard of the propane company in my area that sold for a 10-times multiplier. He had. It sent a chill down my spine. I then anxiously asked if he might be willing to offer his opinion on the value of my company. He wasn't familiar with our present performance and asked me to fill him in, which I did.

As I nervously paced back and forth in my bedroom, I proceeded to give him a detailed background of my business. Careful not to mention what I wanted it to be worth, I didn't want to taint his true, genuine opinion. I filled him in on all the growth we had been experiencing and elaborated on future growth we had in the works. I listed several ongoing projects. It was clear that my business was booming, and, at the rate we were going, my company would be making much more money the upcoming year.

When I had finished, I humbly asked, "So, what do you think? How do you think I'm doing?" "Well, it sounds like you're running an exceptionally clean operation, and you're doing a magnificent job of growing the company. You're running it like one of the Big Boys! Very few small businesses are operating the way you are. I'm sure any of the majors would love to buy a business like yours; you would be a prime candidate for an acquisition," he said. "Well, thank you. That's really encouraging to hear, Frank. So, based on everything I have going on, in your opinion, what would you say my company is worth?" "Well, given the changes that seem to be happening in the industry, and the way you're running things, I don't see why your company wouldn't be worth $25 million by the end of the year," he replied. I stood there, silent, and motionless, in my room with the phone to my ear. It was the moment I had been waiting for. It was the exact amount of money I wanted, and I had an expert telling me my moment had arrived — $25 million! It was here and now, front and center. But it didn't excite me. Hearing Frank say it out loud didn't bring about the flurry of enthusiasm I was expecting. Nothing moved within my spirit. I felt as if $25 million would be selling myself short. My conviction was so strong at that moment, I honestly felt that if someone would have handed me a check for $25 million, I would have handed it right back to them.

While still maintaining my conversation with Frank, I turned around, walked straight over to my big whiteboard on the wall where I had the massive goal of selling my business written in big black letters, "$25 million by May 9th, 2019." And in one clean swipe, I erased the number 25 with the palm of my hand. I then grabbed a marker and instinctively wrote "37" in its place. My new goal, which I had never given any thought whatsoever to, was now $37 million. I pulled it straight out of the ether. After hanging up the phone with Frank, I grabbed my checkbook and wrote myself a new check for $37 million. I also shortened the date by 2 years. I wanted to accomplish this exactly one year from today; May 30th, 2017. I threw the old $25 million check away.

Reflection Point 34

When everyone is involved, everyone knows what to look for. Expressing to the team that I wanted to save money on the cost of our tanks got everyone thinking and engaged. As a result, they paid extra-close attention to the BBQ tanks and kept an eye out for company names and markings we were unfamiliar with. Omar inspected our new tanks, made the discovery, and we hit the jackpot. We were able to reduce costs by eliminating the middleman. Every dollar we saved went straight to the bottom line, and a dollar saved is a dollar earned.

What is an obstacle you feel has been impossible to circumvent?

What approach haven't you tried yet?

Chapter 35:

The Turn of the Century

I was two years into my journey, and things had never been better. I had done or was doing just about everything I ever wanted to do with Prestige Propane Exchange. Then, one day, I woke up and felt as if there was not much left to do. My list of action items was just about all checked off. The business was essentially running on its own and honestly didn't require much, if any, of my time. With Prestige Propane on virtual autopilot, it finally was time to shift my focus. Some much-needed time and attention had to be given to my neglected stepchild, Local Propane, now known as Century Propane.

After acquiring Century Propane in my deal with Danny and putting up a dividing wall between the two operations, I did little else than hire better staff. That gave me some breathing room while I worked on Prestige Propane. Conjointly, Century was upgraded with the same state-of-the-art routing software I had installed at Prestige Propane and received refreshed marketing material and equipment upgrades along the way. But that was about it. Those minor adjustments merely served as a tourniquet so that the better part of my time could be spent on the life-giving organ, Prestige Propane Exchange.

I spent no more time on Century than necessary just enough to ensure it was stable. For the most part, they were on their own. I maintained the operation with a small staff of just seven employees. Surprisingly, the brand had slowly and steadily increased its profits by more than 100% during the two years of my ownership, which goes to show how far a few efficiencies can take you. After stepping in and examining the operation, I knew what I needed to tackle first: **Installations**.

As with most propane companies, Century offered full-service propane installations. Several licensed, independent contractors for hire did this type of work, but most propane companies deemed it to be an integral part of their business. We commonly referred to our team of personnel handling such matters as our *Installation Department.*

Upon request, our employees would provide free installation estimates for potential and existing customers wanting to install propane appliances in their homes or businesses — gas stoves, fryers, dryers, and water heaters.

Although someone was needed to install the gas lines for new customers, our installation department was rarely profitable. Our in-house installers needed to be licensed by the state and possess extensive knowledge of propane. Consequently, they made much more money than any of our drivers. The installers needed expensive, specialized tools and equipment to complete their work, along with specially designed trucks to haul that equipment to job sites. The worst part was, it often took several days and even weeks to complete a single installation, which left us juggling several projects at a time. There were always delays with getting permits and untimely setbacks due to faulty equipment that delayed completion of the work. As a result, Century Propane regularly received its fair share of customer complaints.

When I inquired as to why they were having these issues, the explanation I most frequently heard was something like this: *Installations haven't been completed due to some setbacks. So, we had to pull the delivery drivers off their routes to assist in resolving the installation dilemmas. Then, as a result of the drivers' stepping in to assist with the installations, the deliveries that were supposed to be made, weren't because we didn't have enough drivers to make them. Its a vicious cycle, Boss!*

I had heard different variations of this on multiple occasions. I had just never invested the time to address it adequately. Century Propane hadn't been a priority for me. But it was now. No more Band-Aids; it was time to transform it. I spent hours with the Century staff and our three installers dissecting the operation. I applied a considerable amount of time over several days, thinking of how I might find a way to streamline the process, but, ultimately, I was unsuccessful. The more I learned about it, the more I realized it just wasn't what we were good at. My main focus was on selling and delivering propane, as it had always been. Installations were complicated and confusing, which is why we were losing money. There had to be a better way around this. While I thought of ways to solve this problem in my office, I had one important question on my mind: *How can I continue to offer installations to our existing and future customers without having to employ and manage an entire installation department?*

After some *thinking time*, I had my secretary Vivien contact the state licensing department and ask if it were possible for them to share information on all the licensed contractors in Florida. Much to my delight and surprise, they could. I had an email waiting for me in my inbox within an hour. It contained a detailed list of around 30 licensed installers in our service area.

I began to brainstorm:

If a customer wants to install a propane gas stove in their home, along with a propane tank, and we are only interested in selling them the propane, maybe we could refer the installation work to an independent contractor and just sell the customer the propane, couldn't we? I'd be willing to outsource and let them do the work, as long as we could keep the customer afterward and the customer could pay the independent contractor directly for the installation.

Then we could continue to service them moving forward. That was my first valuable insight.

I then asked my general manager, Omar, to call all of the contractors one by one and conduct a small survey. I wanted to know if they were referring the customers they completed work for to a competing business in the area, and if so, to which businesses and for what incentives?

When Omar finished contacting them all, he reported that many of them weren't referring their customers to anyone. On the entire list of installers Omar spoke to, only two of them were referring their customers to a competing propane company for compensation. They received a 20% commission in return for any business they passed along.

I began to think it over...

So, there are 30 licensed contractors installing propane gas lines in our service area, and only two of them have an allegiance to a competing business for just a 20% commission. Hmm...Interesting.

While he was on the phone with the independent propane contractors, Omar said, several of them asked if we had any 500-gallon or 1,000-gallon tanks in inventory they could purchase from us. He said many installers were having difficulty finding tanks when they needed them because they were expensive and inconvenient for them to store. Most of the contractors worked out of their trucks and didn't have a yard. I made a mental note of that.

As part of our normal business operations, we regularly installed and refilled propane tanks of all sizes. The tanks most commonly installed held 100, 250, 500, and even 1,000 gallons of propane. On many occasions, we even installed multiple 1,000-gallon tanks at a single location but, regardless of what quantities we were delivering it in, we paid the same amount for every gallon of propane. Our salesman's job was to try to sell it for the highest-possible price. That's how we made money.

For example, let's say a gallon of propane was costing us $1. If we had a customer who wanted a 1,000-gallon tank installed, we would quote that customer competitively, according to the market climate to gain their business, but our prices weren't set in stone. The prices we quoted could've been just about any amount —$3.25 a gallon, $2.50 a gallon, $1.99 a gallon, maybe even $1.50 a gallon, whatever they could sell it for. Just about any price reasonably higher than our cost was acceptable to me, as long as we got the account. My orders were consistent: get as much business as possible! Do whatever it takes. I didn't mind if we needed to give a customer lower introductory rates to earn their business, and then increase prices later. As it was written on my whiteboard: We need to sell more gallons! The important thing was to have the customers on our side. Similar to the bird in the hand axiom: "A bird in the hand is worth two in the bush." If we already had the customer on the phone or, even better, in front of us, it was wiser to land the account in that instant, instead of waiting for other business to come along later, which may not come at all. Applying this mentality, we made more from some than others, but it all balanced out. It was dollar-cost-averaging. This method of analysis led me to create something I referred to as *The Contractor Program.*

My idea was simple. By creating an attractive incentive, I turned as many of these contractors as I could into unofficial salesmen for Century Propane.

By adding one more step to their process, I gave them an opportunity to double dip. It was very simple.

Here's how it worked:

The independent contractors already were in contact with customers who inevitably would need to purchase propane. Once their work was completed, most of them couldn't have cared less who the customers bought propane from. This is where we stepped in. I gave them a reason to refer to Century Propane, by offering them 50% of the profit I made on the customer's first delivery. If we were paying $1 for a gallon of propane, the contractor's cost basis would be $1.30 a gallon. I set a 30-cent margin above our true cost to cover our insurance and delivery expenses.

So, let's say a contractor had a customer who needed a 1,000- gallon tank, he still would deliver and install the tank. But now, he also could include initially filling the tank for the customer, turning the contractor's business into a one-stop shop, and by referring us the business, he would make much more money. Century Propane then would have a new customer and keep 100% of the profits afterward.

For example:

Let's assume the contractor gave his customer a market price of $2.50 a gallon.

1,000-gallon tank fill sold at $2.50 = $2,500

Minus contractor cost of propane = - $1,300

That leaves a gross profit of $1,200

The contractor's commission was 50%, which equals $600.

Century Propane kept the other 50%, which was also $600.

That meant, in this scenario, the contractor would make $600 just for referring the customer to us. If the contractor convinced the customer to pay more for the propane, he would make even more. He would be selling the propane at top dollar for us while bringing us a steady stream of business.

In many cases, the contractor's commission was as much or more than he was charging to install the gas lines. This further incentivized the independent contractors to charge as much as possible, making them more money initially and us more money indefinitely. This deal was overly generous but also overly smart. Besides, what did I have to lose? Nothing. What did I have to gain? More and more business. This program got the contractors lining up to give us new revenue.

In addition to all that, I had another play to try to win them over. Going forward, we would offer all independent contractors propane tank inventory at 100% cost. Whatever I paid, they paid. Although this didn't make us any money, that wasn't the intent. I wanted to further gain the attention and eventually the loyalty of the contractors. We already ordered tanks in bulk, so we received preferred pricing. But if we were to order truckloads of tank inventory to keep the contractors' needs met, we would get even better pricing. Which would save the contractors several hundred dollars on the cost of each tank. It was another compelling reason for the independent contractors to come to us. We were offering the most convenient, least- expensive option available to them. Why would they go anyplace else and pay more for the same tanks? I just wanted the customers afterward, and if the contractors came to us for tanks, that meant we were going to gain a new account and sell the customer propane for the lifespan of their contract. Although it would undoubtedly be much longer than that because we rarely lost accounts.

I then assigned two dedicated salesmen to maintain our relationships with the independent gas contractors and gave them 20% of our 50%. So, their commission checks were all but guaranteed. I wanted my account managers to concentrate on forming relationships with the contractors and keeping them happy. They took them coffee and snacks and talked shop with them at job sites. They also coordinated tank deliveries and were sure we maintained healthy inventory levels. Most important, they delivered their commission checks in person with a big smile and a handshake, thanking them for being part of our program. Although, most of the time, the contractors thanked my account managers. After its inception, this program turned out to be our largest source of new accounts at Century Propane, month after month from that time on. It was a slam dunk.

We went on to form lasting relationships with many of the independent gas contractors who were doing this kind of work. From then on, when customers would call for an installation estimate, we would refer them to one of the contractors we were working with. Once they completed the job, we would take over the account, and begin serving the customer. This streamlined our operation immensely and made clear what our staff's objectives were. Now, they all had the same objective: sell more propane!

With those two innovations in place, Century was on the right track. The largest opportunity for propane companies at the time was auto gas. The US government encouraged companies to experiment with alternative fuels. They offered incentive programs with large tax breaks for any companies willing to do so. It appeared to be a golden opportunity for propane companies, with a dominant force behind it. We were able to land a few accounts, which even got us some media coverage.

We converted a small fleet of buses to run on propane gas. This dramatically improved our sales and our profitability at Century. Although I was forced to buy Century Propane and never really wanted it, it appeared to have been a blessing in disguise. There was bankable gold hidden there the entire time. I just hadn't ever given the business a chance. I'm glad I did.

Reflection Point 35

By putting myself in the independent contractors' shoes, I was able to design a program that caught their attention and appealed to them. By creating this attractive opportunity, I all but guaranteed they would continually send us business.

You will have a much greater chance at success if you think things through from every angle.

Whose shoes do you need to put yourself in to gain perspective
and create an advantage?

What would catch their attention?

How can you turn that into a mutually beneficial proposition?

Chapter 36:

Who is the Right Buyer?

It was the end of 2016. I had a full two and a half years back at the helm of my business, and I rarely made time for anything but work. I ate, slept, and breathed propane. I was available only to discuss new business, profitability, efficiency, and company culture. It was all I did. By the end of the year, my profit-and-loss statement said I had made a staggering $3 million in profit. I again had increased profits by $1 million. Everything was going according to plan, and now it was time to start looking for a buyer. But who was it going to be?

I pulled a list out of my drawer that contained the potential buyers for my business, all the people I had spoken to the previous year. The list contained about 18 names of companies and individuals. The candidates ranged from private equities to national propane companies, even some investors I had met from Egypt — apparently, of royal descent who had the means to purchase my entire company out of their petty cash. As I studied the list, I began to envision the daunting task of entertaining these persistent people again. When I previously had spoken to the private equity guys, besides the unappealing deals they offered, which almost always required me to stay in place, I spent more time educating them on the business than trying to sell it to them. I had to show them the value, which in itself was exhausting. Even if we came to an agreement where I wouldn't have to remain involved and not be subject to an earnout, I'm sure there would've been a transition period, and I would have received my money over an extended amount of time. I wasn't interested in that. I needed to turn the tables on this negotiation process. How could I find a way around this?

As I gazed at the list, I began to think and ask myself some of these questions:

What could I do to narrow down this list and not waste my time? I continued to think. *Who could buy this company right now for all cash? No financing needed.* I began to scratch off my list the names of people or companies that couldn't pay cash. I stayed focused and asked myself another question: *Who would I not have to educate on this business?* More names came off the list as I struck a black line through them with my pen. Then came another question, *Who would already see the value in it?* Before answering that one, another question arose: *Who is my company most valuable to?* Now that was a great question. It probably should've been my first. Only three names remained on the list: Empire, Black Bull, and Starlight Propane, the three largest propane companies in the nation. One of them would be my buyer.

Note: Petty cash or the petty cash fund is a small amount of cash on hand used for paying expenses too small to merit writing a check. A petty cash fund can be used for office supplies, cards for customers, flowers, paying for a catered lunch for employees, or reimbursing employees for expenses.

Reminder: What's an earnout payment?

Often, when buyers and sellers want to complete a deal but can't agree on the price, they employ a strategy called an earnout. An earnout is a contingent payment that the seller receives from the buyer only when specific performance targets are met.

Reflection Point 36

By making a habit of asking myself quality questions, I was able to gain clarity and get quality answers in just a few minutes. This exercise may have saved me countless time and effort speaking to unqualified potential buyers. Thanks to this exercise, I knew exactly whom I needed to be speaking to.

Are you asking yourself the RIGHT question?

_____

_____

_____

The answer to what crucial question would save you a
countless amount of time and energy?

_____

_____

_____

_____

_____

_____

_____

Chapter 37:

Thirty-Something

Now that I had a list of the only entities I would deal with, I needed to find someone who could negotiate the deal. So, I sought expert advice. I previously had seen several ads in the back of Propane Magazine USA of business brokers that provided such service; they were all out of state. I began calling them to learn about the process and schedule in-person consultations, if deemed necessary. I gave each one an overview of my business and asked all the same set of prepared questions. While they spoke, I took as many notes as possible, trying to learn as much as I could. I even flew one of the brokers to Miami to meet in person.

When I mentioned the 10-times multiple I had heard of, and my $37 million goal, their responses were similar, asserting that the 10-times multiple was a rare, one-of-a-kind occurrence. The first broker just about laughed me off the phone. He thought that my company might bring a 5–7 times earnings multiple of my $3 million net earnings. I wasn't expecting that reply. Based on his valuation, my company only had a value of $15–$21 million, at most. When I mentioned my friend Frank's estimate of $25 million the previous year, the broker said that was merely an opinion and not reality. I quickly decided to go another route. The second broker, who flew down to meet me, had a much more positive outlook; however, he still estimated my business would command only a 7-times multiple. Under his assumption, my company was worth $21 million, and just might be worth up to $25 million, if, I could find the right buyer. That was more discouraging news. Neither of these brokers had been very persuasive. I respected their opinions but disagreed and, to top it off, if they were successful in negotiating a sale for me, I would have to pay them a 3.5% brokerage fee, which added offence to the already-punishing valuations.

Here's the math: $25,000,000 \times 3.5\% = \$875,000$. No. No way.

They both were nice guys, but there was something that kept gnawing at me: Why do I need a broker? Especially a broker who doesn't see the value in my business or agree with what I felt it was worth. What was such a broker going to be able to negotiate for me, anyway? I would have been hiring the wrong man for the job. Maybe I didn't need a broker after all. I had learned so much about the brokerage process with my questions and note-taking, I felt these men didn't know much more than me. It wasn't rocket science. They definitely didn't know more about my business than I did. After my second encounter, I decided that the right man for the job was me. I believed in my business's value, and I believed I could negotiate my own sale. Why not give it a try?

I was ready to embark on this adventure. It was exciting. I looked up the telephone numbers of the business development departments of all three companies on my list and began calling them to introduce myself. I gave them just enough information to gauge interest, but no more. Black Bull was the first to be scratched from the list. They were having financial troubles, and the company had become unstable, even rumors of bankruptcy. No money equals no deal. We were quickly down to two potential buyers, Starlight and Empire. I first began negotiating with Starlight. I sent them an NDA to sign, and we quickly started negotiations. They requested all of my financial information, which I sent. They seemed impressed. We had several lunch and dinner meetings and many talks over the phone. They were very interested and made me a very generous offer, but it wasn't $37 million. Plus, they wanted me to stay in place and work with them. Why would I sell my company for millions of dollars and get up to work a 9-to-5 desk job the next day? Not happening. I politely declined that offer and ended negotiations. Two down. The last and final option was Empire.

My experience with Empire was far better than the previous two. The representatives of Empire Gas were wonderful people to me, and it was always a pleasure to speak with them. After the formalities, Empire began to research my business in great detail. They seemed quite pleased and impressed with the extent that my financials were in order but needed to dig deeper. A few different representatives dropped in to visit and take a look at our operations. The good news for us was that all was in order. They then phoned around to get facts on our reputation within the industry. We passed all their other preliminary tests. Then they performed an exhaustive review of my businesses financial health; they even brought in a team of forensic accountants. Once satisfied, they wanted to have a conference call to discuss their review and the initial opinion of the value they had arrived at. It sounded to me as if Empire wanted to dip their toes in the water before diving in. They wanted to get a feel for what I believed my company was worth.

This got me thinking. *I know what I want, but how are they seeing it?* I tried to analyze it from their perspective. *How much value does my company have to them, and how can I figure that out?*

I felt that was the right way to proceed, but I wasn't certain. This was my first time selling my business, or any business for that matter; so I wasn't quite sure what to do. I then had a small epiphany: *When I bought Atlas, it had tremendous value to me because I benefited from all the synergies. After I added their accounts, eliminated the competition, and ran it more efficiently, I was able to generate a lot more profit. This is practically an identical situation, except now, I'm the seller! Why not look at it like that?* I knew how valuable my business could be to Empire, especially because I had first-hand experience and understood how valuable purchasing Atlas was for me.

To accomplish this, I would need to use a unique and direct approach to the negotiation. I intended to illustrate not only the value my company had as a standalone business, which spoke for itself, but also to illustrate my company's value to Empire's operations with a synergistic application.

I had our in-house accountant prepare a normalized profit-and-loss statement, removing any non-reoccurring expenses Empire wouldn't have, thus showing more profit. That added a little over $200,000 of profit to our bottom line, bringing our total net earnings slightly over $3.2 million. I then had my accountant create an Excel spreadsheet which added back all the other expenses I was incurring that I knew Empire wouldn't incur. Expenses such as insurance, workman's comp, and any costs related to our production facility. I felt that overhead wouldn't apply to them because they had their own facility and better resources. After eliminating those expenses, my Excel spreadsheet made clear that, by absorbing our company, Empire could turn our $3.2 million-a-year profit into $4.7 million. None of it was fluff. It was all factual. The math favorably illustrated that.

Before finalizing the Excel spreadsheet to send over to Empire Gas, my accountant asked, "Should I calculate the math in two columns: one with the industry standard 7-times multiple, and the other with the 10-times multiple we are hoping for?" My reply was, "No, we're not selling for a 7-times multiple, so leave it out!" I only wanted to bring their attention to the $4.7 million 10-times multiple. Which meant my company would be worth $47 million to them. With numbers like these, I didn't need to sell the company; it sold itself.

The day of the call, there were four reps from Empire on their end and just me and my accountant on the other. My contact at Empire was named Drew, and after some pleasantries, we got right into it. I'd had my accountant send them my Excel spreadsheet before the call, so I knew they had had ample time to review it. They acknowledged that they had received it, and throughout the call, I could hear papers shuffling back and forth, accompanied by light whispering in the background. Not terribly long into the conversation came what you could call toe-dipping time. The first offer they threw out was verbal: "Well, based on what you've got here, it looks like your company could be worth $25 million." Drew said. I laughed light- heartedly, and replied, "Come on now, Drew; you know very well it's worth a lot more than that. Especially to you. You're the right buyer for this company. To you, it's worth $47 million," I said confidently. "Well, I'm not sure it would be worth $47 million to us," he replied. "Well, that's okay, because I don't want to sell it for that much. I just want $37 million," I replied. Drew responded with some good-humored laughter, and I joined him, and we shared a laugh together. "Well, listen, I want to take a trip down there within the next few weeks to visit you, with the intent of coming to an agreement and leaving Miami with a deal in place. Does that sound good to you?" he asked. "Sounds good to me." I replied. "Okay, I'll get back to you with some possible travel dates," he added. I thanked him and everyone on the call for their time and hung up. I was pumped when we got off the phone. He didn't say yes to my $37 million price, but he didn't say no either.

A few days later, I heard back from Drew. He called and asked if we could have our in-person, sit-down meeting at my office. I agreed and prepared for it. I would say we spent extra time ensuring everything was spick and span in preparation for the meeting, but we didn't. The truth was that's just how we kept things. I was actually excited and not nervous.

On the day of the negotiation, we held the meeting after hours, careful not to alarm any of our employees of the potential sale. Drew arrived with an associate from Empire. I believe he was in some sort of financial capacity. I was accompanied by my in-house accountant, who was instructed to offer only the information I requested of him. I didn't want him saying anything out of place. We gave Drew and his associate the nickel tour and then quickly got down to business. The tone of the meeting was easy-going. They were genuinely nice people, and it was a very pleasant experience. But that doesn't mean they came with a check in hand.

After the tour, we grabbed a couple of water bottles, and all took seats in the conference room. As the meeting got underway, Drew took the lead. He asked some questions and pointed out some facts. I responded to most of his queries directly, unless, I needed to defer to my accountant for details. Most of the questions he asked I was prepared for. I had rehearsed this moment in my mind probably a thousand times by that point. The first offer he made was $28 million. That was for my business, all my inventory, and the land the business was on, which surprisingly, had increased to a potential value of about $3 million by that time, though I had previously mentioned to Drew that I didn't want to part with the land. The deal wasn't horribly bad, but obviously it wasn't $37 million, and I wanted to keep the land, so no deal. We calmly and casually continued to debate and negotiate. I was relaxed and in no rush. This was the only place I had to be. It seemed like I was with a couple of friends having a casual conversation over a beer at a weekend get- together. I enjoyed the experience.

Drew and his associate pointed out several other things and made more valid points in a continued attempt to get me down from my $37 million asking price. I would then make valid points of my own, arguing it was worth more than what I was asking for — all based on facts. There were no fantasy claims being thrown out. But that didn't stop him from trying. He would say, "Come on, Max, you know it's not worth that much." And then I would say, "I know it's not worth that much to everyone, but to you and Empire, it's worth much, much more. To you, $37 million is a bargain."

Interrupting our dialogue, they asked for their first break, and requested to have the conference room to themselves, so they could call their superiors, who were somehow part of this negotiation at their headquarters, to fill them in on the progress of the negotiations. When they were ready to resume, their number had increased. Drew and his associate were all smiles when they made me a new offer of $31 million. That offer was for my business, and all my inventory, which we both knew alone was worth $750,000. I got to keep my land as part of this offer, which I valued at $3 million, as long as I agreed to lease it back to them, which was a much better deal, but $31 million plus a $3 million credit for the land, is $34 million. That's still not $37 million. No, no deal.

They again tried to convince me to consider this offer, but I stood firm and insisted it was worth more. Even though I had just declined a $34 million offer, which was bold to say the least, I wasn't nervous. Actually, I felt quite confident. I had taken the time to feel the energy in the room. I knew I was okay. He wasn't going anywhere.

We bantered back and forth, and shortly after, they asked for another break. I had no one I needed to speak to or consult. I knew what my outcome had to be, $37 million. Nothing less. We had been a little over four hours into the negotiation at that point. I could tell they were genuinely getting a bit more flustered. I, on the other hand, was as cool as a cucumber. I knew they wanted to make a deal.

Ready to reconvene, Drew and his associate asked us to join them back in the conference room. This time, he wasn't all smiles. Looking down at notes he had taken from his call with his superiors, he took a deep breath, then exhaled sharply before he began to speak. "Okay, I'm at the end of my rope here, Max. I have a better number for you, but I promise you, it's not going to get any higher than this," Drew declared. I could sense from his tone and his body language that, this time, he truly meant it. We were now five hours into negotiating.

"Empire's final offer is $33,250,000 in cash. You get to keep the land, valued at $3 million, and we also will pay you $750,000 for your inventory. That's a 10.3-times multiple on earnings, and that's the absolute best I can do," he said. I believed him. "Okay, well, give me a second to think about it," I replied. I grabbed my pen and paper and started to add things up.

Cash: $33,250,000

Inventory: + $750,000

Land: + $3,000,000

That, my friends, is **$37,000,000.00**, and that is the end of this story!I stood up and shook Drew's hand, "You've got a deal!"

Reflection Point 37

Believe it or not, the money for the sale of my company was wired to me on June 1, 2017. Which was just two days after I had written out the check to myself. In fact, it was still taped to the wall in my room. Talk about the power of manifestation. I was able to pay off what I owed to the bank, with four years to spare. As part of my ongoing appreciation and commitment to my staff, I decided to tithe 10% of the net proceeds I received to them on that same day. I had approximately 70 employees lined up at the entrance to my office to personally address every one of them. One by one, they made their way in. I explained what was going on and thanked them for their part in our success. I then handed over their bonus. Every employee received a check. Being in the position to do that for my staff felt like it was more of a gift for me than it was for them. For many people, it was a life-changing amount of money. The gratitude they expressed was proof of that. It warmed my soul. I gave out hugs and heartfelt thank-yous to everyone. We laughed, cried, and celebrated as a family, for one last time.

Although I worked extremely hard for the first 12 years of the 15 I was in the propane business, it's important to note that most of the value was created in the final three years. It was the education and strategy I applied that made the biggest impact. I thought things through in much greater detail. I asked better questions to myself and those I associated with. I had adopted a completely different strategy. I knew exactly what I was setting out to accomplish; I wasn't just getting lucky. I tactfully planned for success. If I didn't understand something, it made me uncomfortable. I had to know what I did not know. I persistently studied subjects that I lacked knowledge of. My go-to resource for learning for many years was YouTube. It was simple and effective. While in my car, I

Reflection Point 37

almost stopped listening to music altogether. Instead, I spent that time learning. I listened to inspirational speeches, lectures, and any other form of educational content I was interested in. This was a phenomenal habit. I had developed an insatiable thirst for knowledge. As a result of my efforts, I had the opportunity to retire at just 36 years old.

While I studied with Tony Robbins, I was devoted to learning everything that Tony had to teach. In addition to his work, I attended three more courses with Keith Cunningham. I read books and listened to material by Napoleon Hill, Les Brown, Wayne Dyer, Joel Osteen, T.D. Jakes, and many other men I admired. I used this new outlook on life and what I learned to not only help myself but to help everyone around me. I recommended self-help material to many of my family members, friends, and coworkers, which allowed me to bring them in closer to who I had become. In turn, it gave me an opportunity to give back to them. I became much better at communicating and understanding people in general. Believe in yourself, trust in yourself. Listen to your inner voice. Deep down, you know what you're doing. You've always known!

Sometimes our dreams seem farfetched and unattainable. But what if they weren't?

So, who is
Max Lewis
after all?

Look in
the mirror!

Anyone can be Max Lewis,
and anyone can do the things he did,
even YOU!

Remember those three questions at the beginning of the book? If you never answered them, maybe you should now. If you did, why not try the exercise again and see if any of your answers have changed. It's worth your time; I guarantee it!

1. *What* do you want?

_____

_____

_____

2. *Why* do you want it?

_____

_____

_____

3. *What* are some of the things you can do to get what you want?

_____

_____

Author's Note

A principle I have been applying for most of my life is never to live above my means. I have always been modest with my finances, mainly because, at one time, I knew what it was like to not have money, and how hard I had to work for it. Having experienced that, I rarely overextend myself and continually look for ways to increase my income, rather than cut into my *hard-earned capital,* which I define as money I have had to personally work for. That doesn't mean I don't spoil myself with some things I desire. It just means I'm smart about it. I rarely spend my *hard-earned money* to buy things I want. I let my investments pay for them.

For example: If I want to lease a new car and the payment is $1,000 a month, I produce an income stream for it first. Then I reward myself with the car. Let's use an apartment for an example. Instead of buying the new car outright or making the lease payments with my *hard-earned money,* I will buy an apartment that will generate no less than the $1,000 a month I would need for the lease payment. I then would let the apartment pay for the car. The beauty in this is, after I turn in my lease, I still own the apartment. It likely has appreciated, and I can continue to earn money from it. I can go out and lease another car and *I* will not be paying for it; the apartment will continue paying for it. I could keep that cycle going forever. This way, I'm not working to pay for things I want; my investments are.

Reflection Questions

1. What are your beliefs around money? How has money helped you? *In what ways do you keep track of your finances, and how could you improve them?*

2. What are you planting in your subconscious mind regularly? *What do you need to be planting to get the results you're after?*

3. Who is your target audience, and what strategy have you been using to capture their interest? *Could there be a more effective strategy? If so, what is that strategy?*

4. Is there a situation, person or environment that leads you to continually compromise on what you feel is right for you? *How will things be different next time around?*

5. Have you been ignoring a gut feeling? If so, in what area of your life? *What's something your intuition has been trying to tell you?*

6. Who are the people in your life who motivate and encourage you? *How could you spend more time with them?*

7. Are you giving up at the first sign of an obstacle in a particular area of your life? How could you become part of the solution? *What steps are you taking right now to ensure a better future? What else can you do?*

8. Where have you taken a shortcut that can eventually lead to a setback? *What can you do to correct it?*

9. What closed doors in your life have led to better doors' opening? Have you reached your full potential? *What else are you capable of?*

10. Does your paperwork show what you believe you agreed to? Have you gotten proper legal advice? *What important documents should you personally review?*

11. What is your biggest opportunity? *Why do you see it as an opportunity?* Are you prepared for it? *If not, what do you need to do to be prepared for it?*

12. Are your dreams BIG enough? *What dream do you have that is so BIG it scares you but at the same time EXCITES you? What are some things you can do to get a few steps closer to that dream?*

13. Whose presence are you taking for granted? *How can you express to them how much they truly mean to you?*

14. What is something bold you wish you had the courage to ask someone? *What could you be missing out on by not taking that chance?*

15. Do you listen to understand, or are you listening to respond? *What could you do to be a better listener?*

16. What are the top three things you could do right now to become more efficient and increase your income? *What more will you gain from making these changes?*

17. How often do you evaluate your financial picture? *Where can you trim some fat?*

18. Be honest with yourself. Is all your communication truthful? *How could being 100% sincere improve your relationships?*

19. Are you doing the appropriate amount of research before entering an unfamiliar environment? *How should you be mentally and physically preparing yourself for a new opportunity?*

20. Are you appreciated for what you bring to the table? *Do you need to remove yourself from an unfavorable environment? If so, why?*

21. What steps do you need to take to prove to yourself that your fears are not real? *What brings you peace, and how could you do more of it?*

22. When has losing your cool made things worse? *What will you do differently next time?*

23. What is a strenuous experience you have had that ultimately led to your personal growth? *Have you considered being thankful for it? What about that experience helped shape you?*

24. What is a time-consuming activity you can hand-off to someone else after providing them with the proper training? In what ways will accomplishing this benefit you? *What is a life-changing decision you can make today that can help release you from your past?*

25. How do you organize your thoughts? *How can you improve your strategy? Whose guidance should you seek to help shine a light on your chosen path?*

26. Are your dreams really your dreams? *Are you designing your own future or have you been influenced to pursue something else? What do you want at your core?*

27. Are you spending your time with the right crowd? *What is something you wish you could have learned by now? Without making excuses, what's stopping you?*

28. How do you honestly respond to feedback? How could you improve your response? *What is an existing challenge in your life that might be solved by implementing a unique approach? What could be the solution?*

29. What thought-provoking questions should you be asking yourself before making an important decision? *Starting NOW, what will you do differently going forward?*

30. What is a tough decision you have been putting off? Does it have the potential to set you or someone else free? *How good would it feel to be finally free from it? What would be different?*

31. In your opinion, what is the difference between a boss and a leader? *What kind of environment would you like to create for yourself and others? How can you incorporate more FUN into your life on a daily basis?*

32. Who do you view as an enemy who also has the potential to be your greatest ally? *How can you change the dynamic?*

33. What proactive approach do you take to manifesting your goals? *What are some of the things that would be on your bucket list? What is a time waster you could eliminate to improve your life? Why not try it for a week?*

34. What is an obstacle you feel has been impossible to circumvent? *What approach haven't you tried yet?*

35. Whose shoes do you need to put yourself in to gain perspective and create an advantage? *What would catch their attention? How can you turn that into a mutually beneficial proposition?*

36. Are you asking yourself the RIGHT question? *The answer to what crucial question would save you a countless amount of time and energy?*

37. *What do you want? Why do you want it? What are some of the things you can do to get what you want?*

Creative Exercise

I encourage you to design some quality thinking questions of your own. Remember, you do not want questions that lead to a yes or no answer. You want questions that force you to think. These questions will help guide you when you have a tough or important decision to make.

1._____

_____

_____

_____

2._____

_____

_____

_____

3._____

_____

_____

_____

A few *Thinking Questions*
that have helped me along the way

1. If I was starting over today, what would I do differently?

2. How will I adjust my behavior going forward to create the success I want?

3. What are 3 things I could do right now that could get me closer to my goal?

4. What could I do to make this an absolute no-brainer in the eyes of the consumer?

5. Is what I'm doing right now giving me what I want? If not, what needs to change?

The BEST gift you can give an author is to leave a review.

<u>Please leave a review</u>
on Amazon or wherever you purchased the book.

CONNECT WITH MAX LEWIS ON INSTAGRAM, TWITTER, AND TIKTOK

@WhoisMaxLewis

 For Bookings, Speaking, or Consultations, Email Max@WhoisMaxLewis.com

0001

DATE _____

Pay to _____

WHO
IS
MAX
LEWIS
?

$ [   ]

_____ DOLLARS 🔒

MEMO _____

⑆123456789⑈   ⑆7890⑈5673⑆

What amount would be on *your* check?

What will you *do* to earn it?

www.ingramcontent.com/pod-product-compliance
Lightning Source LLC
Chambersburg PA
CBHW020429130626
46549CB00001B/49